THE SLOW
UNDOING

Stephen H. Lowe

THE SLOW UNDOING

The Federal Courts and the Long Struggle for Civil Rights in South Carolina

THE UNIVERSITY OF
SOUTH CAROLINA PRESS

© 2021 University of South Carolina

Published by the University of South Carolina Press
Columbia, South Carolina 29208

www.uscpress.com

Manufactured in the United States of America

30 29 28 27 26 25 24 23 22 21
10 9 8 7 6 5 4 3 2 1

Library of Congress Cataloging-in-Publication Data
can be found at http://catalog.loc.gov/.

ISBN 978-1-64336-176-5 (hardcover)
ISBN 978-1-64336-205-2 (paperback)
ISBN 978-1-64336-177-2 (ebook)

Portions of chapters six and seven appeared, in different form, as Stephen H. Lowe, "White Subversion of Public School Desegregation in South Carolina, 1963–1970," *American Journal of Legal History* 60 (June 2020): 223–246. Those portions are reprinted here with permission.

To Carmen, Bonnie, and Mattie

CONTENTS

List of Illustrations   viii
Acknowledgments   ix

Introduction   1

CHAPTER 1. "This Couldn't Have Been Ignorance": Challenging the White
Primary in the 1940s   10

CHAPTER 2. Not Equal, but Still Separate: Challenging Jim Crow
Education in the 1940s   30

CHAPTER 3. "Unexampled Courage": School Desegregation in the 1950s   54

CHAPTER 4. "*Plessy* Has Not Been Overturned": Law and Resistance in the
Late 1950s   73

CHAPTER 5. "We Don't Allow Colored People in Here": Segregation to
"Integration with Dignity," 1959–63   92

CHAPTER 6. "We Have Not Yet Run Out of Courts": Desegregation in the
mid-1960s   117

CHAPTER 7. "We've Run Out of Courts, and We've Run Out of Time":
Freedom of Choice and School Desegregation to 1970   150

CHAPTER 8. Desegregation, Not Integration: South Carolina Since 1968   178

Abbreviations   187
Notes   189
Bibliography   223
Index   237

ILLUSTRATIONS

FIG. 1   Judge J. Waties Waring   20

FIG. 2   Pearl Shirer   36

FIG. 3   Senator L. Marion Gressette   57

FIG. 4   J. Arthur Brown   74

FIG. 5   Elloree Training School Teachers   85

FIG. 6   Judge George Bell Timmerman Sr. and Robert M. Cooper   89

FIG. 7   J. Arthur Brown, Matthew J. Perry, Lincoln Jenkins, and
         Hemphill Pride II   98

FIG. 8   Judge Cecil C. Wyche   102

FIG. 9   Mathew J. Perry and Henrie Monteith   121

FIG. 10 Lurma Rackley and Gloria Rackley Blackwell   126

FIG. 11 Judge Robert W. Hemphill   133

ACKNOWLEDGMENTS

Authors inevitably amass debts—always personal, frequently financial—in the course of writing. In my case, those debts have been amassed across nearly thirty years of research and writing. Through multiple drafts and several earlier articles, this book represents the culmination of work that started as a doctoral proposal in the fall of 1990 and became my dissertation in 1999. I owe my fellow students at Michigan State University's graduate program from 1990 to 1996 a degree of gratitude for their encouragement and comradeship. I also thank the faculty of the program as well, especially my doctoral adviser, Barbara Steidle, along with my dissertation committee members, the late David Bailey, Victor Jew, Gordon Stewart, and Stephen Esquith. My thanks also extend to other members of the Michigan State history faculty, particularly Darlene Clark Hine, Wilma King, Sam Thomas, Emily Tabuteau, the late Morgan Sweeney, and the late Harry Reed.

Before Michigan State, I was in a master's degree program at Clemson University, where I not only had the pleasure of working with a wonderful group of faculty members and fellow graduate students but also met my wife, about whom I will write more below. I especially want to mention Alan Schaffer, my MA thesis adviser. He is still missed. Also on my MA committee were Alan Grubb and the late Bill Steirer. My thanks to them and to the other members of the Clemson history faculty, including Beth Carney and Don McKale. I also want to thank Theda Perdue, formerly of Clemson, and Bill Hine, formerly of South Carolina State, for their help and encouragement.

While working on the dissertation, I received a grant from the South Carolina Bar Foundation to do research at the National Archives in Atlanta. That grant was timely and helpful, enabling the last bit of research for the dissertation. Of course, a lot more research had to be done to transform an adequate dissertation into a publishable book. Too many archivists and librarians to even mention helped locate sources and provided assistance and a timely article or document when I was unable to make it to the source. To the staffs of the Clemson Special Collections, the South Caroliniana Library, the National

Archives depositories in Atlanta, College Park, and Philadelphia, and the Moorland-Spingarn Library at Howard University, I offer my sincere gratitude.

Parts of the book were published earlier as articles in the *Avery Review,* the *Proceedings of the South Carolina Historical Association,* and the *American Journal of Legal History.* To those editors and anonymous reviewers, as well as the reviewers of the manuscript, I owe thanks for improving my work immeasurably.

My father, the late Harold B. Lowe, gave me financial assistance and good advice, not often taken, throughout graduate school and well into my postgraduate years. His love for me and my family was deep and abiding. I appreciate him more now than I ever did then.

Before I finished my dissertation, my wife and I welcomed two children into the world—Bonnie, born in 1995 while we were still in Michigan, and Mattie, born in 1998 in South Carolina. They are now grown women, and while the world has not taken the form I would have liked (or anticipated) when they were born, they are working to change it for the better.

Finally my wife, Carmen Harris, a better historian than I by far, edited the manuscript more times than I can count, offered innumerable suggestions for improving my writing, did research when I was not able to, found sources both obscure and meaningful, and encouraged me throughout the long process of getting this work to print. For these reasons and too many others to count, I owe her a debt that can never be repaid. Much of what has made this book worthwhile is due to her. Any errors of fact or judgment are, of course, solely my own.

To Carmen, and to our daughters, Bonnie and Mattie, this book is lovingly dedicated.

INTRODUCTION

This book is a history of civil rights cases African Americans filed in federal district courts in South Carolina, their connection to civil rights activism, and the reaction of White officials and citizens of South Carolina to African American initiative. It contributes to an increasing body of scholarship that argues that despite a relative lack of violence, substantial high-profile Black activism, and White resistance, developments in South Carolina are significant to understanding the unfolding struggles of the long civil rights movement.[1] The role of the federal district courts is another little-studied aspect of the civil rights movement.[2] This work is the first comprehensive study of legal action in a single state beginning in the mid-1930s, when Charles Hamilton Houston established the legal framework for the assault on segregation through the post-*Brown* era. Houston's aim was to overturn *Plessy v. Ferguson,* which underpinned White supremacy. The legal aspects of the civil rights movement include efforts by White people to use the federal district courts to maintain control prior to and well after *Brown v. Board of Education.* These actions demonstrate the importance of litigation as a consequential component of the broader civil rights struggle.

Much of the narrative of the civil rights movement focuses on direct action by African Americans from 1955 through the 1960s. This approach privileges confrontation and certain geographical locations and actors while marginalizing others. Most direct action began or became sustained only after systematic litigation to undermine *Plessy* had succeeded in the Supreme Court but failed to be implemented by federal district courts that were charged with supervision. As the work of both J. W. Peltason and Charles V. Hamilton show, local context influenced many federal district judges to subvert the significance of national rulings. Post-*Brown* direct-action protesters who were arrested or otherwise faced retaliation for civil disobedience added to the caseload of civil rights attorneys, who were using the new jurisprudence to secure favorable rulings to dismantle the structure of segregation issue by issue. It is for these reasons that this work places the district courts as a central intersection of race, law, and civil rights in the Black freedom struggle.

I argue for a reconsideration of the role of federal courts in the civil rights movement by demonstrating that both pre- and post-*Brown,* federal district courts were centrally important to achieving and solidifying civil rights gains. It relies on the entire legal record of actions in the federal district courts of South Carolina from 1940 to 1970 to make the case. It argues that rather than relying on litigation during the pre-*Brown* era and direct action in the post-*Brown* era, African Americans used courts and direct action in tandem to bring down legal segregation throughout the long civil rights era.

The focus is principally on two groups of people. One was a group of Black South Carolinians who—with the help of the NAACP—brought and argued cases in the federal district courts to assert their civil rights and eventually put an end to de jure segregation. Opposing them was a group of White South Carolinians, including politicians and other officials, who struggled equally hard in the courts to prevent or delay equality for all. With the exception of the brief interregnum of "Radical Reconstruction," White supremacy had controlled Black life in South Carolina for nearly three centuries. However, between 1940 and 1970, that historic structure began to unravel as Black and White South Carolinians contended in the state's federal courts over the meanings of the Constitution, justice, equality, and citizenship. This contest revealed the underlying disagreement between Black citizens, White citizens, and the courts regarding equal rights. African American plaintiffs and lawyers from South Carolina, with support of lawyers from the NAACP Legal Defense and Education Fund, brought and argued civil rights lawsuits in the federal courts of South Carolina attempting to equalize, then desegregate, schools, parks, and public life. Meanwhile, White citizens, mostly state politicians and local officials, hired lawyers who crafted new legal theories to defend state practices and forestall Black equality.

With the exception of J. Waties Waring, who became a racial moderate late in his career, South Carolina judges were partisans of segregation and state's rights. Their narrow reading and application of federal judicial decisions protracted the process of desegregation until 1963. Judges born in the nineteenth century especially (Cecil C. Wyche, George Bell Timmerman Sr., and Ashton H. Williams) did not conceal their antipathy for the idea of desegregation. Those born in the twentieth century (Robert Martin, Robert Hemphill, Charles E. Simons), though conservative in mindset, were more sophisticated in their application of jurisprudence, which made their delays of desegregation appear more reasonable.

Ultimately Black South Carolinians endeavored to claim their status as full state and national citizens not only through the courts but also with sit-ins, marches, boycotts, and other nonviolent protests. South

Carolinians—particularly White South Carolinians—had taken pride in the relative lack of direct action or violence their state experienced, but the Orangeburg Massacre—and lesser-known incidents of civil disobedience that preceded it—indicated that South Carolina's facade of racial harmony was weakening under the strain of continued Black resistance to discrimination. The violence that shook Orangeburg in 1968 at South Carolina State College, where Black students protesting ongoing segregation were shot at, and three killed, by officers of the state highway patrol belied the idea that South Carolina could successfully integrat[e] with dignity. Through it all, the legal challenges to segregation continued.

The Landscape before 1940

Between World War I and World War II, life for Black South Carolinians improved, if only slightly, in some areas. According to I. A. Newby, infant and maternal mortality had dropped significantly, and the death rate for Black South Carolinians fell by 18 percent. Most Black citizens were in some way part of the agricultural sector—almost 80 percent lived in rural areas. Debt was increasing, while incomes, especially during the Great Depression, fell. One estimate held that, in addition to other markers of ill health and poverty, only about half of Black children were normal weight and a third suffered from poor nutrition. Black schoolchildren went to school in worse buildings for shorter school terms. Many Black children never attended high school—few were available. On the eve of World War II, the majority of Black South Carolinians could not vote. Black teachers were significantly underpaid compared to their White counterparts. African Americans had limited—at best—access to public facilities, and the access they had was intended to remind them of their inferior status in society. The position of Black citizens in South Carolina was such that it effectively trained each generation for its inferior position in society while simultaneously affirming White supremacy.[3] All that was about to undergo a profound, if prolonged, change.

The leading edge of that change was South Carolina's branches of the NAACP, which came together in 1939 to form a state conference that, under strong leadership, achieved significant civil rights victories over the next three decades. While meaningful progress came only after the unification of the state's NAACP chapters, many of the leaders who rose to prominence in the 1940s and 1950s were already in public view during before 1939. During the 1930s the modern civil rights movement in South Carolina experienced its genesis. Modjeska Simkins, who later became secretary of the state conference and an important civil rights activist in Columbia, spoke out in favor of the federal anti-lynching bill in 1935. In addition to individual leaders, several groups that supported the NAACP or whose members formed the core of future NAACP chapters also came into being during the 1930s.[4]

The 1940s was a pivotal era of legal activism by African Americans in South Carolina. Black South Carolinians began to turn the corner from mere accommodation of—if not submission to—institutionalized and legalized racism to organized and determined resistance. South Carolina became one of several of Houston's laboratories for legal change across the segregated South. Both on their own initiative and in collaboration with the national NAACP, Black South Carolinians became part of a sustained legal resistance to Jim Crow in all its forms. In a span of just a few years in the mid-1940s, Black South Carolinians began fighting in the courts for their right to vote in the state's Democratic primaries and in national elections. When the national NAACP challenged inequalities in teachers' salaries across the South, Black South Carolinians participated. Following the Supreme Court's early decisions dealing with segregated education in law schools, Black South Carolinians attempted to desegregate the state's White law school. When the NAACP turned its attention to desegregating education at all levels, this time Black South Carolinians took the lead, initiating the first case to challenge the constitutionality of segregation in primary and secondary education in the South. When the NAACP began to challenge limitations on access to facilities paid for with tax dollars and businesses serving the public, Black South Carolinians joined in challenging their exclusion from public spaces and filed suit when denied access.

The core belief of White South Carolinians generally was White supremacy —specifically a belief in the naturalness of segregation and the inferiority of Black people. The fear that political equality or economic success would lead to demands for social contact on an equal basis—which would inevitably lead to racial amalgamation (sometimes referred to as "mongrelization")—drove the White majority to develop the legal (and extralegal) means to maintain Jim Crow.[5] Fear, but also what historian Walter Edgar has called "'good order' and 'harmony of the whole community,'" inspired White South Carolinians to support using the courts to resist the end of Jim Crow following the Supreme Court's decision in *Brown*.[6] White supremacy enjoyed support throughout the South, most especially in rural areas, but also in cities such as Charleston that thrived on their Old South traditions. Of particular importance were political figures with ties to rural areas with predominantly Black populations and neofeudal economies and social structures. These rural politicians, like most of their White constituents, were "suspicious of 'progress,' liberal education [and] Yankees." They feared "the threat to state's rights, . . . 'creeping socialism' and the federal bureaucracy" and "sought to suppress the social and ideological aspects of southern change."[7]

Black South Carolinians embraced the "color-blind" construction of Justice John Marshall Harlan and therefore read the Constitution and its promise of justice, equality, and citizenship as an inclusive birthright that when violated could be remedied through the courts. They also recognized that restorative justice had to precede color blindness. White South Carolinians read the Constitution as an exclusionary document, constructed by White people for White people. Only White people had recourse to the courts when violations of their rights occurred. Indeed, court rulings from *Prigg v. Pennsylvania* to *Dred Scott v. Sandford* to the *Civil Rights Cases, Plessy,* and the lesser-known *Williams v. Mississippi* had repeatedly reaffirmed and protected the primacy of White citizenship and rights. In some respects the White leaders who resisted the course of integration and social justice in the courts shared with their Black counterparts a significant trait: a belief in the rule of law. For Black citizens the rule of law meant equality and justice as established in the Fourteenth and Fifteenth Amendments to the Constitution: due process of law, equal protection (and equal treatment), and a sense of fairness that went beyond the written words of the document. For White people the rule of law required a strict reading of the Constitution, and it often required them to ignore the original intent of the Reconstruction amendments, a precedent that had been established in the late nineteenth century. When the courts deviated from their perception, it was legitimate to resist the courts and to question their authority.

White South Carolinians' use of the apparatus of state government, such as the South Carolina School Committee (better known as the Gressette Committee after its leader, state senator L. Marion Gressette), and the legal system as institutionalized forms of massive resistance further illuminates the significance of the courts as a battleground for civil rights. Particularly interesting is the development of White victimization as a judicial strategy, including the use of sociological "evidence" by White lawyers to claim harm to White children to justify the modifications and delays in implementation of court civil rights decisions. Their willingness to use such approaches to legitimize their arguments in an effort to refute the sociological evidence presented in the *Briggs* case signifies an important legal shift toward developing new arguments favoring segregation based on racial differences rather than relying on *Plessy* as precedent.

In the following pages, my objective is to trace the major threads of where and how the law and the struggle for equality intersected in South Carolina. While the book is not biographical in nature, it does introduce several significant individuals, such as plaintiff-activists Gloria Rackley, Arthur Brown, and John Wrighten and Gressette Committee attorney David Robinson, whose contributions to the legal history of civil rights on both sides of the struggle in South Carolina reveal the conflict regarding race, rights, and the law at a personal level. Chapter 1 covers early court challenges to the White primary in South Carolina. A federal prosecution for denial of voting rights in 1942 gave hope to Black South Carolinians but suffered due to an unpredictable witness. The White primary cases in South Carolina that followed the Supreme Court ruling in the Texas case *Smith v. Allwright* (1944) illustrate a recurring theme of the book: the recalcitrance of White officials. who diligently and successfully used litigation to avoid the implementation of Supreme Court decisions and thus to delay progress toward full citizenship for the state's African American population. Two voting rights cases, *Elmore v. Rice* and *Brown v. Baskin,* illustrate both the determination of Black South Carolinians to assert their rights and the determination of White South Carolinians to maintain their hold on political power. In response to *Smith v. Allwright,* South Carolina passed emergency legislation to make the Democratic Party a private club beyond the reach of the law. Black South Carolinians challenged these moves successfully.

Early efforts to establish equality in the field of education were focused on the rights of teachers rather than students. The second chapter addresses Black teachers' lawsuits to gain equal salaries in the 1940s, then segues to the arena of higher education, specifically the case, *Wrighten v. Board of Trustees,* that led to the establishment of a law school at South Carolina State College (now University).[8] Federal judge J. Waties Waring decided the salary case in favor of the teachers but left the door open to merit pay, which also left open the possibility of White duplicity. The establishment of the law school at the only publicly funded college for the state's Black population was also a limited victory. John Wrighten had sued to gain admission to the University of South Carolina's law school, but in keeping with Supreme Court decisions, the state was required only to maintain an equal, though still separate, institution. The law school established at South Carolina State was far from equal to the law school at the University of South Carolina, but it graduated some of the most successful civil rights lawyers in the state, including future federal judge Matthew Perry and future chief justice of the South Carolina Supreme Court Ernest J. Finney.

Chapter 3 recaps the *Briggs v. Elliott* case of the late 1940s and early 1950s but focuses on the reaction of White officials following the filing of the *Briggs* case and the decisions in *Briggs* and *Brown v. Board* a few years later. The establishment of the Gressette Committee was pivotal in the resistance to desegregation by the state's officials. Under Gressette, and more importantly the committee's lead attorney, David W. Robinson Sr., the committee assisted school districts' legal defenses against desegregation suits through the early 1960s by providing research, legal expertise, and trial assistance. Extralegal resistance, such as the establishment of citizens' councils, is also covered in the chapter.

The victory in *Brown v. Board of Education* encouraged African Americans in South Carolina to file several lawsuits seeking to break down barriers to civil equality in areas beyond education. If *Plessy*, a case about segregation in public transportation, was applicable to education, then *Brown*, a case focusing on the field of education, must similarly be applicable outside that field. Chapter 4 explores public accommodations cases starting with Sarah Mae Flemming's lawsuit to desegregate the bus system in Columbia in July 1954, followed by lawsuits filed by other Black citizens to desegregate the Edisto Beach State Park in 1955. White officials, meanwhile, continued their obstruction by closing the park and by passing a resolution asking the US attorney general to place the NAACP on the list of subversive organizations. In 1956 the governor appointed a commission to investigate the group.[9] Several Black faculty members at South Carolina State were not renewed, and several teachers in Orangeburg County, the "Elloree 21," were fired when they refused to sign a statement regarding their membership—or nonmembership—in the NAACP. Meanwhile numerous anti-desegregation bills were passed by the state legislature, and conflicts emerged as segregation policies began to fracture.

School desegregation returns to the forefront in chapter 5. Despite *Brown I* and likely a result of latitude in the *Brown II* ruling, the state made no meaningful effort to move with "deliberate speed" toward desegregation. However, other cases from the late 1950s and early 1960s are considered as well. In *Henry v. Greenville Airport Commission*, the state's federal district courts delved into the issue of interstate travel. Segregationist judge George Bell Timmerman Sr. used one of the classic counterarguments against desegregation when he stated, "the right to equality before the law, to be free from discrimination, invests no one with authority to require others to accept him as a companion or social equal."[10] Other public accommodations cases arose, including cases to desegregate the state's other parks. The bulk of the chapter deals with desegregation in both public k–12 and higher education. As state officials had managed to forestall desegregation, new cases were filed by Black parents in Charleston, Clarendon, Greenville, and Orangeburg Counties to accelerate deliberate speed. After a protracted legal struggle, Harvey Gantt became the first Black student to desegregate public higher education when he entered Clemson University in 1963. The chapter examines the reaction among White students and others to his matriculation. The chapter closes by examining the conventional wisdom that 1963 was a pivotal year in South Carolina's civil rights history. While that argument has merit, I conclude that events over the rest of the decade indicate that while some officials at the highest levels of state politics may have recognized the inevitability of desegregation, they were in no hurry to change, and legal and other resistance continued.

Chapter 6 includes the stories of Irene Williams and Gloria Rackley, teachers in Sumter and Orangeburg Counties, respectively, who were fired for their involvement in civil rights activism. Rackley was effectively driven out of South Carolina, despite ultimately winning her case against Orangeburg schools. The passage of the Civil Rights Act of 1964 and the reaction of White South Carolinians are also central themes in this chapter. Charleston's Roper Hospital managed to maintain segregation well beyond the passage of the Civil Rights Act. Barbecue baron Maurice Bessinger's attempt to assert his (supposed) First Amendment rights to refuse sit-down service to Black South Carolinians represents one of the last efforts of this era by ordinary White citizens to use the courts to contravene federal law.

Chapter 7 addresses the long and problematic transition from piecemeal desegregation to something akin to integration resulting from legal cases that went on for years. South Carolina, like other states, initiated freedom of choice plans as an attempt to delay desegregation. While nearly all of the state's school districts were nominally desegregated by the fall of 1965, most of them had only a token few Black students—usually limited to the named plaintiffs—attending school with their White peers. Pressure on White school districts moved from the courts to the federal Department of Justice and Department of Education. White parents continued to make clear their objections by enrolling their children in segregation academies that were established across the state as a response to desegregation or, in many cases, merely potential desegregation, particularly in the majority-Black region that recently earned the designation as the state's "corridor of shame." The main narrative ends with the mandate, in the fall of 1970, of desegregation of the state's schools resulting from the ruling in *Green v. New Kent County*, a recognition that the state must, in the words of then-governor Robert McNair, "adjust to new circumstances."[11] That adjustment did not come easily. In 1970 a crowd of nearly two hundred White people attacked a bus full of Black students following a boycott of schools by White students.

The legal and social issues arising from decades of inequality and frequent violence were not resolved suddenly in 1970, as the Lamar Riot demonstrates. The brief final chapter follows legal cases in South Carolina since 1970, including the state supreme court's 1999 ruling in *Abbeville County School District v. South Carolina* interpreting the state constitution's "minimally adequate" standard for education in favor of a group of poor, predominantly African

American districts in the corridor of shame. These events demonstrate that the resistance to a new birth of freedom and equality for all born in the post–Civil War era has continued into the present. It also demonstrates that White supremacy, which informed the infrastructure of South Carolina's history since the colonial era, continues to make meaningful change challenging.

1

"THIS COULDN'T HAVE BEEN IGNORANCE"

Challenging the White Primary in the 1940s

In April 1932 a group of relatively well-to-do African American residents of Columbia, South Carolina, including J. G. Stewart, former head of the NAACP in the city, current president R. W. Mance, and E. A. Adams, a future president of that organization, challenged the White primary there by suing the city board of elections in the Court of Common Pleas. Acting through an 1890 law, the city's all-White Democratic executive committee had met in February and decided to allow only those Black citizens who were "known to have voted the Democratic ticket continuously since 1876" (fifty-six years earlier) to vote in the primary.[1] The request for an injunction was denied, and the subsequent appeal to the federal court was dismissed for being filed too late. Their attorney, Nathaniel J. Frederick, had been in practice since 1914. In 1926 he was instrumental in reviving the Columbia NAACP branch, and in 1932 he was appointed to the NAACP's National Legal Committee, which also included Charles Hamilton Houston. Frederick considered building a case to attack the state's Democratic primary, but he delayed acting because he reasonably—and as events in the early 1940s demonstrate, rightly—expected that the state legislature would repeal all the laws relating to the primary should there be a challenge.[2] Though nothing came of the effort, it nevertheless laid a foundation for action in the future. By 1936 African Americans were starting to vote in significant, if not substantial, numbers particularly in urban areas. Within a couple of years, there were about one thousand Black voters in both Columbia and Charleston. The one-dollar poll tax was no longer the impediment that it once had been. Franklin Roosevelt was also an important draw for Black voters, who wanted to vote for him.[3] The role of middle-class Black people at this stage of the movement was key: while working-class Black people were essential to the success of the legal battles that would come, the foundation was laid by the growing political awareness and relative economic independence of the Black middle class. While this may have set the stage for internecine conflict in the

1960s, the focus on the needs of middle-class Black South Carolinians was an important early stage in the growth of the civil rights movement in South Carolina. It signaled the resurrection of Black demands for their rights as citizens.

In July 1939 "unusual numbers" of African Americans began registering to vote in Greenville, South Carolina, perhaps because the mayor and city council refused to implement a program to clear out slums and build low-cost housing, which had been an item of contention for much of the year, as several Greenville businessmen opposed taking an $800,000 federal grant for building government housing.[4] The unusual numbers of registrations by Black voters in Greenville coincided with the establishment of the South Carolina Conference of the NAACP. Over the years leadership in the state chapter was tantamount to leadership of the civil rights movement in South Carolina, where organizations supporting Black rights were few and largely urban. Prominent Black leaders emerged from the NAACP and helped to propel the movement forward when it looked likely to fail. Representatives from chapters in Cheraw, Columbia, Charleston, Florence, Georgetown, Greenville, and Sumter established the state office on November 10, 1939, with Samuel J. McDonald, from Sumter, as the first chair and Reverend Alonzo W. Wright serving as the first president.[5]

Also in July 1939, and not coincidentally, advertisements calling for Klan meetings appeared in the *Greenville News,* and local Ku Klux Klan leader Fred V. Johnson promised that "White Supremacy would be maintained in South Carolina."[6] Johnson went to the registration office and demanded to see the books. As it was during regular business hours, he was refused; he later did get access, most likely from a sympathetic employee or perhaps the registrar himself. US Attorney Oscar H. Doyle, who was from Greenville, refused to prosecute Johnson for interfering with the voter registration efforts, however, as there was no hard evidence that anyone was conspiring with Johnson to deprive anyone of their rights.[7] Hard evidence notwithstanding, it is clear that Johnson colluded with at least one member of the registration board. Klan access to voter rolls fits the pattern of intimidation common throughout the South.[8] In September and October 1939, Johnson's Klan rampaged through Greenville County, intimidating and beating several Black citizens, with no consequences for the hooded villains.[9]

It became clear to Thurgood Marshall and others at the NAACP Legal Defense and Education Fund (LDF) in the early 1940s that federal prosecution of voting rights cases would be half-hearted at best, and thus, perhaps, the LDF was moved to take matters into its own hands. LDF lawyers saw the issue of denial of access to the ballot as a problem of law that the federal courts should handle using legal precedents and federal authority over the states. It was a time-consuming and laborious enterprise often with intangible rewards, but it was beginning to show results.

On hearing of Klansman Johnson's accessing the Greenville voter rolls, Marshall complained to the Civil Liberties Unit of the Justice Department. Assistant Attorney General John Rogge responded that there was nothing the department could do, because Johnson's actions concerned voting in the primary election rather than the general election. NAACP executive director Walter White followed up with a letter to Rogge asserting that there was indeed a federal legal question involved. Rogge had relied on *Newberry v. United States* to justify the department's inaction in Greenville, but White argued that because only one member of the sharply divided *Newberry* Court—Justice James Clark McReynolds—remained on the Supreme Court, the law was ripe for another review.[10]

In October, Marshall wrote Rogge again. Klan activity was ramping up in Greenville, and Marshall was convinced that the Klan would do all it could to prevent African Americans from voting in 1940. Rogge asserted that the "Department of Justice stands ready, *within the limits of its jurisdiction,* to protect the rights of all persons guaranteed and secured by the Constitution. . . . However, the vigilante acts to which [Marshall] referred indicates no violation of a Federal statute to permit the intervention of this Department. Such lawlessness and vandalism are matters of local police duty and should, therefore, be addressed to such authorities."[11] This attitude by federal authorities was typical. Rogge, like others before and after him, avoided federal intervention for fear of antagonizing local authorities and the congressmen and senators who represented them. On lynching, the Justice Department issued a memorandum that could have applied equally to any violation of civil rights in the South, stating that prosecutions "may arouse antagonism on States' rights grounds."[12] The Department relied on the meaningless fiction that local law enforcement officials were enforcers of the law, not merely products of their society.

Except for the Ku Klux Klan, most White South Carolinians did not get involved in the matter of Black voting in the early 1940s. Most efforts at voter registration were easily thwarted, and prosecutions for violating voter rights were pursued only half-heartedly, if at all. The Democratic Party was the only viable political party in the state, and its membership was largely committed to maintaining White supremacy—a task made easier since White people were now a majority of the population. In years past, Johnson's demand to see voter rolls would have been openly and quickly granted. Cross burnings or worse would follow. The late 1930s and early 1940s, as African Americans began to move toward the Democratic Party, led to a shift from extralegal means to institutional ones in the tactics necessary to exclude Black citizens from voting. Instead of violence and fraud, public officials would be encouraged to use their discretion in how they addressed issues of voter eligibility.[13]

The federal criminal trial of White election officials in Gaffney, a textile town in Cherokee County, illustrates the determination of some Black South Carolinians to register and vote and the equal determination of many White citizens to prevent both. When the registration season for 1940 opened, some African Americans in Gaffney attempted to register. "When our turn came to be registered, a part of the board flatly refused to register us because 'Darkies have never registered in South Carolina and especially in Cherokee County.'" Even the county attorney could not persuade the registration board to register the Black citizens of Gaffney. They returned the next day, only to have the door slammed in their faces. On August 25 schoolteacher Lottie Gaffney requested that the NAACP refer the matter to the federal government and to "do whatever in your power to make it safe for us to register" by early September 1940, the registration period for the general election.[14]

The NAACP referred the matter to the Justice Department, asking that the attorney general's office investigate and take action to see that African Americans in the town could register in early September. By September 7 the Attorney General's office had contacted Roy Wilkins, at that time the editor of the NAACP's *Crisis,* to ask whether Lottie Gaffney and the other Black citizens of Gaffney had been permitted to register. They had not. Lottie Gaffney recalled what happened in an affidavit that she and Bernice Bonner submitted on October 8:

> The three members of the Board questioned us as to the reasons for our wanting to vote. They said that we wanted to stir up trouble for them and ourselves. One member said that some God damned son of a bitch Republican put us up to want to vote. If the board would register us it would be dangerous for us—that our houses would be burned; that our heads would be scalped, etc. That if they would register us their heads would be cut of [sic] before night. If we registered it would do no good.

The board members then left the room, even though several White people were waiting to register. The janitor came in and ordered everyone out of the room at 3:00 that afternoon. By 4:30 the board members had returned along with several White people, all of whom were let into the registration room by the janitor. He blocked the entrance to Lottie Gaffney and the others, who were prevented from registering.[15] Although White authorities had succeeded in preventing Black citizens from voting in 1940, US Attorney Doyle continued to work on the case. The 1941 Supreme Court decision in *United States v. Classic* opened the door for federal regulation of primary elections, as primaries were the gateway to final federal elections.[16]

Finally, in early 1942, Doyle believed he had enough evidence to go to trial. In February the Department of Justice prosecuted the members of Cherokee County's Voter Registration Board—F. E. Ellis, John E. Wright, and T. E. Meetze —for criminally conspiring to deprive Lottie Gaffney and three other women of their right to vote. After a short trial, Ellis and the others were acquitted. Accounts of two participants in the aftermath of the trial reveal the problems that the Justice Department had to contend with. The result was obviously un-satisfactory to Lottie Gaffney and the NAACP. She asked Thurgood Marshall about an appeal, even offering to begin "quietly setting up a committee" to supply needed funds for the struggle. Marshall informed her that since this was a criminal action resulting in acquittal, nothing more could be done other than to "lay the groundwork for a civil suit for damages" by having people attempt to register to vote. Upon refusal a civil suit could be filed. Marshall added: "The reason we did not bring an action for damages on the first case was because we had every reason to believe that criminal prosecution would be successful."[17]

The White primary had yet to be ruled unconstitutional, but since the Gaffney case dealt with registration for the general election (unlike the situa-tion in Greenville, where the primary election was at issue), Marshall was con-vinced that Ellis and the other commission members would be found guilty. He had been, he wrote Lottie Gaffney, "repeatedly assured of the whole-hearted support of the local U.S. attorney."[18] Support of the US Attorney's office, however, did not result in convictions of Ellis and the others. Why Marshall, Doyle, or anyone else involved in the case might have expected a conviction is a mystery. An injustice perpetrated against Black citizens by White citizens, with a White male jury sitting in judgment, would not be remedied in this southern town. Marshall and his associates should have expected the result they got.

Lottie Gaffney wrote the national NAACP offices again in June 1942, com-municating that she had lost her job as a result of her participation as a wit-ness for the government in the case—something that would become common for Black plaintiffs. Citing a "frame up" and an "underworld ring" as being responsible for her firing, she outlined how one of the school board trustees admitted that her participation in the case was "the only reason" for her fir-ing.[19] The NAACP referred the matter to the Justice Department, which in turn contacted Oscar Doyle, who had prosecuted the case. Doyle replied that in his opinion Lottie Gaffney was responsible for the acquittals because of her demeanor on the stand and in court. A. B. Caldwell, who had assisted Doyle, concurred with Doyle's assessment of Lottie Gaffney's value as a witness.

Caldwell believed that other teachers who had been involved in the case had been renewed in their annual contracts. Interestingly both Doyle and Caldwell cited Lottie Gaffney's activities as an "agitator in the community" as reasons for wanting her severed from the case from the beginning. Doyle told his supervisor he never wanted to go into court with her again.[20] Lottie Gaffney's reputation among White people may have had as much to do with her firing as anything, and her participation in the case was probably the final straw for the school board. Other participants in the case were not nearly as vocal before, during, and following the trial and were probably more willing to accept the outcome than Lottie Gaffney. For his part Marshall worked with local lawyers Cassandra Maxwell and Harold Boulware to get some relief for Gaffney. Lottie Gaffney went on to be instrumental in the development and organization of the Progressive Democratic Party, founded in 1944.[21]

A few months after the *Ellis* trial, a group of African Americans in Columbia, including NAACP leader James M. Hinton and lawyer Lincoln Jenkins, enrolled successfully in the Democratic Party only to be purged quickly thereafter. As a result they were unable to vote in the primary held on July 25. Under the party's "rule six," voters had to be White to vote in the primary. Clay Rice was among a group of four members of a purging committee for the Richland County Democratic Party. The purging committee ostensibly was responsible for making sure that only people living in a given precinct voted there and for removing the names of people who had been entered "erroneously."[22]

Charles Henry Brown, one of the men whose names had been purged, worried that Benedict College, one of the state's private colleges for African Americans, where he worked, would suffer the loss of "certain funds" if he were to testify in any criminal case. He asked that he not be called as a witness if the case went to federal court. As it turned out, however, Brown's worries were baseless: Claud Sapp, the US attorney for the Eastern District, decided after reviewing the case that there were insufficient grounds for prosecution. Assistant Attorney General Wendell Berge had written Sapp in October 1942, after Hinton and Jenkins wrote to request an investigation. African Americans in four other counties also filed affidavits with the Attorney General's office, and Berge responded by preparing an indictment, which he sent to Sapp. Sapp told Berge that the state legislature or the Democratic Party would soon be "substantially remedying the disenfranchisement of Negroes resulting from the 'white primary' rule," and Berge deferred action. When the state legislature repealed a number of laws relating to primary elections, the Department of Justice made the decision not to prosecute the members of the purging committee.[23] The illusion that local governments were moving toward compliance with federal laws and constitutional standards (when they were merely removing legal control) persuaded the Justice Department to delay action that could have shown White southern officials that the federal government took voting rights seriously. The move also may have been intended to buy time as states across the South waited for the Supreme Court's decision in *Smith v. Allwright*. The failure to prosecute election officials did have one tangible result: Marshall and the LDF would no longer depend on federal criminal prosecution to win rights for Black citizens. If justice were to come, it would be won by the LDF and cooperating attorneys in the civil courts.

Marshall's instincts proved correct. He argued against the Texas White primary before the US Supreme Court, and in 1944 the Court decided *Smith v. Allwright*, which killed the all-White primary, though it was a lingering death. Texas election officials were legally required to refuse ballots to people who did not qualify to vote under Democratic convention rules. In addition the state excluded anyone who had lost in the primary from running in the general election. The Supreme Court ruled that the primary was therefore an integral part of the election and that any restrictions on Black voting during the primary violated the Fifteenth Amendment. The NAACP and their plaintiffs thought the case was a clear victory. Marshall wrote that "once and for all the question of the right of Negroes to participate in primary elections similar to those in Texas" was settled.[24] South Carolina quickly disabused Marshall of the notion that White southerners respected the rule of law. For nearly three-quarters of a century, White people had honed their skills at disfranchising potential Black voters, and the governor and legislature moved quickly to rescue the state's White primary from constitutional oblivion.

Within a few days of the Supreme Court's decision, South Carolina governor Olin D. Johnston, who was then running for the US Senate, called the state legislature into special session for the purpose of removing state control over the Democratic primaries. It was, he said, "absolutely necessary that we repeal all laws pertaining to primaries in order to *maintain white supremacy* in our Democratic primaries in South Carolina. . . . I know that the white Democrats in South Carolina will rally behind you in this matter . . . especially when the protection and the preservation of morals and decency in government is [*sic*] involved." Johnston, not surprisingly, invoked the myth of Black Republican rule during Reconstruction, asking his listeners to recall the dark days of Republican control:

> The records will bear me out that [the] fraud, corruption, immorality, and graft existing during that regime . . . has [*sic*] never been paralleled in the history of our State. They left a stench in the nostrils of the people of South Carolina that will exist for generations to come. The representatives

of these agitators, scalawags and unscrupulous politicians that called themselves white men and used the colored race to further their own course are in our midst today, and history will repeat itself unless we protect ourselves against this new crop of carpetbaggers and scalawags, who would use the colored race to further their own economic and political gain. . . . History has taught us that we must keep our white Democratic primaries pure and unadulterated so that we might protect the welfare and homes of all the people of our state.

Echoing Klan leader Fred Johnson's 1939 pledge, Governor Johnston concluded with a challenge: "White supremacy will be maintained in our primaries. Let the chips fall where they may!"[25] Johnston's speech also recalled Ben Tillman, who said in 1900 that southerners "never believed [the Black man] to be equal to the white man, and [southerners] will not submit to his gratifying his lust on our wives and daughters without lynching him."[26] Nearly fifty years later, Tillman's racist ideology equating the desire for equal citizenship with rape and miscegenation maintained its malevolent influence over most of South Carolina's White population. Johnston's desire to "keep our white Democratic primaries pure and *unadulterated*" parallels Tillman's desire to maintain the purity of White womanhood in a culture where lynching was still accepted as a form of justice.[27]

By using similar language in equating the White primary to the virginal White daughters of South Carolina, Johnston played to the fears and sense of grievance that permeated White southern culture, especially among the working class. Johnston's rhetoric created a heightened sense of urgency within the Democratic legislature, which repealed 150 state laws pertaining to primary elections in less than a week. Included in this fest of legislative action was an act to put repeal of the section of the state constitution mentioning primary elections to a popular vote. The Democratic Party was reimagined as a private club that could control its own membership.[28]

The 1944 primary took place without any major incidents, perhaps due to the recent founding of the Progressive Democratic Party earlier that year, but in August 1946, George Elmore, a businessman and photographer born in Holly Hill and living in Columbia, tried to vote in the Democratic primary. He and several other African Americans requested ballots and were refused, allegedly because of instructions issued by John I. Rice, the chairman of the Richland County Democratic Party and son of Clay Rice, who had served on the Richland County party's purging committee three years earlier.[29]

Elmore turned to the NAACP for assistance, and Columbia attorney Harold Boulware started working on the case, soon joined by Thurgood Marshall and the LDF Boulware, a Howard University Law School graduate and one of few African American attorneys practicing in the state, and Marshall filed suit against Rice and fifty-one other members of the Richland County Democratic Executive Committee and the eight election managers of Elmore's precinct. Marshall, Robert Carter, and a seminar of Columbia University Law School students prepared a brief that followed the Supreme Court's argument in *United States v. Classic,* arguing that primaries, as an integral part of the election machinery, could be regulated. After preparing his brief, Marshall wrote to Fred Folsom, who wrote the memorandum leading to the creation of the Department of Justice's Civil Rights Section and was serving as the assistant chief of the unit. Folsom agreed with Marshall: "If you can establish that the South Carolina primary is, in fact, the election," wrote Folsom, "then by force of the *Classic* opinion, the Federally-secured right to vote for Federal officers attaches to that primary."[30] It was clear to any observer that this was the case. The winners of the Democratic primary had consistently won in the general election since 1875. Since 1880, and especially after adoption of the new state constitution in 1895, the South Carolina popular vote for president was overwhelmingly Democratic. Even greater differences could be found in congressional, senatorial, and gubernatorial elections over the same period. In 1946, 290,223 votes were cast in the first primary election for governor, and 253,589 were cast in the second primary. Only 26,326 votes were cast in the general election. Marshall and Boulware argued that since the general election was so lopsidedly Democratic, the primary election was essentially the only one in which a meaningful vote could be cast. The Democratic Party historically had also produced the ballots for the general election, constituting an essential state function that was subject to regulation.[31]

The complaint also challenged the governor's and legislature's attempts "to evade and circumvent the decision of the Supreme Court."[32] Flouting the Court's decision reveals the extent to which White South Carolinians were willing to retain white supremacy. This challenge to the rule of law indicates a mindset among many southern politicians and their supporters that White supremacy was more important than what the Supreme Court ruled—when they disagreed. The White southern interpretation of the Constitution had not evolved since *Dred Scott:* African Americans had no rights that White men were obliged to recognize. This ideology—reiterated by the Court in *Plessy*—remained integral to the view that the United States was a White man's country.[33]

The defendants predictably responded by arguing that the Democratic primary was outside the boundaries of state law. The Democratic Party was "a private voluntary association of individuals, mutually acceptable to each other," and nothing more. They denied the significance of the Democratic primary in deciding the eventual election and even avoided using the word *election* when referring to the primary. The eight defendants from the precinct committee were managers of the primary, not, as the *Elmore* complaint called them, "election managers." This semantic difference was intended simply to avoid any association of the defendants with an election that would indicate official responsibility in light of *Smith v. Allwright*. The defense also rejected Elmore's claim to status as a qualified elector. He "was not qualified according to the rules of the Party and was not a White Democrat and not duly enrolled." Other denials followed: qualifications for electors laid out in the state constitution did not apply to the primaries but only to the general election; the Democratic primary did not "control the choice" of eventual officeholders; *Smith v. Allwright* was not applicable to the case, because the primary was essentially different since that decision; and the plaintiffs could just as easily organize their own political party, equally free from state statutory regulation.[34] These denials had essentially been dealt with in *Smith*, but repeating them in the *Elmore* response speaks to a pattern that South Carolina's defenders of state's rights continued for most of the civil rights years.

There were of course no differences between the old state-sanctioned party and the new "private club." At the trial, though, the defense tried to emphasize the minimal technical differences between the pre- and post-*Smith* Democratic Party, arguing that those small differences were significant changes. The 1942 party rules required voters to "support the nominees of such party, state and national." The new rules for 1944 dropped only the reference to the "state and national" electoral level while still requiring voter support. The mechanism for selecting officers, committeemen, and delegates remained unchanged. The party renamed itself the Democratic Party of South Carolina and, using the 1942 rules as a template, wrote a new set of rules to incorporate the new reality. The new rules allowed for voting machines, changed municipal election guidelines, and changed the procedures for absentee balloting. The 1946 rules were substantially unchanged from those of 1944, except that they provided for eighteen-year-olds to vote in the primary. Under the old statutes, penalties for perjury and fraud concerning elections were severe, but because the party was no longer part of the state, the only consequence one could face was expulsion from the party. The new rules required an additional oath from national congressional candidates, requiring them to "support the political principles and policies of the Democratic party of South Carolina" during their time in office.[35] The "political principles and policies" that the candidate would be upholding included White supremacy and segregation. This new loyalty oath was not merely a requirement for potential national officeholders. It was also a jab at national Democratic Party trends that culminated in the adoption of a civil

Judge J. Waties Waring (Courtesy
of South Caroliniana Library,
University of South Carolina)

rights plank in 1948, at the Supreme Court, and at African Americans in South
Carolina. The state party was making it clear that their intent was to maintain
White supremacy in their party and in South Carolina politics.

In July 1947 Judge J. Waties Waring found that, despite allowing voting
machines and lowering the voting age to eighteen, very little had changed since
1944 in the conduct of elections.[36] The most important thing that the party did
not change in 1944 or 1946 was the requirement that party members must be
White.

"It is true," wrote Waring, "that the General Assembly . . . repealed all laws
relating to and governing primaries, and the Democratic Party in this State is
not under statutory control, but to say that there is any material difference in
the governance of the Democratic Party . . . is pure sophistry." The party organization, from club meetings to the preparation of ballots, was the same in
1946 as it had been before the legislature removed all those laws in 1944. Governor Johnston had made no attempt in 1944 to conceal the reason for erasing the
primary election from the statute books of the state, and Waring saw no reason
to pretend that there was any reason under the law, other than the exclusion
of Black South Carolinians, to defend the actions of the legislature. "It is time
for [the United States] to take stock of our internal affairs," he wrote, echoing
those who agreed that the United States, as leader of the free world, must live
up to its historical and constitutional ideals. "It is time for South Carolina to
rejoin the Union. It is time to fall in step with the other states and to adopt the
American way of conducting elections."[37]

Judge Waring was in his own right a key figure in the civil rights movement in South Carolina. Descended from the earliest Charlestonians, Waring became an advocate for Black rights following his second marriage, to a twice-divorced northerner named Elizabeth Avery Mills Hoffman.[38] Waring's ruling was a shock to the operation of the federal district courts of South Carolina. However, his fellow judge, and vehement segregationist, George Bell Timmerman was not, however, willing to rejoin the Union. In late August he issued a temporary stay of Waring's order, and the state Democratic Party filed an appeal in October. The White Democrats focused on three arguments: first, the *Smith* and *Classic* precedents depended on statutory rather than private regulation of political primaries; second, no state action was involved in the *Elmore* case; and third, the party was a private organization. Waring had "misread" the precedents and "seem[ed] to have been influenced by a speech made by President Truman," because he quoted the speech in his opinion. The White Democrats argued that the principle of allowing "several hundred thousand" African Americans to vote in the White primary was equivalent to giving people the right to go into each other's homes and express political opinions, even if the homeowner were not willing to listen.[39] This argument, ridiculous as it may sound, illustrates the tortured logic that White officials put forth in an effort to achieve their constitutionally suspect ends. The party was willing to use any argument, no matter how weak or specious, to support the contention that the primary was not really an election and certainly was not *the* election. This was done to preserve their inherited belief that Black South Carolinians were not part of the body politic.

When George Elmore focused solely on discrimination against himself and other people of color, White Democrats "earnestly submitted" that his case threatened their own rights. The response in the *Elmore* case reveals White people's belief that it was their own rights that needed protection. Analogizing the party apparatus to a private home was an example of this, as was the reliance on the First Amendment's assertion of free association. Since the party was a private organization, its members' right to associate was being sacrificed by the Supreme Court—and by Judge Waring more immediately—in order to grant rights to African Americans to which they had no legitimate claim.[40] The right of free association was as important, if not more so, than Elmore's right to impose himself on a group of voters with different political and social views in the name of political equality. Under their *"theory of government, appellants have a perfect right to organize their political party and limit the members thereof to white persons who sympathize with their political views. . . . How can the appellee be accorded the right to vote in such a primary without destroying the basic rights of the members of such party to freedom* of political action, freedom of thought, freedom of speech and freedom of assembly?"[41] The constitutional doctrine under which the White Democrats were operating favored the status quo. Anyone seeking to change the political paradigm would have to organize a new political party (a right the White Democrats were quick to concede to African Americans).

Elmore v. Rice highlighted these discordant views of the Constitution. White South Carolina Democrats adjusted the late eighteenth-century theory of the union as a voluntary confederation of states as a justification to resist externally mandated policies designed to guarantee individual rights. However, during the legal crisis surrounding the Fugitive Slave Act in the 1850s, *Dred Scott*, the *Civil Rights Cases,* and *Plessy v. Ferguson,* all of which upheld a subordinate position for persons of African descent, South Carolina constitutional theorists took the view that a Supreme Court ruling establishing a national standard was a good one.[42] Elmore's legal team countered that the "Constitution is a living instrument. The rights protected have never been fully enumerated. . . . This deliberate effort to circumvent the decisions of the United States Supreme Court is another challenge to our ability as a nation to protect the rights of all of our citizens in practice rather than in theory."[43] It came down to a view of whose rights the Constitution protected. African Americans believed that all Americans were entitled to the same rights, while South Carolina's White Democrats believed their own rights were paramount.

When the court of appeals confirmed Waring's decision in the *Elmore* case in December 1947, it seemed like "the lid [was] nailed down on the coffin of the white primary."[44] South Carolina's Democratic leaders had other plans. Since the party remained a private club, the 1948 party convention decided to allow African Americans only "qualified participation in the primary." In addition to requiring potential Black voters, but not White voters, to present their general election voting certificates, the convention required voters to swear an oath that they "believe[d] in and will support the social and educational separation of races" and "the principles of States' Rights," as well as their opposition to the Fair Employment Practices Commission law.[45] This new oath, they hoped, would not only reinforce the ideals of the party but also deter Black citizens from even trying to vote in the primary.

Harold Boulware reported "a continuation of, but with more efficiency of a hitherto established policy of holding to a bare minimum the number of qualified electors among Negro citizens." There were problems in every part of the state. Boulware accused officials in the Lowcountry counties of Berkeley and Dorchester of breaking state law by writing certificates for White party members from the roll books while potential Black voters were forced to wait in silence. In Marion County a young Black veteran and college graduate was turned down for a certificate for reading too fast, while a teacher with thirteen years' experience was turned down for not reading well enough. In Clarendon County the tax assessor began omitting the poll tax from the property tax bill, which then required a specific effort from people to pay the tax. The audit books mysteriously disappeared when people went to pay their poll taxes, only to reappear after local Black citizens filed a lawsuit. Union County registration board members were somehow unable to meet together on registration day, even though White people were still somehow managing to get their certificates. In Jasper County, where both White people and African Americans were required to have certificates to vote in the primary, the committee managed to run out of certificate forms after "about 25 or 50" African Americans qualified on the first day of registration.[46] These methods of preventing African Americans from voting were not new, of course, but Boulware saw a heightened devotion to such subterfuge in the wake of the *Elmore* case.

While African Americans could vote upon presenting certificates and taking the oath, the new rules technically prevented them from becoming full members of the Democratic Party. Party membership was an important requisite for the exercise of power in the political universe of South Carolina. Membership in the Democratic Party "club" allowed one to vote for local and county party officers, attend the biannual party convention, and otherwise participate in the party machinery. By being denied party membership, African Americans were effectively excluded from everything but the actual election. Even then the existence of the oath made voting in the primary problematic for most African Americans.

In July 1948, a month before the scheduled primary, the NAACP filed a second suit against the state party. The plaintiff, David Brown, was a fifty-six-year-old service station operator from Beaufort County who had always voted for the Democratic candidate (of course there was little choice), but the county party had purged his name from the rolls. *Brown v. Baskin* took on the oath now required from each voter, attacking the conspiracy that White leaders of the Democratic Party entered in order to undermine the constitutional rights of Black voters.[47]

The hearing on the preliminary injunction in *Brown v. Baskin* took place on July 16, 1948, while the Democratic National Convention was being held in Philadelphia. There, southern White Democrats walked out of the proceedings, led by South Carolina governor J. Strom Thurmond. They were protesting the administration of Harry S. Truman, whose integration of the armed forces, sponsorship of the panel that wrote *To Secure These Rights*, and growing vigor in supporting civil rights were anathema to southern White Democrats. Thurmond stated at the time "that there's not enough troops in the army to force the southern people to break down segregation and admit the Negro race into our theaters, into our swimming pools, into our homes, and into our churches."[48]

Brown v. Baskin led to several small-scale defections from the state Democratic Party. Party chairmen from several counties filed motions to be released from the lawsuit on the grounds that, contrary to the rules of the party, African Americans were being enrolled as members in those counties without swearing the oath. Despite the defections of county operatives in Greenville, Pickens, Jasper, and Laurens Counties, the vast majority of county committees remained loyal to the state convention's rules. The general response of most defendants was simply to deny all the allegations on the complaint and to contend that the ruling in *Elmore v. Rice* was being followed. The defense asserted that the requirement that Black voters must present general election certificates to vote in the primary actually put them in "a position of advantage to that occupied by white democratic members." White voters were required to "enroll at particular places and within limited time," had to pass literacy tests, and be able to interpret the Constitution. Baskin's attorneys defended the oath as reflective of the political and social beliefs of most South Carolinians. The Constitution of the United States notwithstanding, South Carolina's leadership, embodied in the Democratic Party, asserted White supremacy as an "established principle of government" for the state.[49]

Soon into the July 16 hearing, Waring dismissed the case against the county chairmen from Greenville, Pickens, and Laurens Counties. Waring was "extremely gratif[ied]" that three counties, at least, had seen fit to follow his earlier orders but "quite ashamed" at the fact that only three of forty-six county governing boards had "sense enough, . . . nerve enough, and . . . patriotism enough to make a true, fair, and just decision." Waring then thanked the attorney for the three counties "on behalf of the government—on behalf of the American people."[50] Waring congratulated the Jasper County committee for abandoning the state party by getting rid of enrollment books altogether but kept them in the case to be sure that the county would be bound by any ruling that might be issued regarding the oath.

On the stand David Brown attested to the purging of his name from the party books in Beaufort prior to the 1948 primary. Brown's alleged membership in the Progressive Democratic Party, which several prominent African Americans in the state had organized in 1944 to enable Black participation in politics, came up early as Marshall tried to defuse that issue. Brown stated that he was not a member of the Progressive Democrats and had never voted for any candidate in the general election other than the nominee of the Democratic Party, but on cross-examination he admitted that he had participated in meetings of the Progressive Democrats, had voted for Osceola McKaine, the Progressive candidate for US Senate in 1944, and had given money to that party. Marshall's redirect examination redeemed Brown, however. Marshall asked if the Democratic Party had ever asked Brown to participate in any of their meetings and whether there was "any other Democratic organization that [he] could participate in other than the Progressive group." When Marshall asked him why he went to enroll as a Democrat, Brown simply responded, "To be able to elect anyone I think is qualified towards running the city."[51]

Marshall's examination of W. P. Baskin recalled his earlier examination of Baskin in the *Elmore* case. He explored the organization and functioning of the state Democratic Party, including the mechanism for the biannual changes in the party rules. No changes in the rules for party membership had been made from 1946 to 1948: African Americans were still not allowed to be members of the party, now organized as clubs at the county level. Baskin admitted that, as chairman of the state executive committee, he had changed some of the rules after the convention, striking out the word *understand* from the oath. Now prospective voters did not have to understand the party's principles in order to support them. Judge Waring and Baskin then argued over whether striking out the word was a substantive change in the oath—if it were, then the executive committee theoretically had the power to change the oath in other ways, such as removing the requirement to support segregation. Baskin consistently denied that removing *understand* meant anything more than a cosmetic change. Of course, belief without understanding was one of the mainstays of the Democratic Party in South Carolina. Waring was skeptical.[52]

Ultimately the matter rested on whether the party was in compliance with the ruling in *Elmore v. Rice,* which entitled African Americans to be enrolled on the party books. Waring questioned Baskin at length regarding his role as chairman of the party in adopting rules for 1948 that directly conflicted with the *Elmore* decision. Despite objections from Baskin's lawyer, Sidney S. Tison, Waring insisted on getting some response from Baskin on the question. Baskin claimed that he was overruled by the convention and then by the committee, and he had "never made a statement . . . that a Negro could not be enrolled, and I have never made a statement he should be purged. I have been requested for statements along that line, but I have never made one."[53] Some African Americans had even been enrolled and not subsequently purged in Baskin's own Lee County.

One important element of the defense held that the Progressive Democratic Party, which held meetings in African American churches and attempted to seat delegates at the national Democratic convention in Philadelphia in 1948 as they had in 1944, was a separate entity from the state Democratic Party. As such its membership could be considered the same kind of private club as the White Democratic Party in the state. Baskin asserted that the two parties were separate entities. In a demonstration of circular reasoning, he argued that Black members of the Progressive Democrats could not have participated in the state's Democratic primary because, being Black, they could not be members of the Democratic Party in South Carolina.[54]

After testimony concluded, Judge Waring asked for an explanation of the mindset existing behind the party rule, only to be disappointed when no one stepped forward to explain it. Waring lectured Tison at length over the apparent attempt by party bosses to "evade the spirit of the opinion [in *Elmore v. Rice*]." Waring complained that the leaders of the party merely followed the order in *Elmore* rather than paying heed to the spirit behind the decision. "I think," he said, "they should have considered themselves bound by the opinion, not as a matter of law but as a matter of common sense, to know what the courts would do in the future."

> The leaders of the party, or a majority of the leaders apparently, choose to follow the order and not look in to [*sic*] the opinion, the rationale or the spirit. This couldn't have been ignorance. If it was ignorance, it was ignorance so crass as to seem unbelievable in a body of several hundred men who are practiced politicians and have been running the Democratic party in this state for many years. . . . It couldn't have been just immature, juvenile smartness, because I couldn't accuse them of that. And, therefore, it must have been deliberate.

Waring granted a preliminary injunction, taking to task the Democratic leadership of the state. He declared that his opinion would "say to the people of South Carolina that the time has come when racial discrimination in political affairs has got to stop. . . . I say thank God for Pickens and Laurens and Greenville and Jasper [Counties], some men that put their feet on the ground and stood up in public and said, 'We are Americans, we are going to obey the law.' Now the rest of the state is going to obey the law." He then made it clear that any violation of his order or the "letter and spirit" of the opinion would be considered contempt of court.[55] Waring commanded the defendants to enroll African Americans as members of the local clubs and prevented them from requiring either the presentation of election certificates or the swearing of any oath other than one requiring the voter to support the primary winners in the general election. Finally, in keeping with the original injunction, Waring ordered the enrollment books to remain open until the end of July 1948.[56]

Still hoping to defeat a permanent injunction, Baskin's lawyers answered the charges later in July. Brown's alleged membership in the Progressive Democratic Party continued to be central to the defense. The Progressives did not support White supremacy, went the South Carolina Democratic Party argument, so they could not be members of the party. The members of the South Carolina Democratic Party had every right to limit membership to "those who are in sympathy with its principles and the purpose of fostering and effectuating them."[57]

The defense tried to force Waring to recuse himself on grounds of favoritism toward the plaintiff. On October 20 defense lawyers filed an affidavit by John Stansfield, one of the defendants, alleging personal bias by the judge on the basis of statements made during the original hearing and a newspaper report of a Waring speech at the Black National Lawyers Guild. At that event Waring had said, "The problem is to change the feeling, the sentiment, the creed, of the great body of white people of the South that a Negro is not an American citizen."[58]

In the October hearing on the recusal, Waring said, "The address [to the Lawyers Guild] was to the effect that I was in favor of enforcing the law. I assume that if I had made a speech that I believed in enforcing the law against murder, I would have to disqualify myself from trying a murder case on this theory. . . . There is nothing to the motion." On November 26 Waring issued his final order in the case, reiterating his earlier preliminary injunction. The party could not require an oath, keep African Americans off the enrollment books, or otherwise maintain different requirements for voting based on race or religion.[59] Waring's decision prompted South Carolina congressman Bryan Dorn, who represented Waring's Charleston district, to call for an investigation into Waring's "conduct in office." It would not be the last time that Waring would face reprisals for his actions. Once the appellate court affirmed the decision in 1949, the White primary came to an official end. Robert McC. Figg, former solicitor for the state's Ninth Circuit and now in private practice, wrote the clerk of the Fourth Circuit Court of Appeals to tell him in June that the state executive committee had met and decided not to appeal the case or request a stay.[60]

The defendants' actions—spurious arguments and long-shot appeals—are emblematic of White South Carolinians' civil rights resistance strategies. Although African Americans began to vote in small numbers in the aftermath of the *Elmore* and *Brown* decisions—in August 1948 about thirty-five thousand African Americans voted in the state primary—their victory was short-lived.[61] In 1950 the state legislature again began regulating primary elections but refused to act to protect Black voters' rights. As a result fraud, physical and economic intimidation, and discrimination in registration continued. In areas of the state that were predominantly Black, African Americans voting remained very limited.[62]

Voting continued to be a dangerous business for African Americans, as Archie Ware was about to discover. Ware was born in 1882 and had lived in Abbeville County all his life. He grew to an imposing 6 feet 4 inches, and by 1948 owned a grocery store and was pastor at four separate African American Baptist churches, one of them since 1913. After Judge Waring opened up the Democratic primary, Ware registered to vote, and on August 10 he voted in the primary election. When he left the polling place, John Black, a candidate for county magistrate, and four other men attacked Ware with knives and a club. Black hit Ware in the head at least twice, hard enough to require stitches. Two nearby police officers did nothing to assist Ware as his assailants continued their attack. In all Ware received an eight-inch scar across the right side of his stomach, a five- to six-inch-long scar on his left thigh, and a stab wound on his back left shoulder. Following the attack, Ware moved to Illinois to live with his sister. He had been beaten just after casting his vote for John Black.[63]

Other African American voters in Abbeville never went to the polls that day. Ware, from his new home in Evanston, Illinois, alleged that they were intimidated, though all who were interviewed denied anything more than "friendly" warnings from White people. Not one of them wished to be a witness if any case ever came to court. Lack of evidence against Black and the other assailants led the FBI to close their case at the end of October 1948. When Assistant US Attorney General Alexander Campbell suggested calling a grand jury to investigate the matter further, Oscar Doyle responded that he doubted whether any further investigation could turn up anything new. Besides, he argued, turning the "good people" of this "most backward section of South Carolina" against the institution of the grand jury would be counterproductive.[64]

The attack on Ware cast a pall over the victory won in Judge Waring's court. Winning the White primary cases in Texas and South Carolina did not pave the way for masses of African Americans to vote in primaries or elections. In addition to the threat of violence, which was never far from the mind of Black southerners, southern states relied on other means of restricting the African American vote, such as the 1890 Mississippi plan, which managed to disfranchise most Black voters and leave most White voters eligible, while ostensibly treating both equally in literacy testing qualifications for voting. While most other southern states refused to abandon legislative control over primaries, they did manage to develop strategies to prevent Black participation. Alabamians by a narrow margin passed the so-called Boswell amendment, which required a literacy test or property qualification for voting. In Georgia the legislature resorted to a plan like South Carolina's, but it failed when Herman Talmadge lost a legal challenge for the governorship to Melvin Thompson, who vetoed the legislation.[65]

After the passage of the 1957 Civil Rights Act, voting rights were no longer a target for NAACP litigation. The cases had been difficult all along, and southern states remained adept at preventing massive influxes of Black voters. The Justice Department could directly involve itself in the protection of voting rights by suing to prevent the misuse of registration laws or investigating voting practices. The act also established a Commission on Civil Rights empowered to investigate and publicize violations of civil rights. However, only about 60,000 Black voters registered throughout the South prior to the 1958 election. Numbers more than doubled between 1958 and 1964; in 1960 Black voters helped John F. Kennedy carry South Carolina, and in 1966, the year following the passage of the Voting Rights Act of 1965, they helped to elect Ernest F. Hollings to the US Senate. By 1970 there were 213,000 registered Black voters in South Carolina, but that number was still less than a quarter of the total number of voters in the state.[66] Another consequence was the rise of a Republican Party, with Albert Watson and Strom Thurmond leading disaffected South Carolina Democrats. The majority of White South Carolinians ultimately surrendered the Democratic Party to Black South Carolinians, while the Republican Party has become the dominant political party in the state.

2

NOT EQUAL, BUT STILL SEPARATE

Challenging Jim Crow Education in the 1940s

Control of Black South Carolinians' education was one of many tools that White South Carolinians used to secure White supremacy. In the 1940s Black South Carolinians, assisted by the national NAACP, began to challenge Jim Crow education. Thurgood Marshall, who became chief counsel of the NAACP Legal Defense and Education Fund (LDF) in 1940, continued Charles Hamilton Houston's conservative strategy designed to bring about equity within the segregated system. Equitable segregation as a tactical response to the larger problem of Jim Crow ran the risk of strengthening the system that the NAACP was attempting to destroy. Given the backwardness of the southern state economies, it could, however, lead White citizens to abandon segregation when it simply became too expensive, which is what the NAACP hoped would happen. Had White South Carolinians done in the 1940s what they tried to accomplish in the early 1950s—taxing their way into an environment in which resources were closer to equal but still segregated—segregation might have lasted longer. By the 1950s it was too late for such an attempt to succeed, but in the early 1940s the White power structure in South Carolina was still intent on maintaining an unequal segregated system.[1]

Unable to find plaintiffs, the LDF deliberately avoided elementary and secondary education equalization in the 1930s and early 1940s. Two areas of segregated education, salary equity for Black public-school teachers and in-state access to postbaccalaureate education for Black southerners, became the focus of the LDF's litigation. The large number of potential clients for salary equalization appealed to the LDF lawyers, and similar cases had enjoyed some success, at least at first. Black teachers throughout the South were grossly underpaid compared to their White counterparts. Estimates in 1941 called for $26 million per year to equalize salaries in the region, plus an additional $9 million to reduce class size to bring teacher–student ratios in line with those of White schools. Black teachers in North Carolina had attempted to bring a case back in 1933, but divisions in the Black community weakened support, and the case went nowhere. Ultimately North Carolina began to equalize salaries without having to deal with lawsuits in 1939. In Maryland the legal recourse was more successful. The state began equalization efforts in July 1937 following the settlement of a case filed in October 1936. Not all was well in Maryland, however, as cases in Prince Georges and Anne Arundel Counties dragged on. Ultimately the Anne Arundel case provided Marshall and the NAACP the precedent they needed to carry the salary cases to other states. Richland County, South Carolina, in fact, adopted a plan designed to equalize salaries gradually following a case from Norfolk, Virginia, in 1940.[2] By the mid-1940s more than thirty cases were active in twelve states, including South Carolina. Some states equalized salaries, but in some cases White officials developed merit-based salary systems to thwart equalization, making it more difficult for Black teachers to realize real gains. Consequently Black teachers' salaries rose only to about 65 percent of White teachers' salaries, up from around 55 percent. The NAACP also faced problems with limited resources. The requirement to focus legal resources where they could do the most good meant that they only sued larger, urban school districts, leaving rural districts free to continue discrimination.[3]

On September 13, 1937, Marshall wrote a memorandum for branch presidents and enclosed a report, referencing the *Gibbs* case from Maryland, outlining the results of that case and setting a strategy for salary cases going forward.[4] Starting in 1938 Marshall began corresponding with the Palmetto State Teachers' Association regarding the salary issue, but even by 1939 the organization had not joined the fight for equalization. The state conference of the NAACP became involved as well. State conference meetings were scheduled in June so teachers could attend. Osceola McKaine, associate editor of the *Lighthouse and Informer* newspaper and a leader of the Sumter branch of the NAACP, began to put out feelers to build a case in 1940. He also attempted to raise money to finance a suit. James M. Hinton, leader of the state conference, agreed to offer support but refused to offer financial assistance. Hinton thought that, since teachers were the best-paid Black workers in the state, they should finance their own suit. At a meeting of the state conference board of directors, Marshall reaffirmed that NAACP money could not be used to support the case but encouraged the group to solicit support for a suit among the state's Black teachers. Fundraising continued, but it was not until three years later that a suitable plaintiff was found in Charleston. Malissa Smith would probably have been a good plaintiff, but Boulware delayed filing the case, and when school began in September, Smith disappeared for a week to get married. She was subsequently dismissed. Eugene Hunt was going to be the next plaintiff, but fears that he would be drafted sooner if he filed suit led to his replacement. Finally Burke High School science teacher Viola Duvall agreed to carry the case forward in October.[5]

As the case progressed, it became clear that the Black teachers were going to win, and the district agreed to a consent decree under which salaries would be equalized over a three-year period. Georgetown's state senator Olin Sawyer expressed the defiance that many White South Carolina politicians felt when he asked, "Are they going to send the army to South Carolina to make us [raise Black teachers' salaries]? The state legislature reacted by establishing a complex administrative system for challenging pay disparities. We are running this government."[6] Under the new law, any dispute would have to be heard by the county school board, then the state board of education, before going to state courts. Later that year in Columbia, Albert N. Thompson petitioned the school board of Richland County District 1 to enforce its own policy of equal pay for all teachers in the system. Because of the advancement policy initiated there in 1941, the school board denied Thompson's petition. All teachers, according to the board, had "equal opportunity to advance both in pay and in position. Such advancement [was] based primarily on demonstrated teaching ability and efficiency and also upon worth to his or her superiors—not necessarily on length of service." Officials referred to the policy as the "worth-minimum plan."[7]

District 1 officials claimed that the worth-minimum plan had raised the salaries of Black teachers in Columbia. In fact the state-mandated minimum salary had risen by 1944 to $900 per year, so the district plan did not have much impact. The effective maximum pay for Black teachers in Columbia's School District 1 was less than the state minimum. Salary tables for that fall indicate that most White teachers at Wardlaw Junior High received $1,089 for the academic year, while Black teachers at Booker T. Washington High School were still being paid below the state minimum of $900. Most were to receive $882 for the year, none was to receive more, and some earned as little as $623.25. A later list of new teachers submitted by the school district lists the average salary for new Black teachers in Columbia as $1,026.25 in 1944–45, while the average salary for new White teachers was $1,425.85. The White teachers, on average, had more experience, but nearly all the teachers, Black and White, came to their jobs with college degrees. Figures for earlier years going back to 1941 reveal similar disparities in average salaries.[8]

The school board's decision regarding Thompson's petition admitted that salary disparities still existed. The board maintained, however, that any remaining disparity was due to differences in qualifications rather than race. On November 18, 1944, the board denied Thompson's petition. The school board's position was that it was not a matter of equal pay for equal work: it was a matter of "performing essentially the same duties *with equal proficiency to that of the white teachers.*"[9] The board argued that Black teachers in general performed their duties less ably than White teachers; consequently their "worth" was less than that of their White counterparts. Such reasoning was common among White officials: concentrating on the "here and now." They were willing to ignore the historic disparities that caused the difference in "performance": a significant number of Black teachers came from South Carolina State College, the only public college for Black citizens in the state, which was notoriously underfunded. The South Carolina public schools in which South Carolina State's graduates had been taught were also grossly underfunded, and a significant number of their students were economically and socially disadvantaged. These factors did not matter to White officials, who pointed to measures of performance such as test scores and the numbers of students pursuing higher education that indicated the "proficiency" upon which their legal arguments depended. This emphasis on present disparities, while ignoring historical and social policies and structures that caused them, became part of the argument for delaying desegregation through the next two decades. White people understood performance differences as evidence of Black inferiority. Black people saw them as consequences of their history.

Thompson, with legal assistance by the state NAACP, took his case from the school board directly to federal court, despite the state law requiring salary appeals to be taken to state court first.[10] His complaint sought to circumvent the law requiring appeals to the state superintendent of education and other state venues by arguing that it would delay any remedy.[11] Since local White citizens controlled all other avenues of appeal, any effort to petition those agencies would have been a waste of time and energy, a fact that was lost on neither side in the matter, to be sure.

The complaint filed on February 6, 1945, by Thompson's attorney, Shadrack Morgan, and joined by Marshall pointed out the salary disparities that existed in the district. White teachers received higher minimum and maximum salaries, intermediate salaries were higher for White teachers, and salary increases for White teachers were consistently higher than those offered Black teachers. The complaint avoided mentioning the subjective efficiency or proficiency, instead concentrating on qualifications and experience.[12]

The defense depended on the state law circumscribing appeals to dispose of the matter. Challenging Thompson's standing, school district attorneys contended that if the school board had dealt with the case, and no appeal taken in accordance with state law, no controversy could exist. The defense also noted that a new system of certification and recertification, along with a race-neutral salary scale, was scheduled to be put into effect on July 1, 1945. New teachers with a bachelor's degree would receive $105 per month at the highest grade level, to be determined by his or her score on the National Teacher Exam. A teacher with fourteen years' experience and a master's degree would receive $185 per month. As part of the state's recertification plan for teachers, South Carolina required them to take the National Teacher Exam, the results of which would be arranged in a four-tiered salary scale based on performance on the test. Those in the top 25 percent would get an A, those in the middle 50 percent would get a B, those in the next 15 percent would get a C, and the bottom 10 percent would get a D. Pretesting indicated that 90 percent of White teachers but only 27 percent of Black teachers would receive the higher two grades on the test. The NTE pretest suggested that nearly three-quarters of the Black teachers would rank in the bottom half, thereby mostly preserving discrimination through "nondiscriminatory" means.[13]

NAACP lawyers asserted that from 1941 through April 1945, new Black teachers had been paid the minimum salaries for their positions, while all new White teachers were paid more than the minimum. The defense refused to admit any of this and attempted to force damaging admissions from the plaintiff. Among the points that the defense sought to make was that District 1 "paid salaries to teachers and principals in excess of the minimum based on individual qualifications, capacities and abilities." The defense elaborated on the teacher recertification plan by noting that the qualifications for a new teacher included an evaluation of the college from which they graduated. They could thus discriminate against Black teachers by holding their college ties against them. Ultimately the defense promised that the salary scale for the upcoming academic year would be based on experience and that all teachers would be paid equivalently.[14]

On May 26, Judge Waring, invoking the *Alston* case from Virginia, issued the injunction Thompson had sought. "Subsequent to [1941], the Board has made a study and has alleviated the condition to a certain extent, but there is still a disparity between white and negro teachers of equal education and experience." Waring noted that despite board assurances that the disparities would be remedied, the new state law only applied to money coming from the state for teachers' pay. It did not apply to the county portion. Therefore any county could continue to discriminate in teacher pay while still operating well within state law. Waring enjoined Richland District 1 school commissioners from paying Black teachers and principals "less than the salary paid white teachers and/or principals of the same qualifications and experience and performing substantially the same duties, on account of race or color," but he left the door open by concluding that local school districts could still make decisions about individual teachers based on their merit.[15]

The inventive responses of White South Carolinians to the rulings in *Thompson v. Gibbes, Rice v. Elmore,* and *Brown v. Baskin* made it clear that winning cases was easier than enforcing decisions. Waring had yet to reach the point he would a few years later, when he realized the importance of challenging segregation head-on. Instead, while he may have been more forward-thinking than many of his colleagues on the bench, he still seemed to have some inherent trust in the White power structure. As such Waring's latitude on merit in the teacher salary case left the door open to discrimination at the individual level and, in a way, made racial discrimination against the group easier to disguise. Those Black teachers whose professional training had been substandard but who were allowed to work because their salaries were so low now faced high stakes tests to secure a living wage.

In February 1949 approximately 5,000 people, of whom around 2,400 were Black, took the National Teacher Exam in South Carolina. About a quarter of the Black teachers who took the test were subsequently accused of cheating. The accusations were based on reports from several Columbia-area schools, where several room examiners confiscated materials that had allegedly been used for cheating. These materials were used to make a composite key, which was used by the Educational Testing Service in Princeton as a template to compare to the South Carolina exams. In total 801 tests "compared to a substantial extent" with the master key that had been compiled from the confiscated "cheat sheets."[16]

Among those accused of cheating was Pearl Green Shirer, a twelve-year veteran teacher from Charleston. Shirer had not been caught with the answer key, but the investigation by the Educational Testing Service revealed her to be among the teachers whose answers corresponded to the master fraudulent key that had been assembled. The state Board of Education summoned Shirer and others to a hearing before an investigating committee and presented them with evidence of cheating. Although in Shirer's case, the only evidence consisted of the correlation of her answers to the fraudulent key, this was enough to justify the board's decision to revoke her teacher's license. Shirer responded by filing a complaint against Jesse T. Anderson, the state superintendent of education, along with the rest of the state education board and Charleston superintendent G. Creighton Frampton. The decision of the two-member investigating committee amounted to a finding of fact from which there was no appeal, and as such she argued that she had been denied due process and equal protection.[17]

Many of the Black teachers who had been accused of cheating had been offered the chance to continue teaching under a temporary license. Shirer and her attorney argued that offering the temporary licenses amounted to a transparent means of paying Black teachers less than their White counterparts. Shirer said

Pearl Shirer (courtesy of Janice
Shirer Broughton, Charleston, South
Carolina)

that she had been offered a lower-salary permit in exchange for an admission of
wrongdoing and information on who had given her the fraudulent key, but this
placed her in a catch-22: since Shirer knew nothing of the cheating, there could
be no way for her to join the quid pro quo. Although 188 individuals (of those
the Board of Education had had time to interview in the aftermath of the scandal) had already confessed to cheating on the test, the evidence against Shirer
was only circumstantial. Eighteen of the accused teachers admitted cheating
during the hearings held by the Board of Education in October 1949; 59 teachers subsequently admitted their cheating after having their teaching certificates
revoked. Two hundred thirty-two of the accused teachers continued to deny
their guilt up to the date the answer was filed. An additional 76 who had taken
the test while still college students admitted to cheating. Finally 32 individuals
admitted preparing or disseminating the fraudulent keys.[18]

Circuit judge John J. Parker and district judges Waring and George Bell
Timmerman Sr. heard the case on January 23, 1950. At issue was the constitutionality of the state statute that allowed the state board of education to
terminate teachers who had acted immorally or unprofessionally without any
specific right of appeal. The state contended that the lack of a specific stipula-
tion of the right of appeal did not necessarily mean that all legal recourse had
been exhausted with the board of education hearing. In fact one teacher, Julia
Pettiford, had been granted a writ of certiorari from the state courts. That case,

Pettiford v. State Board of Education, had been decided (against Pettiford) by the Richland County Circuit Court and was pending appeal in the state supreme court.[19]

Shirer testified that upon receiving letters asking her to appear before the State Department of Education, she went to Columbia to confer with Ellison M. Smith, the chair of the state recertification program. According to Shirer, Smith asked her to admit cheating, and in return he would allow her to continue teaching with a temporary permit, which meant a greatly reduced salary. If she would not admit cheating, Smith threatened, Shirer would not be allowed to teach in any city or state for the rest of her life. J. Means McFadden, attorney for the state, asked Shirer why she wanted the results of the 1949 test thrown out and the results of her 1947 test counted. Shirer had previously taken the test twice, scoring first a D and subsequently a C in 1947. Her score on the 1949 test, on which she had allegedly cheated, was a B. Shirer responded, "I would rather have that than nothing at all."[20]

Shirer's attorneys called John A. McHugh, a teacher at Booker T. Washington High School who had voluntarily appeared before the state board of education and admitted having a fraudulent key to the NTE. While he had never received a temporary permit, McHugh testified that his salary had been reduced as a result of his admission of guilt, but only because the local school board anticipated later action by the state board. McHugh also testified as to the origin of the fraudulent key. He had been approached before the examination and offered the key for "a certain fee." Later several teachers met at his house and copied the key, and McHugh was to pay part of the fee for the correct answers.[21] McHugh never implicated Shirer.

Trying to show that the accusations of cheating were no more than an effort to lower salaries of Black teachers, Shirer's attorneys called other teachers and questioned them on the specifics of their present employment. Daisy Louise Greenlee consistently denied ever using a key in the examination, up to and including the hearing before the state Board of Education. Greenlee claimed that Smith had offered her promises like those he offered Shirer. "He said if I would tell him who was selling the examination key and admit [cheating], he would help me, but if I didn't admit it I would be out of a job because my certificate would be revoked." In her meeting with Smith, Greenlee denied using the key and subsequently was called before the state board, which revoked her teaching certificate on November 18, 1949. Samuel Williams admitted using the key and continued to work; in fact he had not even suffered a reduction in salary. His superintendent, G. C. Frampton, had advised him to write a letter asking to remain in his job as principal of the Baptist Hill High School until the matter was cleared up, and he had done so.[22] Ellison Smith denied ever having offered anyone a permit to teach in exchange for an admission of guilt. In fact, Smith argued, neither he nor the state board could promise a permit without a request from the local school board. Every permit that had been issued, including those for teachers who had testified for the plaintiff, was issued at the request of the local school board.[23] This was disingenuous at best, as "advice" from the state board would probably go a long way toward securing a job for someone. In the end the judges unanimously held that because Shirer's answers matched up well with the fraudulent key, the board had acted justifiably. Shirer's fate was left in the hands of the school board.[24]

Shirer's case represents a shift in attitudes among Black South Carolinians. Without significant constitutional issues at stake, the case is like many that escape the scrutiny of constitutional scholars. Nevertheless it is significant because of the symbolic changes that it represents. Like David Brown, Albert Thompson, and Viola Duval, Pearl Shirer was willing to stand up to the injustices she perceived. Although it was ultimately futile, her challenging of the White establishment would have been unheard of just a decade earlier. The scandal itself is a manifestation of White South Carolinians' intent to maintain a racially hierarchical system by using law and bureaucracy to ensure that the playing field remained tilted toward White people. So long as it was legal to discriminate on the basis of race, the quality of Black teachers did not matter. In an era before the recognition of cultural bias in testing, the use of this test as indicative of merit disadvantaged Black teachers. The salary cases left aside the glaring issue of the racial disparity in school quality at all levels, which was a corollary to low teacher pay.

Graduate education was another of the pillars of Houston's three-point program. The first NAACP attack on segregated educational institutions challenged the law school at the University of Maryland. In December 1934, while Marshall was still in private practice, Donald Murray applied for admission to the school and was summarily rejected. Like the states of West Virginia and Missouri, Maryland provided scholarships to out-of-state schools for African Americans who wished to pursue their graduate studies. When the case came to Marshall's attention, he eagerly took part, beginning what would become a long career of attacking segregation and discrimination. The case moved quickly through the Maryland courts in the spring and summer of 1935, and Murray emerged victorious. Despite attempts by the state to accelerate the appeal in the hope that the trial court would be overturned, Murray was admitted to the university's law school in September. Ultimately the state court of appeals agreed that Murray would be denied a substantially equal legal education since the scholarship aid only covered tuition and, most significantly, since Murray would not be able to study the law of the state in which he planned to practice.[25] Murray's case, since it ended with the state court of appeals, had no legal authority outside Maryland.

Lloyd Gaines, a Missouri native and a graduate of that state's all-Black Lincoln University, wanted to go to law school and had applied to the University of Missouri Law School in 1936. His application was rejected, and he was offered two options: he could go out of state under Missouri's scholarship plan, or he could go to law school at Lincoln University, where a law school would be built if he chose that option. He refused both options and sued the state. Charles Houston, in his last major case for the NAACP, argued that the scholarship program was unconstitutional and that the state must build the new law school. The new school could then be challenged on the basis that it was not equal to the main law school at the University of Missouri. The US Supreme Court ruled that Missouri must admit Gaines to the White law school or build a separate one. The state chose the latter option, leading to further legal action on the issue of equality of the schools. However, by the time the hearing on equality came up, Gaines had disappeared, and the NAACP had to accept the half-victory of the Supreme Court's decision.[26] Legally the most that any state would be required to do if a Black college graduate desired to pursue a legal education would be to build a separate law school. In South Carolina, George Bailey applied to the University of South Carolina Law School in 1938, but over two years the university took no action. Bailey considered a case and corresponded with Marshall and others at the NAACP offices. The legislature considered creating a law school for African Americans in 1939 but let the issue drop, thinking that Bailey's application would fade away. Bailey took a job with the postal service in Columbia.[27]

South Carolina's 1895 constitution required that the state's educational institutions, from elementary through professional schools, be segregated.[28] The University of South Carolina, founded in 1801 as South Carolina College and integrated for a while during Reconstruction, became White-only once again under an 1887 act of the state legislature.[29] Before 1895, when South Carolina State College was created, the state had given money to Claflin College, a Methodist-supported school for African Americans that was also in Orangeburg.[30] By 1945 South Carolina State enrolled 35 percent of the state's Black college students, while the six public colleges for White students enrolled more than half the White college students in the state. Most students at South Carolina State trained for the teaching profession, although less than half of the school's graduates received teaching certificates for 1947–48.[31] Although a liberal arts university, medical school, law school, and military school were provided at public expense for White students, none was provided for Black students.

White South Carolinians, even in the face of precedent from other states, were not about to give up and let Black students attend "their" schools. Although the issue at hand was the right of Black South Carolinians to secure graduate and professional education in their home state, White South Carolina's response to the *Gaines* and *Sipuel* cases was to establish its own out-of-state scholarship program. Having abandoned the idea of a law school for Black South Carolinians in 1938, White lawmakers returned to the idea, in addition to setting in motion the process of creating a graduate school for Black South Carolinians. Six years after *Gaines,* the state legislature authorized South Carolina State to establish graduate programs in law and medicine but appropriated no money for the new programs. In 1946 the legislature authorized twenty thousand dollars for the graduate school and five thousand dollars for tuition grants.[32] Thus when Charleston native John H. Wrighten applied for admission to the University of South Carolina's law school in June 1946, he was summarily rejected.

Wrighten appealed to the state NAACP for help, and in turn South Carolina NAACP president James M. Hinton appealed to the national office. By November, having had no response, Hinton's urgency increased. He wrote to Marshall in New York:

> Is it possible to get some action on our 'Graduate and Professional['] case? Attorney H.R. Bouleware [*sic*] claims to have done everything, requested of him, and this matter has been hanging since about May of this year. . . . Our State Conference is losing ground in South Carolina because we cannot get action on anything. We felt that the graduate suit would save our face, since we can get nothing on the voting case. . . . It is becoming embarrassing to us.

Robert Carter, the NAACP's assistant special counsel, apologized for the delay and accepted the blame, since Marshall had been out of commission for some time while recovering from an illness. Although he was preparing to go to Birmingham for several trials, Carter promised to write the complaint for South Carolina as soon as possible. Hinton remained nervous, however, because the state NAACP desired to file the case before January 4, the start of the state legislative session, and because the Palmetto State Teachers' Association was beginning to feel let down by the NAACP in the salary case. Wrighten was getting "jittery" himself; he would later cause several headaches for Marshall and others.[33]

Wrighten's suit against the University of South Carolina was finally filed in January 1947. Because of Marshall's continuing illness, Carter took charge of the case. The complaint was straightforward: he asked the court to enjoin the university to admit Wrighten and to declare that the policy of refusing to admit African Americans to the law school was an unconstitutional violation of the Fourteenth Amendment.[34]

The state responded that South Carolina State was the institution of higher education for Black South Carolinians and that the state constitution, which required separate schools for the "white and colored races," forbade Wrighten from enrolling at the University of South Carolina. The state rejected the equal protection argument because the "plaintiff and others similarly situate[d]" could go to law school at South Carolina State, where a law school would be established if there were demand. This legal education would be "substantially equal" to what they could receive at the law school at the University of South Carolina."[35]

The state legislature had already passed a law requiring South Carolina State "to establish a graduate law department." A similar law passed in the 1945 session as well. Had Wrighten applied to State's nonexistent law school then, a law school would have been created there. Since Wrighten had what state officials argued was a legitimate chance to go to law school, there could be no injury done to him, and his rights had not been violated.[36]

The state also argued that Wrighten's suit was not in good faith:

> [The] true purpose of the present suit is not the seeking of a legal educa-
> tion by the plaintiff . . . but is rather an attempt by the plaintiff and those
> associated with him in the maintenance of the present suit, to break down
> and disrupt the established policy of the State . . . and of its people to
> provide a separation of the races in the educational institutions of the
> State for the mutual benefit of both races. [The] policy [of segregated
> education] has been sanctioned, recognized and approved for a long period
> of time by both the white and Negro citizens of the State and has been
> adhered to by both races with the knowledge that it is the best system un-
> der which peace and good order can be maintained, the reciprocal rights
> and friendly relationships between the races preserved, and their honored
> traditions perpetuated.[37]

White South Carolinians justified the perpetuation of discrimination by argu-ing that segregation was consensual, an argument that was used into the 1960s, even as the lawsuits Black citizens filed, which required lawmakers to enact laws to shore up White supremacy, signified dissent.

At a pretrial conference held on May 15, 1947, Judge Waring, who heard the case because Judge Timmerman was a university trustee, immediately brought up the issue of the law school—or lack thereof—at South Carolina State. The opposing sides had interpreted the issue differently, and Waring wanted clarification. Lead counsel for the state, David W. Robinson, discussed a few minor issues then raised a key question: Was this a case about the lack of a "comparable law school" or in fact about the constitutionality of segregation in education?

Carter argued that "we haven't as yet brought into issue the question of segregation. This case can be decided . . . on the doctrine . . . that with qualifications, education for Negroes must be equal or comparable—as it is for whites. We don't feel in this suit it's necessary to go further [but] if you're asking merely how we feel about it, our contention is segregation is discriminatory." Carter was quick to make sure that the legal questions went much further than just the provision of a law school for Black students—he reserved the right to address whether the school approached equal quality to the existing law school. He noted that "segregation itself can [not] be maintained at this time unless a school is provided for Negroes." Waring responded by asking whether an "adequate" school, even if not at the university, would satisfy the plaintiffs, but Carter demurred, saying that it would come down to an issue of fact— whether the schools were in fact equal. Waring agreed, noting that "the mere fact there's a declaration that there's a law school in Moncks Corner or Jedburg doesn't mean it ends this case." Carter reiterated this point in a letter to Waring later that month. He argued that "even under a theory of segregation full protection of plaintiff's constitutional rights would require his admission to the Law School at the University of South Carolina." Waring responded that the only issues he would allow into the trial were those of sufficiency and quality.[38] Robinson and Waring both thought that the case revolved around the narrower issue.[39] The time was not yet ripe, at least in Waring's mind, for a full-blown review of segregated education.

On May 31, 1947, the parties met at the Richland County Court House in Columbia. Miller F. Whittaker, the president of South Carolina State; Norman M. Smith, the president of the University of South Carolina and a defendant in the case; and Samuel Prince, dean of the university law school and also a defendant, were scheduled to give pretrial depositions. Whittaker testified that the college's budget of $364,909 for 1946–47 had already been substantially used up, without the creation of a law school, with one more month left in the fiscal year. There were no buildings available for use as a law school, no area outside the main library for law students to study (in fact the campus was already overcrowded), and no offices for law professors.[40]

The budget for 1947–48, however, was substantially larger ($545,000), and the college was now required to establish law, medicine, and other professional programs. The sum of $180,000 to create a law school and a medical school was not going to be sufficient, and Marshall tried to establish this by engaging

Whittaker in a discussion about law libraries. Marshall argued that a minimum of ten thousand books would be required to form an effective law library, and when Whittaker estimated that just $50,000 would be required to establish a law school, Marshall challenged the figure: "Do you think you could set up a law school with four full-time professors, a library, building, equipment, and a library of at least ten thousand carefully selected law books on fifty thousand dollars?" Whittaker had to answer that he did not think so. Later Whittaker added that the amount was intended to fund scholarships for students to study out of state as well. Marshall established that the only progress that had been made toward the establishment of a law school was the formation of a committee to study the problem of creating a law school at the campus, and that committee had not yet reported to South Carolina State College's all-White board of trustees.[41]

When Marshall questioned Samuel Prince, the issue turned to the adequacy of the new law school. Prince admitted that it took two years for the Association of American Law Schools to approve a school for accreditation. James H. Price, co-counsel for the state, objected on the grounds that the new law school would provide a "reasonably comparable" legal education for Black South Carolinians. Thus whether the school was accredited or not was of no consequence. Nevertheless Marshall hammered the question home, noting that credits could transfer from one accredited school to another without an examination. When Marshall asked if an "unaccredited law school [was] equal to an accredited law school," Prince tried to deflect the question—"You mean, is comparable to a . . ."—at which point Marshall reminded him that the question was not about comparability but equality. Prince recovered well, arguing that the quality of the legal education one might receive could be equal, even without accreditation. The discussion continued along the same line for several minutes; Prince even once argued that rather than going to an accredited school, he would "go where [he] knew some professor that [he] wanted to follow." The state's argument centered on the idea that they could create out of whole cloth a law school that was essentially equal to the law school at the university, which had been a member of Association of American Law Schools since 1924 and accredited by the American Bar Association since 1925. Such an argument, though clearly ridiculous, was the stuff of which White South Carolinians' need to maintain segregation was made.[42]

A few days later, Wrighten's lawyers argued that since South Carolina only had one law school, it must allow Black applicants to matriculate. The South Carolina case, Wrighten's lawyers argued, was like the Missouri case since there was no law school for Black applicants in the state when Wrighten applied to the university. Though South Carolina had expressed willingness to fund such a law school should there be a need, the facts of the cases were essentially the same. Two men, both qualified for admission to the White law school of their respective states, had been denied the right to a legal education at a White-only law school. In Maryland, since there was only one law school, Donald Murray had to be admitted to the White school. The Maryland precedent did not apply in Missouri, the state argued, because it had declared its intent to create a law school at Lincoln University. The Supreme Court disagreed: "The policy of establishing a law school at Lincoln University had not yet ripened into an actual establishment, and it cannot be said that a mere declaration of purpose . . . is enough."[43]

The trial was held over two days in Columbia in early June 1947. Marshall's first witness was Whittaker, who testified briefly to the effect that no law school existed at South Carolina State at the current time or when Wrighten was applying to law school at the University of South Carolina, nor was there any other facility where Black students could receive a legal education in the state. On cross-examination by Robinson, Whittaker told the court of John Wrighten's expressed interest in a law school at State College. Wrighten had written Whittaker in February 1947, after initiating the lawsuit, to inquire about the existence of a law school at State College, and Whittaker had responded that there was none. Later that month Whittaker wrote Wrighten to inform him of the state legislature's appropriations for a law school at State College. Whittaker asked if he could consider Wrighten's initial letter a letter of application, since the establishment of a law school was still contingent on having student interest. Wrighten told him no, since he had not yet consulted with his attorney, Harold Boulware.[44]

As it turned out, several other graduates of South Carolina State as well as other Black South Carolinians studying out of state had written Whittaker about the possibility of receiving state aid on the basis that there was no graduate training available to African Americans in the state. Whittaker replied to each that no money was currently available but that in the 1947–48 appropriation, the legislature had set aside money for the establishment of a law school at South Carolina State and that he would correspond further with them. This meant that the sixty-thousand-dollar appropriation for the law school and other graduate programs in 1947–48 was also intended to fund aid for Black South Carolinians studying out of state.[45] The already small pool of money was rapidly shrinking.

Robinson established that money had—at least technically—been appropriated to the law school. In 1945–46 the appropriation for South Carolina State was a lump sum, and the legislature had authorized the establishment of a law school, so some of the money could technically have been used for the creation of a law school. In 1946–47, $25,000 had been designated for graduate and law programs, but the lack of law school applications caused the money to be diverted to the graduate program. An additional appropriation of $350,000 as part of a surplus appropriation bill was on the governor's desk awaiting his action, and part of that money was earmarked for a new graduate building at State. Marshall noted before Whittaker was dismissed that "this [was] a theoretical building."[46]

When Robinson moved on to the possible creation of a law school at South Carolina State by September, Marshall vigorously objected. Wrighten was not interested in what might happen in the future, said Marshall, but in getting a legal education today. Waring interjected, asking, "Suppose they came in and showed there was a law school running now that would satisfy the requirements?" Waring had hinted at his ultimate decision: he was not going to be the judge to force the first state in the Deep South to desegregate its schools, and he was looking for a way to avoid doing just that. Marshall insisted that the state had to show it had a law school for Black citizens right then, but Waring argued that "the Court has power to admit them to a law school and fix the time. . . . I think a Court of equity has a right to make a reasonable time to do anything of that sort."[47] Waring's thinking was going along the lines of the *Gaines* precedent rather than the nonbinding Maryland case.

After President Smith confirmed that Wrighten's race was the only reason that he had been excluded from the University of South Carolina, Marshall rested his case. Attorney Price called John Wrighten as his first witness. Price's first substantive question concerned whether Wrighten would attend a law school at South Carolina State if it provided a "reasonably and substantially . . . comparable legal education." Marshall immediately objected: Price was asking about what might possibly happen in the future and, in addition, was missing the whole issue of the defense's case. The law school at State must be "completely equal," not "substantially comparable." Waring agreed but gave Price some wiggle room by allowing him to use the phrase "substantially equivalent—on a parity."

Wrighten balked. It was "a question [he could] not answer." Price was incredulous, and when Wrighten said it would take him some time to answer the question, Price offered to "wait right now for a minute or two and let [Wrighten] think." Wrighten finally responded that "if it's equal in all respects to the University of South Carolina, I'll attend [a separate law school]. That is, if it's equal in all respects." Though he tried with his answer to stay within the boundaries that Marshall had set, Wrighten probably damaged his own case by admitting that he would attend a separate school. Marshall tried to object, but in the absence of a jury, Waring was willing to allow the answer to stand.[48] The fact that Black South Carolinians had been routinely and historically subjected to conditions ranging from grossly inhumane and discriminatorily racist belied South Carolina's reputation for southern gentility and hospitality.

W. C. Bethea, the secretary of the all-White South Carolina State Board of Trustees and a member of the committee studying the establishment of a law school, testified that even if only one student attended, State would open a law school in September. He told the court that President Whittaker had already been searching for a dean for the law school, and that Dean Prince of the university's law school was advising South Carolina State regarding building a law library for the new school. Bethea also testified that if Wrighten had applied for admission to South Carolina State for February 1947 rather than to the university for September 1946, he could have been accommodated easily. Not only would Wrighten have access to a law school at State, argued Bethea, but the board of trustees would also "strive to make it better [than the University of South Carolina Law School]." Bethea admitted that it would have been impossible to build a new building in such a short time, but that space—while limited—was available. Faculty members could have been assembled; the question of law books was one he could not answer. Bethea hoped to have a dean on board the week following the trial: "One of our old students. He'll be all right, I believe, if he'll accept." He may have been referring to a lawyer in Chicago who had been Harold Boulware's college roommate, but reportedly he wanted $50,000 a year to take the South Carolina State job. Boulware himself intimated that he was a candidate, but he wanted $15,000 per year. The dean at the University of South Carolina Law School was making $5,500 per year at the time.[49]

Prince probably weakened Wrighten's case further. His descriptions of the university law school made it easy to imagine that a comparable school could be set up on just about any campus in the state. The only real office belonged to the dean; faculty had no separate offices. Students had no lounge space and no study area. Two or three thousand of the library's twenty-five thousand books were stacked on floors due to insufficient space for the volumes they had. The only testimony Prince offered on direct examination that could have been helpful to Wrighten was that the law school's budget was more than $53,000, with receipts surpassing $65,000. The new law school at State could not be expected to meet its goals—including buying books for the library—with less than $60,000. The state budget set aside $10,000 of the $60,000 for scholarships for medical and pharmaceutical education. However, Prince had studied the problem of acquiring books for the new library and had come up with a price of $24,289 for 7,500 secondhand volumes. David Robinson also asked Prince his opinions on class size and educational quality as well, to portray the inevitably smaller classes at State as an advantage over the classes at the university.[50]

Marshall quickly got to the point when it was his turn to examine Prince. Graduates of the university law school were automatically admitted to the state bar, so Marshall asked Prince if admission to the bar should be a requirement if the law school at State were to be considered equal to the university's. Prince, a former member of the board of bar examiners, dodged the question by arguing that admission to the bar right out of law school was in fact a detriment, since he believed that law graduates should take the bar exam.

Marshall turned to the impact of accreditation on the admission of non–University of South Carolina graduates to the South Carolina bar. South Carolina law automatically admitted to the bar not just graduates of the university's law school but graduates of any law school accredited by the Association of American Law Schools. Marshall moved to admit the association's standards into evidence, but attorney Price objected (even though the university law school was accredited by that body): "We don't care what some crowd of professors in New York or Massachusetts have ruled about." Despite Dean Prince's position in favor of requiring the bar exam, the fact was that graduates of accredited law schools were automatically admitted to the bar, and Judge Waring admitted the association's standards into evidence.[51]

The defense's first witness was South Carolina native Jack Lott, former dean of the law school at the University of Louisville. Robinson explored the relative merits of small versus large classes with Lott. Marshall soon objected, given that the questions dealt with a matter that was outside the current dispute: small classes might be an issue, if there had been a small law school in the state, and Marshall was prepared to assemble witnesses on the point of small versus large classes, if it came to that. Judge Waring agreed with Marshall. The only conclusion this line of questioning could lead to was that the university law school was not particularly good, so Waring ruled it irrelevant. Nevertheless Waring allowed Lott to answer to establish a record. J. W. Hicks, former dean of Furman University's law school, which had closed its doors in 1930, agreed that small classes were better for law students. Following Marshall's brief cross-examination of Hicks, the defense rested, and Judge Waring gave each side ten days to prepare final briefs.[52]

Waring deliberated for about three weeks after the last words of the attorneys. His order, filed on July 12, 1947, essentially followed *Gaines*. Noting that educational segregation was a "political rather than a judicial problem," he chose not to discuss the legality of segregation. He concluded that Wrighten was indeed "entitled" to a legal education in South Carolina. Since state officials had assured the court that the segregated law school would be fully operational by that fall, Waring decided that if the law school at South Carolina State were opened and "on a substantial parity in all respects" with the law school at the University of South Carolina, that would be a "proper solution." If the new law school were not on parity, Wrighten and others would have the right to admission to the university's law school. Waring offered a third alternative: the state could choose not to offer legal education to anyone in the state.[53]

Before Wrighten applied to the University of South Carolina, in late 1945 Ada Lois Sipuel, an Oklahoma native and a graduate of Langston University, decided to sue the University of Oklahoma rather than attend the Jim Crow law school established at her alma mater. The OU law school had rejected her application to the law school because of her race. As Wrighten's case moved through Judge Waring's court during 1947, the *Sipuel* case in Oklahoma was moving through the appellate courts on its way to the US Supreme Court. Sipuel's case went to the Supreme Court in 1948, but the Court dodged the main intention of her argument—that the law school for African Americans established in Oklahoma was so inferior to the University of Oklahoma's as to be a sham. The Court decided that the state of Oklahoma must provide Sipuel with a legal education "as soon as it does for applicants of any other group." Instead of taking a stand, the Court sent the case back to Oklahoma for further review. While many believed that the decision required Sipuel's admission to the University of Oklahoma, the regents decided to take the *Gaines* option of opening a separate Black law school, this time by setting aside three rooms in the state capitol. As in the *Wrighten* case, Marshall attempted to challenge separate but equal directly, but the Supreme Court rejected his appeal since he had not challenged the doctrine in the state courts. Sipuel refused to apply to the segregated law school at Langston, possibly because her husband was a federal employee working in personnel at Tinker Air Force Base. Ultimately the Black law school in Oklahoma remained open only eighteen months; during that time there was only one student. The school closed in 1949, and Ada Sipuel was admitted to the University of Oklahoma Law School, from which she graduated three years later.[54]

After Waring's ruling in his case, Wrighten found himself in a difficult situation. "The case is won, but what shall I do? I was told to enter the law school at SC State College, and I was told not to enter, because it is not equal to that of the University of SC." By September, Wrighten decided to enter the law school at South Carolina State but had been dissuaded from doing so by Marshall, who wanted to push for desegregation instead of equalization. "When I returned to SC and told the people here that I was not going to the law school, and the reasons why I was not going they almost curse[d] me out, and thats [sic] the opinion of some of the members and officials of the N.A.A.C.P. here." Members of the Charleston NAACP branch were pressuring Wrighten to go to the new law school, and he had given up a job teaching at the Avery Institute there. Marshall was incredulous as to why Wrighten would want to "accept a $10,000 law school in a $1.50 university," given that plaintiffs in Texas were standing their ground and refusing to "accept a $100,000 law school in a three and a half million dollar university." After Marshall advised him not to go to the new law school, Wrighten found himself out of a job. He was married and had a child by now as well. He pleaded to Marshall, "I haven't done anything since I have been here [back in South Carolina], and I can't get any help from these people. I am asking you to please explain your reasons to them for telling me to withdraw from the law school, and see if you can get some help for me until I can fin[d] something to do." Marshall's response was fiery. He would, he wrote, "personally file charges against [any] member or officer" who violated the organization's committed policy of opposition to segregation, and he asked Wrighten for the names of the individuals who had "cursed [him] out." Meanwhile, Marshall tried to reassure Wrighten that the national and local NAACP would stand behind him, and that there must be several Black-owned businesses where he could apply for work. Marshall then followed up his letter to Wrighten with a memo to Hinton, Boulware, and Rev. Jesse Beard, the president of the Charleston branch of the NAACP, in which he demanded a special meeting with the state executive committee to find out exactly where everyone stood.[55]

On October 1, Wrighten wrote Marshall again. He had met with the executive committee of the Charleston branch to ask for their assistance in finding work or funding, and "they told me that they did not have anything to do with the case." Hinton had not responded to a letter he sent a week earlier, and Wrighten was growing more impatient with the local and state branches. "To me I have been treated wrong by these people, but I am willing to fight on regardless to their opinion of me and the case." On October 6, however, Wrighten wrote that he had reenlisted in the army, having run out of alternatives and money. "Please don't think hard of me for doing this, but since I could not fine [sic] any kind of jobs here I decided to do something for my self." He still had not received a response from Hinton and no longer "care[d] if I hear from him, because he has not lived up to his word." Two days later he wrote Hinton again, explaining to him his reasons for wanting to withdraw from the case. "It's better for me to drop the whole thing before I get into something else without the backing that I was assured when I made application to the university." However, before Wrighten could sign the last papers for his reenlistment, Boulware and others were able to talk him out of his plans and get him to wait a little while longer. Having achieved the creation of a law school for Black South Carolinians at State College, many local Black leaders wanted Wrighten to attend to avoid "the ill feeling that might develop among the whites."[56]

Marshall by March 1948 was convinced that Wrighten was unreliable. He asked Boulware to withdraw the motion for further relief filed the previous October and to leave the case where it stood. Wrighten had, Marshall wrote, "demonstrated that he is not the type of reliable plaintiff necessary to proceed in this type of case." Marshall was confident that the defendants' request to vacate the declaratory judgment in Wrighten's favor would fail, but he no longer felt it would be advisable to pursue any further relief or damages for him.[57] The state's appeal to the Fourth Circuit was abandoned when Waring, at a second hearing, ruled that the conditions of his ruling had been met. The law school at South Carolina State would open as planned.

Although Wrighten did not matriculate in September 1947, nine others did. It soon became clear that the General Assembly was willing to invest in the law school to maintain segregation. In 1948 they appropriated two hundred thousand dollars for a building and thirty thousand dollars for books, and it was clear that the college was a going concern.[58] In February 1949, Wrighten, still desiring to go to law school, wrote to Judge Waring's wife to ask for her help in securing funding to attend the law school at State College. Judge Waring replied that it would be inappropriate for him to assist Wrighten and forwarded a copy of Wrighten's letter to Marshall in New York. Marshall wrote Wrighten a scathing letter, chastising him for his "bad taste" in writing the wife of the judge who had tried the case and reminding him that he should always consult with his lawyers before doing anything concerning it.[59] Wrighten entered the South Carolina State Law School in the fall of 1949 and, despite the acrimony that Marshall appeared to hold toward him, eventually became the lead attorney in several civil rights cases in South Carolina.

Judge Waring's rulings in education cases in the 1940s were moderate at best and demonstrate a deference to racial disparities that White South Carolinians had built into a world shaped by *Plessy*. Events following the *Wrighten* ruling illustrate the formidable protections that White South Carolinians had crafted. Since 1895 Black South Carolinians had faced the choice of taking crumbs or getting nothing in the Jim Crow system. Waring's rulings in *Thompson, Shirer,* and *Wrighten* show that the destruction of Jim Crow was not a given and that the results of challenges might not always be beneficial.

Wrighten v. Board of Trustees also illustrates the many difficulties that African Americans faced as they attempted to use the courts to win their rights. A conservative court system, from the federal district courts all the way up to the US Supreme Court, which still relied on the controlling precedent of *Plessy*— not to mention conservative state courts across the South—did not help the situation. Wrighten, frustrated at almost every turn by the slowness of the developing case, the lack of help from local NAACP branches, and his inability to support himself following his bold stance in attempting to integrate the law school at the University of South Carolina, was caught between the aggressive strategies of the national and state NAACP and the more conciliatory attitudes of some Black leaders in the state. Ultimately it came down to what Wrighten truly wanted: a legal education. Had Wrighten been willing to forego his legal education, even while the new law school operated at State College, Marshall may never have had occasion to become so frustrated with his client. However, Wrighten wanted access to a law school in his home state more than he wanted a law degree from the University of South Carolina.

The dean of the new law school at South Carolina State was Benner C. Turner, who became president of the school in 1950. Turner was an accommodationist in race relations and worked with state politicians to ensure continued and increased appropriations for the law school and later the college. He cracked down on student demonstrations in the 1950s, and Gov. James F. Byrnes rewarded him with help in securing grants as well as increased appropriations. By rewarding Turner, Byrnes believed he was undermining some of the more militant Black leaders at Allen University and Benedict College, both of which Byrnes and other White leaders regarded as NAACP strongholds.[60]

For White South Carolinians, legal victories by Black plaintiffs—no matter how symbolic—indicated that segregated institutions were threatened. After the *Wrighten* case was concluded, Clemson College moved to preempt the prospect of forced desegregation. In February 1948, Clemson registrar G. E. Metz wrote a long memorandum to the board of trustees. Without mentioning the *Wrighten* case, he instead focused on the application to Auburn of an African American student and World War II veteran who was attending State Teachers College in Montgomery, Alabama.[61] Metz noted that it was "almost impossible . . . to anticipate just how or when a definite application will be received from a Negro applicant" and asked the board to provide advice in the event of an application.[62] In fact Clemson had accidentally admitted a Black Kentuckian in September 1947, though nothing came of it once the Clemson administration realized their error. Metz did not have to wait much longer for another application. In April 1948, Spencer M. Bracey, a student at South Carolina State, applied to Clemson's graduate school for architectural engineering, and Spencer's brother Edward wrote three days later requesting an undergraduate transfer to Clemson for the fall of 1948.[63] R. F. Poole, Clemson's president, blamed the NAACP for putting the older Bracey up to it. James M. Hinton denied any knowledge of Bracey's actions, saying that Bracey's "application was as much a surprise to us, as to you."[64]

At least one Clemson alumnus was not unhappy with the prospect. Daniel Moorer, a 1940 graduate, wrote Poole to recommend admission to the Braceys.

Moorer argued that "a graceful act on the part of an institution of one of the allegedly backward States would . . . exert a benign influence on the whole problem. . . . Such an act would require no small measure of courage in those on whom the responsibility of decision rests."[65] There was no more courage among Clemson's leaders than there was among the rest of the White leadership of the state. The only semblance of courage at the time came from T. B. Young, a member of Clemson's board of trustees, who wanted Clemson to "be honest in our real reasons for not accepting them."[66] Clemson's official explanation was that the programs of study desired by the Bracey brothers were not available at Clemson, but of course they were not available at South Carolina State, either, though State's board did approve an undergraduate program in civil engineering starting in the fall of 1948.[67]

Clemson's board met in June 1948 and decided to send Spencer and Edward letters stating that, since South Carolina State offered programs that would be equally useful, including an architectural engineering graduate program that South Carolina State did not, in fact, offer, they should remain there. The proposed letters did eventually get to the point: while the state had a policy of providing "separate and comparable [not equal, interestingly] facilities" for Black and White education, Clemson did not have a "right" under state law to consider applications from Black students. It is arguable whether Clemson would have looked favorably on the admission of the Braceys even if the institution did have a "right" to look at their application.[68]

Nationally desegregation of higher education had been won in the case of *Sweatt v. Painter* in 1950, though the Supreme Court relied on the fact that the law school created in Houston was "not substantially equal" to the law school at the University of Texas. While there was still room for interpretation, desegregation in higher education became a lower priority for both the state and national NAACP through the 1950s, as the organization and the nation turned its attention to the integration of primary and secondary education. Locally the pragmatic acceptance of Wrighten's limited victory and the willingness of Black South Carolinians to enroll at South Carolina State Law School put the problem on the shelf until the early 1960s.

Black South Carolinians' cautious attempts to crack the wall of segregation that proscribed their lives offers a case study in why segregation lasted so long. White South Carolinians showed the sophistication built through generations of practice beginning as early as the founding of the colony in building laws and policies to establish White dominance and limit Black advancement. When policy failed, White officials were willing to pay for their racism. The money set aside for the law and graduate programs at South Carolina State foreshadowed the school building program designed to prevent desegregation in the 1950s. The acumen of these officials enabled them to remain within the boundaries of the constitutional jurisprudence while elevating state power to maintain White supremacy. Some efforts—privatizing the Democratic Party, for example—were clumsy and easily recognized for the subterfuges they were. Other efforts—such as the development of a merit-based pay system for teachers or creating a separate law school at great expense—could appear to be conciliation to new realities that theoretically opened opportunities to all. The success of these strategies in the teachers' salary cases and in the Wrighten case laid a foundation for further delay and obfuscation.

3

"UNEXAMPLED COURAGE"

School Desegregation in the 1950s

While some partial desegregation had occurred in some areas of the South, public school segregation remained in force in South Carolina through the 1950s. Even so, national victories in cases dealing with voting rights and higher education as well as national and local victories in salary cases encouraged Black South Carolinians.[1] Given that Waring's ruling in John Wrighten's case required either equality in segregated education or desegregation and that before his lawsuit Black South Carolinians who wanted to practice law either had to read law or attend law school out of state, the case, along with the others already discussed, established Black South Carolinians' claims to their rights. While the South Carolina cases so far had come from the cities of Charleston and Columbia, the case that would ultimately undermine segregation in the state emerged from what might seem the unlikeliest part of the state. In rural Clarendon County, Black people outnumbered White people by two to one but owned less than 15 percent of the land. Most Black citizens grew cotton on White-owned land and earned less than one thousand dollars per year for their effort.[2] The county was one of the most impoverished counties in the state, if not the South, in the late 1940s, yet it was there that Black South Carolinians attempted to secure funding to operate a secondhand school bus they bought for their children by pooling their meager resources before seeking to equalize, then to desegregate, public education.

In March 1948, after several months of dealing with White authorities with no success, African Americans in Clarendon County filed suit in federal court in an attempt to equalize transportation by forcing their district to provide school buses for Black children. Although ultimately the case was dismissed on a technicality, as the first case filed in the modern civil rights era to challenge the segregation of Black children, *Levi Pearson v. Clarendon County Board of Education and School District No. 26* set the stage for *Briggs v. Elliott*, the landmark suit that ultimately led to desegregation.[3]

The dismissal of the *Pearson* case was dispiriting, but not enough so to keep the small group of determined parents from trying again. Less than a year following the *Pearson* dismissal, a group of Black parents led by the Reverend J. A. De Laine organized to petition the school board of Clarendon County for better school facilities, and when the board refused to act on their petition, the families sued. The lead plaintiff, Harry Briggs, worked as a service station attendant. His five children attended the Scott's Branch school, a ten-room building that combined all grades from elementary through high school for African Americans. Despite the reprisals that Levi Pearson had faced because of his earlier suit, Briggs and the other plaintiffs stood their ground. While advantageous for the case, the rural setting had disadvantages for rural plaintiffs who, unlike landowner Pearson, were dependent on economic entanglements with White people. Briggs and his wife, Liza, both lost their jobs as a result of his signing of the equalization petition. Eventually, after the 1954 Supreme Court decision in *Brown*, the Briggs family had to leave the state.[4]

Ironically, a rural district was likely more fertile ground to challenge "separate but equal," as disparities could not be remedied as quickly as they could in cities where Black schools, while not equal, were more modern than what was found in rural counties. As the *Briggs* case moved toward its first hearing, state officials took note. They believed that moving quickly to equalize, or at least to improve, Black schools would make the impending case moot, just as the promise of a law school at South Carolina State had resulted in a conservative decision in the *Wrighten* case. In June 1950 a six-man committee formed by the House of Representatives in the South Carolina General Assembly began meeting to discuss a new state sales tax with the purpose of improving the schools with the proceeds. Officials drastically reduced the number of school districts from 1,200 to 102, and the state assumed greater authority over both financial and educational policy.

Former Supreme Court associate justice James F. Byrnes, elected governor without opposition in November 1950 following an overwhelming victory in the Democratic primary that summer, declared, "Whatever is necessary to continue the separation of the races in the schools of South Carolina is going to be done by the white people of the state. That is my ticket as a private citizen. It will be my ticket [as governor]."[5]

When the *Briggs* case came before Judge Waties Waring for a pretrial conference in November 1950, Thurgood Marshall was certain of getting a fair hearing. Waring had already been contacted by Walter White, the national director of the NAACP. White told Waring of his fears that Marshall was reluctant (perhaps because of Waring's ruling in *Wrighten*) to join the judge in moving toward genuine desegregation. Waring was fully aware of the dangers of going with precedent and settling for equalization as he done in *Wrighten*—especially since the state could argue that the improvements taking place would lead to substantial comparability within a reasonable time. Not wanting the case to be moot on those grounds before it could be effectively heard in court, Waring as much as ordered Marshall to drop the case and refile a new complaint directly attacking segregation. The unfortunate immediate result of Waring's action meant that the case would have to be heard by a three-judge panel made up of arch segregationist George Bell Timmerman Sr. and North Carolina native John J. Parker, chief judge of the Fourth Circuit Court of Appeals, whose position was uncertain because he had occasionally sided with African Americans in cases on appeal but had not done anything to break new ground when it came to their rights.[6]

Waring's direction probably convinced Byrnes and the General Assembly that more coordinated action was necessary. A month before the *Briggs* case was to be heard in district court, the state legislature in April 1951 authorized a fifteen-member School Segregation Committee (usually called the Gressette Committee after its leader, Calhoun County senator L. Marion Gressette) "to study and report on the advisable course to be pursued by the State in respect to its educational facilities in the event that the federal courts nullify the provisions of the state constitution requiring the establishment of separate schools for children of the white and colored races."[7] The committee's purpose was to recommend new laws to ensure the perpetuation of segregation. Later the committee's legal team assisted school districts in their defenses against desegregation lawsuits.

The trial in *Briggs v. Elliott* began on May 28, 1951. Robert McC. Figg, who had written some of Strom Thurmond's Dixiecrat speeches, represented Clarendon County and its superintendent, R. W. Elliott. Figg began the proceedings with a stunning announcement: they stipulated, as the state had in *Wrighten*, that the Black schools of the district were in fact unequal to the White schools. Furthermore, because of the proposed new sales tax designed to end the disparities between Black and White schools in the state, Figg asked the court to delay the proceedings to allow the state sufficient time to put the plan into effect. Marshall was unwilling to concede that ending disparities in infrastructure was sufficient, however, and Judge Parker allowed him to proceed with his argument.[8]

Marshall's case depended substantially on the testimony of expert witnesses such as Matthew Whitehead, a Howard University professor of education. Whitehead had examined the schools of Clarendon County and found them not just inadequate but terrible. His report to the Legal Defense Fund

Senator L. Marion Gressette (courtesy of Richland Library, Columbia, South Carolina)

following his visit to the schools in April 1951 detailed the horrible conditions that Black children suffered just to get what little education was afforded them. The White schools were all brick or stucco, while the Black schools were all wood. Teacher to student ratios were 67 percent higher at Black schools: forty-seven to one as opposed to twenty-eight to one. The Black high school's curriculum consisted of agriculture and home economics. White students took classes in typing or biology. Black schools sometimes lacked running water or electricity, and no Black school benefited from indoor toilets. There were other problems as well, ranging from the lack of transportation, lunchrooms, and janitorial services to, at one Black school, a complete lack of desks.[9]

Harold McNally of Columbia University's Teachers College testified that there was no way that students in conditions such as those outlined by Whitehead could receive an adequate education. Per-pupil expenditures and teacher-student ratios both had important effects on the quality of education. Ellis O. Knox, like Whitehead also of Howard, reinforced McNally's testimony. McNally, however, had to admit under Figg's cross-examination that he had no experience studying segregated school systems, so presumably he could not testify that segregation itself caused lower achievement among Black students. Knox, however, did have such experience, and he testified that even in substantially equal situations, segregation would lead to unequal educational achievement.[10]

After spending the morning with the educational experts, Robert Carter, who was handling the examinations for the Legal Defense Fund, introduced his key witness. Kenneth Clark was a social psychologist who had worked on the effects of segregation on the self-awareness of Black children. In Clarendon County he had found that Black children often identified White dolls as "nice" and that when asked to identify the doll that most accurately resembled themselves, they chose a White doll instead of a Black one. He had examined sixteen children at Scott's Branch school, and the numbers of children who preferred White dolls to Black dolls mirrored those he had found in earlier experiments he and his wife had conducted in Washington, DC, and New York City.[11]

The next day Marshall delivered the closing argument. The facts were no longer at issue: the state admitted the disparity in facilities and, in so doing, destroyed an essential lie built on the foundation of *Plessy v. Ferguson:* that separate somehow automatically meant equal. The *Plessy* court had said that the segregation was not a mark of inferiority, but Clark's tests had suggested otherwise. Now what remained at issue was the law. Segregation was not a reasonable application of the law, and the plaintiffs had proved that the institution had caused significant psychological and social damage. Figg responded by arguing that precedent allowed states to run their educational systems as they saw fit, but when pressed by Judge Parker, he vacillated on what kind of decree should be issued. Vaguely he asked for "a reasonable time" to prepare the plans for the school equalization program. There would be a time in some undefined future when the "problem" of segregation would "disappear," but Figg did not elaborate. Following a final statement by Marshall, the panel adjourned, and the three judges met to consider their response.[12]

The decision came within a month: Parker, joined by Timmerman, ruled that the issue was properly a legislative one. Since there were strong arguments on either side of the segregation controversy, he reasoned, legislatures must be let alone to hash it out, although the Supreme Court had backed away from *Plessy* as the precedent on which state legislatures operated regarding graduate education. Recent Supreme Court precedents in *Sweatt* and *McLaurin* dealing with higher education did not apply, because education at the lower levels was compulsory, because it could conceivably be as good in a segregated lower school (although Whitehead's report demonstrated that was not the case in Clarendon), and because professional contacts were not as important as they were in a law school. Parker's majority decision put the status of *Plessy* to the side, because "railroad matters" were not being considered.

In dissent Waring issued his final major opinion from the bench: a twenty-page excoriation of segregation and a passionate argument for its demise.

While his declaration that "segregation, per se, is inequality" is widely quoted, the contour of his dissent thoroughly dismantled the argument for segregation both judicially and socially. He ridiculed the state for its admission of inequalities, when, in their answer to the filing five months before the trial, they had declared that none existed. "Subsequent to the institution of this suit, James F. Byrnes, the Governor of South Carolina, had stated in his inaugural address that the State must take steps to provide money for improving educational facilities and that thereafter, the Legislature had adopted certain legislation. They stated that they hoped that in time they would obtain money as a result of the foregoing and improve the school situation." Waring argued that ignoring the "primary purpose of the suit" would show that the efforts and expense of the sixty-six plaintiffs, their six attorneys, and eleven witnesses—many in the latter two groups came from out of state—would be in vain. Waring lauded the "unexampled courage" of the plaintiffs, who persisted against a "long established and age-old pattern of [the state's] way of life." He continued, "If a case of this magnitude can be turned aside and a court refused to hear these basic issues by the mere device of admission that some buildings, blackboards, lighting fixtures and toilet facilities are unequal but that they may be remedied by the spending of a few dollars, then, indeed people in the plight in which these plaintiffs are, have no adequate remedy or forum in which to air their wrongs." Waring predicted that if the case was turned aside, the Black struggle for equality would continue for generations. "They are entitled to have these rights now and not in the future. And no excuse can be made to deny them these rights which are theirs under the Constitution and laws of America by the use of the false doctrine and patter called 'separate but equal' and it is the duty of the Court to meet these issues simply and factually and without fear, sophistry and evasion." Waring declared that he wanted "no part" of further evading the issue. He declared that the nation must, "without evasion or equivocation, face the issue of whether school segregation was legal or not under the Fourteenth Amendment."

Waring went on to discuss how the Supreme Court had used the Fourteenth Amendment, while prohibitory, to create a body of law that asserted African American citizens' rights beginning in 1880 with *Strauder v. West Virginia* through recent higher education rulings. He then turned his sights on *Plessy*, the "real rock on which the defendants base their case." Waring pointed out that the state's intent in the recently decided *McLaurin* case was to satisfy its own segregation laws rather than comply with the national standard, quoting, "State-imposed restrictions which produce such inequalities cannot be sustained." After discussing the plaintiff's witnesses' finding of the damage that segregation caused to *all* children, Waring attacked racial prejudice:

When do we get our first ideas of religion, nationality and the other basic ideologies? The vast number of individuals follow religious and political groups because of their childhood training. And it is difficult and nearly impossible to change and eradicate these early prejudices, however strong may be the appeal to reason. There is absolutely no reasonable explanation for racial prejudice. It is all caused by unreasoning emotional reactions and these are gained in early childhood. Let the little child's mind be poisoned by prejudice of this kind and it is practically impossible to ever remove these impressions however many years he may have of teaching by philosophers, religious leaders or patriotic citizens. If segregation is wrong then the place to stop it is in the first grade and not in graduate colleges.

Waring continued, "From their testimony, it was clearly apparent, as it should be to any thoughtful person, irrespective of having such expert testimony, that segregation in education can never produce equality and that it is an evil that must be eradicated." He declared that segregated education in South Carolina must go "now." "If the courts of this land are to render justice under the laws without fear or favor, justice for all men and all kinds of men, the time to do it is now and the place is in the elementary schools where our future citizens learn their first lesson to respect the dignity of the individual in a democracy."[13] Soon thereafter, however, Waring retired and left the state, never to return until his burial in 1968.

After Waring's scathing rebuke, just eight days later, on July 1, 1951, a 3 percent sales tax—the first in the state's history—went into effect. By September 1954 legislators had appropriated more than $100 million in sales tax for the improvement and construction of schools. Byrnes also sought close cooperation among southern states to resist federal intervention.[14] He called for the other states to follow South Carolina's lead and acknowledge inequality that existed in segregation and commit to reform. Like a military strategy, it was hoped, this commitment would leave the South impregnable to attack from without by the federal government or by Black citizens from within.

In the early years of the equalization program, the money spent on Black schools was nearly two-thirds of all expenditures, even though political expediency required significant spending on White schools as well. George Bell Timmerman Jr., son of the judge, who was elected as governor in 1954, stated in his 1955 inaugural that "our building program has substantially equalized school buildings for Negro children. Many of them attend finer school houses than do many white children."[15] In Clarendon County more than $2.1 million was spent by 1956, compared to $770,576 for White schools. By early 1956 the school equalization program was 95 percent complete in Orangeburg County.

Spending in that county, which had an enrollment of 6,254 White students and 12,859 Black students, totaled $5.3 million, of which $3.9 million went to Black schools.[16] The program had standardized school buildings and led to a boom in school construction, but despite the huge gains in school expenditures in the early 1950s, South Carolina still lagged behind many of its southern neighbors in spending. South Carolina's spending on education increased by 253 percent between 1940 and 1952, but similar jumps throughout the region kept the state behind. In 1952, for example, South Carolina trailed every state but Arkansas in spending for instruction and total education spending. South Carolina also lagged behind all other southern states in the ratio of spending for Black and White students: in 1940 Black students received thirty cents for every dollar spent on White students; by 1952 the amount had risen to sixty cents—but it was still the lowest percentage in the South. South Carolina's Black teachers were the third lowest paid in the region as well, trailing only Mississippi and Arkansas.[17] Even though the original plan was designed to "equalize" Black schools, by 1963 White schools had received 53.9 percent of the equalization money. Black South Carolinians continued to press for desegregation as well, so the plan failed on multiple levels despite the improvements that took place.

Like the teacher salary cases, the school equalization program was never intended to be a means of securing social justice for Black South Carolinians. Rather it was intended all along to undermine or delay desegregation under the guise of moving toward compliance. The school building program was certainly successful in decreasing some of the disparities in infrastructure between Black and White schools. In 1950–51 there were 1,300 one- or two-teacher schools for Black South Carolinians and only 377 for their White counterparts. By the end of the 1954–55 school year, South Carolina still had 339 of the tiny schools serving Black students and 96 serving White students. By the 1956–57 school year, the numbers had been drastically reduced even further: 54 one- or two-teacher schools remained for White students and only 79 for Black students. In 1956 there were 236 White high schools and 131 Black high schools in the state.[18] However, spending did nothing to overturn decades of curricular and economic disparities that resulted in lower educational attainment for Black students. Black students averaged only 4.3 years of schooling, while White students averaged 7.6. While both were below the national average of 9.3 years, clearly the state had not lived up to the promise of equality while offering separate educational opportunities to Black students.[19]

In January 1952, Governor Byrnes recommended repeal of the section of the 1895 state constitution that required the state to operate public schools. In the November 1952 elections, South Carolina voters by a margin of more than two-to-one approved the repeal of the constitutional requirement for public schools. Although never acted upon—in fact the repeal amendment was not ratified until March 1954—the repeal would have allowed the General Assembly to eliminate the entire system of public education, thereby eliminating the legal issue.

By the time the Supreme Court sent *Briggs* back to the district court for an update on Clarendon's equalization, the panel was made up only of Parker and Timmerman, who ruled that adequate progress was underway in March 1952.[20] The NAACP again appealed. As the case made its way back to the Supreme Court in December, Robert Figg speculated that it would uphold the lower court decision.[21] Combined with cases from Kansas, Virginia, the District of Columbia, and Delaware, the South Carolina case led to the Supreme Court's opinion in *Brown v. Board of Education,* a decision that led to more than twenty years of conflict in the courts and ultimately in the streets of South Carolina and other states. In the immediate aftermath of the decision, however, the only thing that changed was the intensification of rhetoric.

Reaction to the decision from the public was swift. Letters from White South Carolinians to state senator Edgar A. Brown offered support for resistance to desegregation. One of the first letters Brown received came from Jack Hightower, writing from New York. Hightower, a transplanted southerner from North Carolina, was vice president and general manager of the Greyhound Bus Corporation. "I trust this finds you in good health," he wrote, "and in the frame of mind to insist that the State of South Carolina tell the Supreme Court to go to hell." He asked in a postscript, "Why in the hell don't we secede again? We control all the good Bourbon, so the damyankees [*sic*] would die of thirst!"[22] Brown responded, as he did to several other correspondents, by sharing his conviction that the decision set back Southern life by "fifty years and has done the colored people untold and irreparable injury. The rank and file of the colored people in the South want Segregation."[23] Columbia attorney Irvine Belser wrote to Brown suggesting that people who wanted desegregation be required to set up "voluntary associations or corporations modelled along the lines of Electric and Telephone Cooperative corporations."[24] Brown's response to Belser revealed the strategy that White South Carolina would use for the next decade. Since only Clarendon County was affected by the decision, supposedly, "if we forced the court to refer the Clarendon County case back to the District Court and then the NAACP had to take up every other district, because each is a separate situation, and with separate conditions, it would take a life-time to ever substantially uproot our present public school system."[25] Interestingly, Waring had anticipated such a strategy in his dissent, and perhaps it was the source of Brown's inspiration. Waring wrote: "If this be the measure of justice to be meted out to them, then, indeed, hundreds, nay thousands, of cases will have to be brought and in each case thousands of dollars will have to be spent for the employment of legal talent and scientific testimony and then the cases will be turned aside, postponed or eliminated by devices such as this."[26]

It did not take a lifetime, but for many African Americans, it probably seemed that way. The strategy of delay was not, as many apologists for White leaders have argued, merely a means of preparing White South Carolinians for the inevitable. Rather it was a strategy to maintain segregation and to keep Black South Carolinians in the unequal circumstances in which they lived by wearing down the resolve of their challengers or having them age out. The argument that White leaders were preparing their White constituents for change is patently false given the years of calculated delay and segregationist rhetoric that followed.

There were some White people who offered moderate or progressive opinions. From Hilda, South Carolina, Evermae B. Robertson wrote that she "cannot see [herself] teaching negro children" but suggested that desegregation should be done on a grade-by-grade basis starting with first grade, an idea that was frequently proposed throughout the desegregation period. Nevertheless she looked forward to retirement.[27] Clara Annie Childs, a former teacher "now studying at Duke University," wrote with a different point of view. Worried about the prospect of closing public schools, Childs called for leadership from state politicians and also suggested a "long range program of trial enrollment beginning at the first grade." She, unlike many others in and out of positions of leadership, recognized "the temporary motives of politics" and the "emotionalism over chimeras" that overblown rhetoric over the *Brown* decision could lead to.[28]

Black South Carolinians reacted in different ways to the Supreme Court's first decision in *Brown*. On May 25, 1954, some parents of Black students in North Augusta submitted a petition requesting the continuation of segregation. In Mullins about one hundred "patrons" of a Black school argued for segregation's continuation as well.[29] In Florence in the summer of 1955, following economic reprisals and the threat of reprisals, many parents asked to withdraw from a petition to desegregate their schools.[30] The threat, and reality, of economic reprisals likely had something to do with their desire to withdraw their names from the petitions. Interestingly George Elmore, who had fought for Black voting rights in the 1940s, opposed the *Brown* decision. However, it is possible that much of Elmore's discontent arose from his inability to acquire an office with the NAACP.[31]

Despite isolated opposition, most Black South Carolinians favored desegregation. James M. Hinton, the state NAACP president, said that local action would be taken in school districts to urge desegregation, and in Sumter the board of directors of Morris College for Negroes, a Baptist school, officially de-segregated by ordering the admission of all qualified students—the first school in the state to desegregate officially since the imposition of Jim Crow.[32] In early November the state's White Methodists and the White teachers' professional organization, the South Carolina Education Association, recommended the continuation of segregation. In response to the move by the White association, the parallel Black teachers' professional organization, the Palmetto Education Association, which had supported John Wrighten's efforts to desegregate the University of South Carolina Law School, promised "to work unceasingly to uphold" the *Brown* ruling.[33]

The Supreme Court's refusal to uphold the separate but equal doctrine required state leaders to go on the attack. Byrnes, a former Supreme Court justice, wrote an article for *U.S. News and World Report* castigating the Supreme Court and demanding that it be "curbed."[34] On May 20 he froze the school construction program, demonstrating White belief that Black South Carolinians did not deserve decent schools unless they were willing to accept segregation, as well as a willingness to punish all South Carolina children for the Supreme Court's actions. The shutdown only lasted a couple of months, as the Gressette Committee recommended in July, following an appraisal of the system, that the program be restarted. The recommendation came primarily because the committee members feared that shutting down the program would merely give impetus for African Americans to intensify demands for desegregated schools.[35]

David Robinson—who in addition to serving as lead attorney for the Gressette Committee was also, ironically, the former leader of the state's Committee for Interracial Cooperation—argued that the money should be released to local school boards. They should be given "broad powers in the assignment of pupils [since] the best chance of evolving something satisfactory is to leave the problem in local hands." Releasing the funds would allow the local school boards to have something to work with as they undoubtedly would continue to assign students on the basis of race: "If we decline funds for a negro high school in a school district, the Trustees will have no alternative but to mix the children. If we provide the high school, the chances are great that most of the negroes will prefer their children to go to this new school."[36] It also meant that more money would be available for building or improving White schools. Funds were released at the end of August. Following the centralizing efforts of the early 1950s, the new push to allow local districts more control had legal ramifications. Giving local district boards more control meant that instead of suing a county board of education, plaintiffs would have to sue individual district boards of trustees, creating a more protracted process.

Robinson explored a variety of responses to the *Brown* decision. In early June 1954, he proposed that the Court's decision should be reframed as one that emphasized individual rights, thereby considering the child's or parents' wishes to attend a desegregated school. Such a policy would theoretically include a "restricted" right to petition for transfers to different schools. Some of the restrictions Robinson proposed eventually came to pass, such as requiring the petition to be filed a certain amount of time before school started in the fall. Other proposals, such as a requirement that only lawyers admitted to the state bar and who lived in the state could represent students wishing to transfer— clearly aimed at NAACP attorneys from New York—were never implemented. While his later writings often took a harder line on desegregation, Robinson's responses were moderate, befitting the former chair of the Committee for Interracial Cooperation, at least for the time and circumstances. While he believed that "most of the parents prefer their children to go to segregated school," he also believed "that a few negro children in the white schools would not create a serious problem."[37] State attorney general T. C. Callison agreed with Robinson that rights not "exercised or demanded by the individual" should not be enforced by the courts but acknowledged that the *Brown* case would work as a class action and control the situation for everyone.[38]

Robinson wrote of the "strong disagreement" felt in South Carolina regarding the Supreme Court's decision in *Brown*. The decision, he argued, was erroneous in relying extensively on Topeka, where segregation was optional, and Delaware, where the Black population was small, rather than on Virginia and South Carolina, where segregation was required and the Black population was quite large. Nevertheless, he wrote, "we must recognize that when reduced to decree form it becomes the law of the land. . . . [However,] in the absence of a decree . . . final decisions must be postponed." Robinson called for "calm, considered thinking" but said that the schools should be operated just as they had been in 1953–54. Regardless, there were only two alternatives in the long run. The only advantage, if it were one at all, to closing the schools altogether, would be "some exodus of our Negro population," leading to an estimated reduction to 10 percent from the current 40 percent. Some people thought that "Negroes deserve to lose their public education facilities because of their part in the segregation litigation," but Robinson considered such an attitude "short sighted": "Our Negroes should be educated into responsible, efficient, tax-paying citizens, not left as unskilled recipients of social security benefits." The other alternative Robinson foresaw was equally unattractive: "Mixing the races in the schools . . . [would] retard rather than advance the education of both races." In addition, "many Negro school teachers would be without jobs."[39] The solution would require a holding by the courts that "trustees cannot be forced to integrate the schools on . . . a geographical basis, [in which case] the Negro parent [would be] relegated to his right to petition to have his own child admitted to the white school upon the ground that there is no reason other than race upon which the Board can exclude him." Robinson thought this was the best way to limit the number of Black students applying to White schools.[40] Debate over school closing continued well into the 1960s. Had African Americans been successful at integrating schools in the late 1950s, parts of South Carolina might have followed the disastrous course followed in Prince Edward County, Virginia, but by the time minimal desegregation came to South Carolina in 1963, few political leaders were willing to resort to that extreme measure.

Still, in the fall of 1954, no Black students attempted to enroll in any of the White schools of the state. However, a Catholic school in Rock Hill opened its doors to Black students for the first time. On the first day of school, twenty-nine White children and five Black children were enrolled. At the same time, the Presbyterian Synod that included South Carolina voted to continue segregation in its institutions. The vote affected Presbyterian College and Thornwell Orphanage, both in Clinton, South Carolina, and a seminary and a college in Georgia and North Carolina, respectively.[41]

On taking office in January 1955, before the court had even heard arguments in the remedy stage of *Brown*, newly elected governor Timmerman reiterated his campaign position that freedom of choice was the only acceptable answer to the quandary posed by the Supreme Court's decision in *Brown*. Timmerman also proposed removing public school issues from the jurisdiction of the federal courts, arguing that such "judicial infringement upon . . . freedom" must be stopped. Timmerman became the spokesman for White dissent against the Supreme Court's ruling. He criticized President Eisenhower for daring to suggest that individuals should be "judged and measured by what he is, rather than by his color, race or religion." "Never before," said Timmerman, "has a national administration proclaimed as unimportant a person's race and religion."

Meanwhile the Gressette Committee offered its own suggestions on how best to delay segregation. First the legislature should remove all compulsory attendance laws from the books. Then it should authorize the devolution of the power to open and close schools to the district boards of trustees from the county boards of education. The legislature should also allow pupils to transfer across county lines and allow trustees to lease or even sell school property. In March the legislature passed several laws based on those recommendations, including a repeal of the compulsory education law. Timmerman declared that the repeal was "a pledge of good faith to the [White] people of South

Carolina that they will not be forced to send their children to mixed schools."
In an address to the convention of the South Carolina Education Association,
the governor said that "never before has anyone seriously proposed that the
children of two biologically different races should be compelled to mix socially.
. . . It is new. It is novel. It is contrary to the divine order of things. Only an evil
mind could conceive it. Only a foolish mind can accept it." Thomas R. Waring,
nephew of the judge and editor of the *Charleston News and Courier,* wrote
in *Harper's* of White fears: the worry that Black underachievement would undermine school quality was a major cause of dread for White parents, but in
addition "there's no use to tell them that it is unlikely that anyone will catch
venereal disease from a toilet seat. They just don't want to take risks of any
kind with their children."[42]

Recognizing that even requiring cases to be filed district by district might
not be sufficient discouragement, in April the legislature, in an amendment
to the annual appropriations bill, provided that state money would be cut off
for any school ordered to integrate by a court order. Several counties, including Clarendon, followed suit by adopting complementary measures for their
localities. The state legislature also acted to end the practice of automatically
rehiring teachers, thereby giving local trustees more power over their teaching
staff. Following other conservatives, the state's two US senators, Strom Thurmond and Olin D. Johnston, proposed national legislation to reduce the scope
of federal court jurisdiction over education.[43]

The next month the Supreme Court rendered its decision regarding the
process of desegregation in *Brown II.* Unfortunately the Court came up with
the phrase "all deliberate speed" to describe how the process of desegregation
should proceed and directed the federal courts in the states to take the lead in
the process. When *Briggs v. Elliott* was remanded to the three-judge panel for
further review on orders from the Supreme Court in *Brown II,* Judge John J.
Parker pounced on the opportunity to interpret the High Court's decision.[44]
The Court had not, Parker decided, struck down all constitutional law supporting segregation. While *Plessy* might be invalid, the *Civil Rights Cases* decision
still held. State action to enforce segregation might be illegal, but a private decision to segregate remained sacrosanct.[45] Parker's dictum—often referred to in
the literature as the *Briggs* dictum—guided much of the legal thinking of many
White lawyers and judges in South Carolina for years to come.

While the actual decree enjoined the Clarendon County school board from
excluding Black children from White schools, the language of Parker's dictum
caused trouble for more than a decade. His words, put to use by districts and
other officials to secure White supremacy, delayed all desegregation until the

early 1960s and prevented meaningful levels of desegregation until the fall of 1970. Thus, as dozens of southern communities in several states began the process of desegregation following *Brown II*, South Carolina remained one of the states where forcing plaintiffs to sue by school district to enforce *Brown* predominated.

"Many people are coming to realize," Timmerman said in November, "that integration, politics and sociology are poor substitutes for Christianity." "I am convinced the great majority of our Negro people oppose racial mixing," he continued, adding a list of what some White people would have called "good Negroes" to his diatribe. It was in this same speech that Timmerman, building on the same straw man argument that White southerners relied on throughout the civil rights era, attacked the NAACP's role in the aftermath of the brutal killing of Emmett Till. "There was nothing in the case to warrant the notorious publicity," Timmerman said. "It was given notoriety only because it happened in Mississippi. The *alleged* body of Till was taken to Chicago . . . [and] placed on public exhibition in one of the most uncivilized displays of desecration in modern times."[46]

Thurgood Marshall remained optimistic following *Brown II*, declaring in an interview with the *Southern School News* that the policy of the NAACP was "desegregation in most areas of the South by not later than September 1956." Black South Carolinians across the state's urban areas—Beaufort, Columbia, Greenville, Florence, and Spartanburg—either submitted petitions or were planning to do so.[47] Meanwhile the NAACP reached a pragmatic decision regarding Clarendon County. The case had been made that school segregation was unconstitutional, but White people in the county made it abundantly clear to Marshall when he visited the county in 1955 that they would have no problem closing the schools if push came to shove. NAACP executive secretary Roy Wilkins stated that "from a practical standpoint," it did not matter "if Clarendon [County] is not integrated for 99 years."[48] The organization thus made the difficult decision to leave Clarendon County to its own devices. Additional legal action beginning in 1960 and lasting most of that decade was required before desegregation took place.

Despite Marshall's initial optimism, the fact that *Brown II* placed direct authority over desegregation under the federal district courts provided the infrastructure for delay. Though *Brown II* was decided in May 1955, by September 1956 only 723 of 10,000 southern school districts had any measure of desegregation. In Charleston, as in other cities and towns in South Carolina, African Americans became increasingly impatient and began to organize. Students at Burke High School met with teachers for planning sessions. One of those students was Harvey Gantt, who later integrated Clemson University. One of the leaders of Charleston's movement was J. Arthur Brown, a Realtor who was well known in the African American community. Under his leadership the city's NAACP membership rose from 300 to almost 1,500 within a few months of his assuming the reins.[49] While White South Carolinians began to organize actively against desegregation, Black citizens were beginning to move equally quickly to challenge segregation.

One observer noted that "resistance to desegregation [was] increasing in South Carolina" and that it took several forms. When Black parents in Charleston County organized petition drives, signers' names were published in the *News and Courier*, and Thomas Waring suggested that White readers "study carefully" the list of names. White parents in Moultrie District, across the Cooper River from Charleston, organized in response to a petition by Black parents there and went "on record as being in favor of the closing down of the schools before any school in the district is permitted to operate on a non-segregated basis." In all there were more than one thousand White attendees at three different meetings in response to petitions from Black citizens in the county.[50] Following the lead of their counterparts in Mississippi, Alabama, and Louisiana, and usually in response to Black assertiveness, White South Carolinians began to form citizens' councils to supplement legislative and legal resistance by exerting economic and political pressure to force Black citizens to back down. In Orangeburg County a petition signed by thirty-six Black citizens led to the formation of the Elloree Citizens' Council, and three more citizens' councils were formed by the end of August in that county alone.

The council movement in South Carolina thrived especially in the low-country and piedmont and enjoyed the approval, if not the direct participation, of many members of the state's power structure. Members of the so-called Committee of 52, which cooperated with the councils, included several prominent businessmen. Local politicians regularly spoke at council meetings. Unlike the councils in other states, however, the South Carolina citizens' councils did not have very much legislative influence. The most influential politicos did not associate with the councils, though Emory Rogers, who had represented Clarendon County in the *Briggs* case, served as the first executive secretary of the statewide group. The citizens' council movement in South Carolina peaked in 1956, and though new chapters were formed into the 1960s, membership began to dwindle thereafter. Following Rogers's retirement at the end of 1956, the South Carolina Association had no cohesive leadership. Dedicated segregationist William D. Workman charged that the Ku Klux Klan had infiltrated the citizens' councils, a charge that indirectly led to the resignation of Baxter

Graham, the third chairman of the state association in as many years. Subsequent leaders were content to make sure that local governments were aware of the problems that desegregation brought and were never dedicated to expanding the organization's membership.[51]

Despite the variation in the councils' fortunes, their efforts met with some success. Several African Americans who signed the Orangeburg petition were dismissed from their jobs or told not to return as tenant farmers or sharecroppers the next season. Several African Americans responded by requesting that their names be removed from the petitions they had signed. Some, like Wilhelmenia Jones, claimed they did not know what they were signing. In all more than thirty signers asked to have their names removed from the petition. In Clarendon County, J. H. Richburg asked that his and his son's names be removed from the list of people added to the list of plaintiffs in *Briggs v. Elliott* because his daughters and daughter-in-law were having trouble getting their teaching jobs renewed.[52]

Orangeburg County state representative Jerry M. Hughes proposed investigating NAACP activities at South Carolina State, where students went on strike in 1956. In October, Lt. Gov. Ernest F. Hollings declared that the NAACP should be declared "subversive and illegal." In November it was revealed that Dean Chester C. Travelstead of the University of South Carolina's School of Education had been dismissed for favoring desegregation. For many White people, opposition to desegregation remained the priority, and even the minimal authority of religious leaders was insufficient to move them toward moderation. Reverend John V. Murray, under pressure from local Methodists because of his anti-segregation ideas, was removed from his position and transferred. In Batesburg, Governor Timmerman's own pastor, G. Jackson Stafford, resigned from his position in the First Baptist Church over the issue. He had voted for a resolution adopted in the Southern Baptist Convention favoring the Supreme Court's decision in *Brown,* and opposition quickly arose against him among his congregation, culminating in the deacon board, of which Judge Timmerman was chair, forcing him out.[53]

In December 1955, the Gressette Committee issued its third annual report, calling for "every legal means" to be employed to maintain school segregation. The Supreme Court, according to the committee's interpretation (certainly informed by Judge Parker's decision in the 1955 *Briggs* action), "did not intend to force integration on an unwilling people." In the January 1956 session of the state legislature, several legislators introduced new bills designed to cement the state's commitment to segregation or to prevent the operation of the NAACP. Joining other southern legislatures including those of Virginia and Texas, South Carolina's General Assembly passed laws attempting to restrict the activities of the NAACP and to otherwise ensconce massive resistance into state law. Among the new bills were proposals to give county sheriffs the power to reassign students in case of potential violence; to bar teachers from being members of the Communist Party or the NAACP (though not the citizens' councils); to forbid state employees from membership in the NAACP or the KKK; to remove the tax-exempt status of churches that allowed their buildings to be used for meetings of the Communist Party or the NAACP; and to study the effects of disposing of state-owned property that might be abandoned if integration were ordered. The legislature passed all but the latter bill by April 1956.

Burnet R. Maybank Jr., son of the late US senator whom Strom Thurmond had replaced in 1954, proposed a bill to provide state income-tax credits for people who sent their children to private schools in the state. It would allow relief for 30 percent of tuition, which could grow to 100 percent if integration were ordered. Maybank also explored relief from local property taxes, which supported public schools, for the same group.[54] There was even a resolution of interposition, hearkening back to the days of John C. Calhoun and the Nullification Crisis. New laws included requirements to close South Carolina State and any White college involved if desegregation were ever ordered, though an early draft of that bill would only have affected the White school involved.[55]

It was the year of the Southern Manifesto, in which the vast majority of the southern legislative delegation in the US Congress praised the *Plessy* case and subsequent supporting interpretations for their "humanity and common-sense." The manifesto, written largely by recently elected South Carolina senator Strom Thurmond, set forth the southern constitutional principle that the Supreme Court was allowing their personal opinions to interfere with the good order of society and with established constitutional doctrine.[56]

On the heels of Thurmond's manifesto, his home state legislature passed a joint resolution "condemning and protesting the usurpation and encroachment on the reserved powers of the states by the Supreme Court of the United States." Outlining the state's constitutional theory upon which segregation was based, the resolution emphasized South Carolina's reliance upon the Tenth Amendment, reserving powers not delegated to the national government to the states. The Supreme Court did not have the power to rule on the rights of the states, and the right of states to have segregated schools was not prohibited under the Fourteenth Amendment. "The action of the Supreme Court . . . constitutes a deliberate, palpable, and dangerous attempt to change the true intent and meaning of the Constitution," the legislature resolved. Approved on February 14, 1956, this "love letter" to the Constitution, or at least a White supremacist version of it, argued that the state should "judge for itself of the infractions and . . . take such other legal measures as it may deem appropriate to protect its sovereignty and the rights of its people."[57] Clearly only the "rights" of one segment of the people were being protected. Those legal measures would stall desegregation for another seven years and prevent any significant desegregation in South Carolina for another seven years beyond that.

4

"*PLESSY* HAS NOT BEEN OVERTURNED"

Law and Resistance in the Late 1950s

Despite White South Carolinians' rejection of *Brown,* Black South Carolinians worked to build on the precedent as they brought new issues to the courts in the second half of the 1950s. Attacking segregation in public accommodation enabled South Carolina's NAACP chapters to broaden the constitutional principles outlined in the *Brown* decision into South Carolina society. While the Court had not specifically overruled *Plessy v. Ferguson* beyond public education, individuals challenged the principles upon which *Plessy* rested, namely that segregated accommodations would be acceptable as long as they were "equal." White South Carolinians responded with political and legal measures, economic reprisals, and sometimes violence. The White community—even those in federal positions—was largely united in its efforts to nullify desegregation and clearly saw the school cases and other desegregation cases as inherently intertwined. Changes in the law would not translate into changes in their attitudes.

In July 1954, a year and a half before Rosa Parks was arrested in Montgomery, Alabama, for refusing to relinquish her seat on a city bus, Sarah Mae Flemming of Columbia sued the South Carolina Electric and Gas Company, which operated the city's bus system, for segregating her on the city's buses. The case came before Judge George Bell Timmerman in February 1955, and he quickly dismissed it, ruling that Flemming's case had no standing, since the state codes in question were constitutional. *Brown v. Board of Education,* he wrote, "is not applicable in the *field of public transportation.* . . . One's education and personality is [*sic*] not developed on a city bus. . . . To hold that the *Brown* decision extends to the field of public transportation would be an unwarranted enlargement of the doctrine announced in that decision and an unreasonable restriction on the police power of the state."[1] Flemming appealed in July 1955.

A couple of months earlier, a group of African Americans in Charleston County had met at NAACP chapter president J. Arthur Brown's office to discuss getting permission to use the Edisto Beach State Park, the only one

J. Arthur Brown at an NAACP meeting, September 15, 1963 (courtesy of
Richland Library, Columbia, South Carolina)

of twenty-one state parks that was closed to African Americans by law. One
park (Pleasant Ridge, in Greenville County) was designated for use by African
Americans exclusively, while four other parks had areas set aside for use by
Black citizens.[2] Although Black people in the Charleston area had threatened
to sue for some years, they had taken no action, and the issue had been on the
back burner since 1952, when a group of Black business owners and professionals from Charleston pressed the county to open a beach for Black citizens in
the area.[3] Now, with *Brown* the law of the land, the time seemed ripe to reopen
the issue. Etta Mae Clark, the second vice president of the Charleston branch
of the NAACP, was among the participants, as were John Chisolm and Charles
Mason, both of whom were on the local executive board of the NAACP. Clark
worked with her brother Richard at Richard's grocery store; Chisolm was
J. Arthur Brown's business partner; Mason was an executive at the Fielding
funeral home.[4] As such all had a certain amount of economic independence
from White people, making it less likely that any reprisals would have an effect.
Clark initiated the meeting because she "was going to have some friends down
in June and . . . wanted a place to take them, which we do not have, and [she]
went to [her] friends and asked about the Edisto Beach Park. . . . They said they
don't see any reason why we shouldn't write and ask for admission. We were
not going down, but we wanted to find out what was legal or right for us to do."

Clark and the others wrote J. M. Pope, the superintendent of the park, asking for permission to use the park's facilities on May 25. Pope's successor, Donald Cooler, responded: "This park was established in 1935 for the exclusive use of white persons, and based on custom and precedence we will have to deny your request." Cooler informed the group that "several of the state parks in South Carolina are designated for Negro use only. One park in this area, Hunting Island, has separate white and Negro areas. I suggest that you visit that park where you will be most welcome." Clark and the others used Cooler's response to sue him, state forester C. H. Flory, and state park director C. West Jacocks. They argued that sections 51–181 through 51–184 of the 1952 state Code of Laws specifically limited the use of the Edisto Beach State Park to White citizens, which violated the Fourteenth Amendment.[5]

The state's answer to the suit derived from *Plessy*'s assertion that the Fourteenth Amendment "could not have been intended to abolish distinctions based upon color, or to enforce social, as distinguished from political, equality, or a commingling of the two races upon terms unsatisfactory to either."

> [T]he purpose of the Park is to provide wholesome relaxation and recreation for those of all ages and sexes using the facilities, without compulsion and voluntarily, but that due to the natural inclination of each race at this time to associate with members of its own race, and to the present natural, historical, cultural and deep-rooted mental attitudes and feelings of each race against the social and sexual mixing of the races, there exists potential and definite dangers of unpleasantries, social friction, breaches of the peace and other events leading to riot and bloodshed.[6]

In addition to arguing that segregation was mutually agreed upon, the defense also relied on asserting that the rights of White citizens who might want to use the park without Black people being around were being violated. Ending segregation would be "a denial of equal protection under the law to the majority in favor of the gratification of a small vocal portion of the minority group." As in the law school case and the school equalization program, White people were willing to pay to maintain segregation. They accused the plaintiffs of "blocking the establishment" of a separate park for Black people, for which the state had appropriated fifty thousand dollars, because of "plaintiffs' objection to any segregated system, no matter how equal, and their insistence upon full integration, irrespective of the detrimental affects [sic] which will result from such a policy to members of their own and of the white race."[7] White people were victims of desegregation, not perpetrators of segregation.

At the first hearing in the case, held on August 23, 1955, presiding federal district judge Ashton H. Williams asked John Wrighten, the plaintiffs' attorney, whether it might not be a better idea if the plaintiffs accepted money to build their own beach. He wondered "whether or not [Wrighten] would rather see this beach closed altogether and the state surrender it [to private sale], rather than to accept the $50,000 and build a beach of your own." Wrighten demurred, citing Supreme Court case law, but Williams persisted: "We have got an unusual and extra-ordinary situation in Charleston County and in this section of the state, and I think that you are practical enough to realize that."[8]

Williams continued, citing at length an article by Frank Porter Graham, former US senator from North Carolina and president of the University of North Carolina. Graham, "the most enthusiastic supporter that you [African Americans] have in the United States," had argued that "a reasonable time is needed in the Deep South for the stages and ways of profound adjustment of the inner spirit of the people for the outer and sincere fulfillment of the new law of the land [*Brown v. Board of Education*]." Williams concluded by noting his duties as a judge to enforce the laws, but he remained "tremendously impressed" by Graham's argument "that the Deep South [states] . . . were the very last places that the people who had won the fight should attempt to press to victory." Segregation was too ingrained in the Deep South for Black citizens to have the temerity to demand what *Brown* required. He overtly disagreed with the decisions he was tasked to enforce: "If I had been sitting on the Supreme Court, I wouldn't have signed the opinions that were signed on May 17, 1954 and May 31, 1955."

The judge was not finished. He advised Wrighten, and the rest of South Carolina's Black population as well: "Don't be glib. Don't be too jubilant. Don't crow too much. Don't let your national secretary [of the NAACP] ever come back to South Carolina and make a speech over the radio. I listened to him. It was the worst speech I have ever heard in my life. It was the worst thing that could ever happen to the colored people."[9] Williams warned the plaintiffs to avoid "unwise action" that might "destroy, if you do it too quickly, the things you hope to accomplish." The parties then agreed to let the state supreme court decide the matter, with the federal court maintaining jurisdiction. In an unusual move, Williams added a dictum that had nothing to do with any of the legal issues involved. After warning the Ku Klux Klan of the dangers of coming into conflict with the decisions of the Supreme Court, Williams cited the NAACP as the second of

> two organizations whose apparent purposes and aims are to win by any means. . . . This organization, along with the Klu [*sic*] Klux Klan are the real enemies to any progress in the school cases, or in any other like cases. It is my belief that no progress can be made unless and until both the Klan

and the NAACP are eliminated from the picture in South Carolina. . . . I shall scrutinize all cases coming before me most carefully, and if it appears that either the Klan or the NAACP have been guilty of improper and illegal practices, I shall not hesitate to take the proper steps.[10]

In December 1955 a similar case in Maryland had been decided in favor of a group of Black people seeking access to a state park there, and under the agreements reached the previous August, the Maryland case controlled the issue in South Carolina.[11] However, since the state supreme court did not address the facts of the Maryland case, it remained unclear to the state's attorneys that the Edisto Park should automatically be opened to African Americans. The parties agreed to a trial in the federal district court, and the date was set for February 6, 1956.

At the trial Assistant State Attorney General James S. Verner questioned Etta Clark at length. After first establishing the NAACP membership of the principals, he questioned Clark about the fifty thousand dollars that the state legislature had set aside to establish a private park for African Americans. Clark declared that she had no knowledge of any such effort beyond having read about it. Verner then asked Clark a key question: "Suppose that the state would put a park for the Negro people and one for the white people, would you be satisfied with that, or do you want only one park open to all?" Clark responded concisely: "As of today, I want one. . . . Any place that is open and supported by tax money, I would like to be allowed to go."[12] Verner seemed incredulous: "You are perfectly willing for the park to be shut down so long and no matter how much other people sought it, so long as a Negro cannot go to any park, no matter where it is or what it is, is that correct?" Clark's response went well beyond the question: "They never cared how I felt. I never had any place to go."[13]

Verner moved on to explore Clark's membership in the NAACP and the issue of her "representation" of Black Charlestonians in the case. Of the 35,000 to 40,000 African Americans in Charleston County, only 1,400 belonged to the local branch of the NAACP. There had never been a vote among the membership concerning the issue of segregated parks. Verner asked whether the group had conferred with Thurgood Marshall or any other lawyers prior to writing the letters to the state park. He then established that Wrighten was the NAACP counsel for Charleston. Given Judge Williams's earlier tirade against the national NAACP, Verner's strategy of painting the lawsuit as a conspiracy by leaders of the Charleston branch, with possible connections to Marshall, was clever. However, Clark continued to insist that no one had conferred with any lawyer before writing the letters asking for admission to Edisto Park.

Nevertheless the connections to the local branch were clear. In the absence of anything more than a coincidental connection, Verner's attempt to paint the lawsuit as a conspiracy failed.

When J. Arthur Brown took the stand, South Carolina State Law School graduate W. Newton Pough, the co-counsel for the plaintiffs, established that the local NAACP had had some conferences about the matter and had hired an attorney to investigate it. Brown also noted that there had been efforts to investigate buying other areas for a recreational beach for Black people in Charleston County, though nothing had ever come of the efforts. On cross-examination attorney Verner asked whether Brown and the others' reasoning behind trying to get access to the beach for Black people was just "to put this matter to a test and get justice, if you call it justice, and get it over with," instead of truly desiring, after forty-one years of life in Charleston County, finally to go to the beach for fun. Verner also questioned whether racial peace in the county could continue with an integrated park system. When asked if he thought the racial situation was "disintegrating due to the present pressures that are being exerted," Brown responded, "I feel that if agitation is not brought about by some hot-heads, that people will get along together." Verner attempted to paint Brown as one of the local hot-heads on racial policy. Brown had been involved in petition drives calling for the integration of local school districts in Charleston County. He had also typed the letters to the park superintendent, though he insisted that he did not ask anyone to sign the letters—that was a purely voluntary matter.[14]

Judge Williams speculated that criminal activity in an integrated park would increase. "Now, we might as well be perfectly frank with each other, and we know that there is a greater criminal tendency in Charleston among the Negroes than there is among the white people." Williams also noted that he was comfortable with the wider discretion that the Supreme Court had given federal judges for dealing with the school situation but was concerned that no such rules applied for parks. Nevertheless Williams was willing "to lay down the rule and have the Supreme Court pass on it at a later time."[15]

Verner appealed to tradition invoking South Carolina's long heritage of racial segregation—the "spirit of the state"—to bolster his argument against suddenly integrating the state's institutions. He and Williams attempted to get Brown to work out a compromise in which the court could issue an order allowing the beach authorities to set aside a portion of the beach for use by Black people. Despite repeated assurances from Brown that any violence would be the result of individual disagreements rather than racial animosity, Williams remained unconvinced. Not surprisingly Williams also remained concerned that the beach would be "abandoned" by White people if he opened the beach to everyone, though it apparently escaped him that such an abandonment would be voluntary and therefore fine under the *Plessy* theory. Verner claimed that "that practically happened in the Maryland case. When it was opened, the whites quit using it in Maryland to a large extent." Brown insisted that once the park was opened, it may very well take a transition period in which White people would refuse to come to the park, but like other facilities in Charleston, the beach would eventually be integrated as they began to return. "I think that when those people find out that being around Negroes, that we aren't any type of creature who will eat them or try to tear them apart . . . and that we are just another group of human beings [things will return to normal]." Verner remained skeptical.[16]

In a final exchange, Judge Williams and state attorney general T. C. Callison discussed the relevance of the case to *Plessy v. Ferguson* and *Brown v. Board,* reluctantly concluding that "the State has itself to blame somewhat for not having made some provision years ago."[17] Now, with *Brown* as the law of the land, the court's hands were tied. During the trial the General Assembly passed legislation to withdraw state funding from any school or park that was ordered to be integrated.

The court adjourned so Williams could consider his opinion, but on February 8 the State Forestry Commission "jumped the guns on the legislature" and ordered the park closed. State senator Edgar A. Brown knew that Judge Williams had his hands tied by the Maryland case and decided that the best way to deal with the Edisto case would be to close the park. Special legislation was prepared and rushed through the legislature. Commissioner Flory got wind of the legislature's move, probably through the governor, and preempted it.[18]

The legislature continued with its actions. The park would remain open to White visitors, though: it was little used in winter anyway, except by fishers. The *Columbia State* noted that Flory had said that any fishers who showed up could go right ahead and fish—if they were White. On February 9 the state senate began consideration of the bill to close the park officially, pending the legislature's determination of how to deal with state funding for the park system. There was already a provision in the appropriations bill to continue funding the park system only if it continued to be operated on a segregated basis. Ultimately, in addition to confirming the Forestry Commission's closing of the Edisto Beach State Park, the legislature amended the state Code of Laws to require segregation in all state parks.[19]

On March 2, 1956, Judge Williams decided that, since the legislature had passed the law closing the park, there was "no further question to be considered in the Park case." He ordered a hearing on March 21 on the question of dismissal.[20] In the meantime, on March 8 Governor Timmerman signed the act closing the park altogether. The plaintiffs refused to remove their complaint: the issue was not whether the state had the power to close the park but whether the statutes that mandated segregation in the park violated the Fifth and Fourteenth Amendments. Since the commission and legislature had closed the park, they could immediately reopen it if the plaintiffs withdrew.[21]

Because the legislature would have to act—and because that would take at least a year—the state argued that the case before the court was moot and hypothetical. The US Supreme Court had ruled the statutes in question unconstitutional in the Maryland case. So if all the plaintiffs wanted was a declaration that the laws were unconstitutional, they had it—though not from Judge Williams. The only issue left was whether the judge would order the park opened to all, and since there was no park left to open, the issue had dissolved. Closing of parks—or schools—in the face of desegregation orders was a new form of White resistance that relied on the state action doctrine. If the state were not, in fact, acting to enforce segregation, there could be no legal foundation for a case challenging segregation.

Williams refused to issue any ruling concerning all the state parks in South Carolina. Only the Edisto park was at issue in the case, and since no Black citizens had applied for admission to any of the other parks and may never do so as far as Judge Williams knew, there was no reason to issue a blanket ruling. However, he was prepared to "state here and now that the Supreme Court of the United States has already ruled that [the] plaintiffs have a right to use the Edisto Beach if it is ever used as a public place."[22] Williams then spoke at length with attorneys Callison, Verner, Pough, and Wrighten regarding whether to issue a formal ruling or to dismiss the case. Ultimately he decided to defer action, keeping the case open but undecided. Noting appeals by leaders of both national political parties, Williams called for a "common sense" solution, lest South Carolinians of both races find themselves not only without parks but without schools as well. The state legislature was "playing for keeps," said Williams, and he did not want to be the judge responsible for the closure of the state's schools.[23]

Williams and other federal judges in South Carolina played a vital role in maintaining segregation. By limiting rulings as much as possible and adhering to sometimes antiquated precedents, they often managed to drag cases out longer than necessary. After the court of appeals overturned Timmerman's decision in the *Flemming* case, he remained defiant. He argued that *Plessy* had not been overturned. It was mid-1956, and he had just dismissed Sarah Mae Flemming's case for the second time, this time after a two-day hearing where she and other witnesses on her behalf testified. Since *Plessy* had been the controlling precedent at the time Flemming filed her original case, that precedent continued to drive Timmerman's rulings, even though the appellate court clearly held otherwise. Flemming's attorney was Philip Wittenberg, a Columbia attorney who had attended the University of Michigan as an undergraduate and stayed for law school.[24] Wittenberg wrote Arthur Caldwell, the head of the Civil Rights Section of the Justice Department, who opined that Timmerman was unfit to sit on the bench and predicted that "the time is not far off when some drastic action may have to be taken with regard to him." Nevertheless the Civil Rights Section did not involve itself in the case for technically narrow reasons. Wittenberg, who was Jewish, ultimately resigned from the case after a cross was burned in his yard and he received numerous threatening telephone calls.[25]

In May 1956 the state Public Service Commission issued its own opinion supporting Timmerman's decision. The commissioners quoted at length from *Plessy*, a decision that had "guided their lives . . . for sixty years. It has never been over-ruled. It states eternal truth." The eternal truth of *Plessy* led the commissioners to believe that "the United States Supreme Court should [not] or would [not] reverse the decision in the above cited *Plessy v. Ferguson* case." Citing communist involvement for good measure, the commissioners argued that, instead of reversing *Plessy*, the recent school cases should be the ones reviewed by the Supreme Court for possible reversal. They authorized the commission's counsel to file an amicus brief in the case.[26]

Flemming appealed again following Timmerman's second dismissal of the case. In November the Fourth Circuit sent the case back to Timmerman again. This time, in June 1957, there would be a trial. Paralleling what happened to Rosa Parks, the trial was held before an all-male, all-White jury, which took about half an hour to find for SCE&G. There would be no appeal, as the Supreme Court had already decided in the Alabama case that segregation in local bus systems was unconstitutional.[27] Sarah Mae Flemming thus became a footnote in the history of the movement to desegregate public accommodations, despite the importance of her case to the movement in South Carolina.

While these cases were being litigated, the General Assembly continued its efforts to negate the civil rights movement and push the NAACP into irrelevance in South Carolina through the legislative process. On February 8, 1956, state representative Charles G. Garrett of Greenville County introduced a bill that would bar members of the NAACP from holding any state, county, or city job in South Carolina. The *Columbia State* printed the brief bill in its entirety. Garrett's measure charged that the organization "disturbed the peace and tranquility which has long existed between the White and Negro races, and [was] so insidious in its propaganda and the fostering of those ideas designed to produce a constant state of turmoil between the races, that membership in such

an organization is wholly incompatible with the peace, tranquility and progress that all citizens have a right to enjoy."[28] Two weeks later the House sent
the bill to the state senate, and it was approved on March 17.[29] The NAACP
lost little time in preparing to file a lawsuit to prevent its enforcement and to
have it declared unconstitutional. James M. Hinton confidently asserted that
1944—when Judge Waring overturned the state's continued efforts to maintain
the White primary—would be repeated in this case.[30]

Both houses also jointly resolved to petition the US attorney general to
put the NAACP on the list of subversive organizations.[31] The joint resolution
cited fifty-three members of the NAACP who had come to the attention of
the House Committee on Un-American Activities for alleged communist, or
similarly un-American, activity. South Carolina state representative John C.
Hart of Union, the author of the joint resolution, argued that the only reason
the attorney general had not already placed the NAACP on the subversive list
was "political expediency." Roy Wilkins, the national executive secretary of the
organization, countered those accusations. The NAACP, he said, had a record
of "constitutional procedure," and any action to undermine it was "designed
to confuse the people on the racial issue facing the South. That issue is whether
the politicians of [the South] will recognize the authority of the U.S. government or join the communists in efforts to subvert our constitutional system."[32]

In January 1957 new proposals to delay integration, including bills to close
any desegregated school automatically and give the governor the power to
authorize tuition grants for transfers to private schools, to prevent state police
officers from aiding federal officers, and to prevent the use of state jails to house
federal detainees charged with opposing integration, were among prefiled bills.
State appropriations for parks and schools explicitly stated they were contingent on racial segregation. When Clemson University accepted ninety-nine
thousand dollars in grants from the Atomic Energy Commission in June 1957,
Governor Timmerman threatened to sue the college unless they returned the
money. The government contract contained a nondiscrimination clause that
would, Timmerman believed, open the college to admitting Black people and
communists.[33] In addition, South Carolina's Code of Laws required Clemson
to close its doors if any person were admitted to the school under court order.
As noted earlier, state law also required South Carolina State to close if any
Black person were admitted to any public college other than South Carolina
State under court order.[34] After the closing of the Edisto park, few doubted that
the state would follow through on such a threat.

Other laws were proposed to prevent bringing civil rights cases under the
heading of barratry (the bringing of frivolous or groundless lawsuits) and to
require local chapters of the NAACP to file membership lists with the secretary

of state. The anti-barratry bill passed in February 1957. In addition to those mentioned above, which were still pending, there were bills that would require public transportation carriers in Florence County to mark their restrooms "white" or "colored," to require blood banks operating in the state to mark their blood by race, as well as other less "colorful" laws all with the goals of maintaining a racial demarcation and of restricting the operation of the NAACP and those sympathetic to it.

While the official doctrine of the state remained true to its segregationist values, there were isolated places where African Americans were able to enjoy facilities that had been kept from them. On the morning of January 26, 1957, a train carrying a group of military inductees was delayed in Rock Hill. Mrs. M. T. Neal and her husband owned two restaurants in the city. The Neals had not owned the restaurants for long when Mrs. Neal agreed to feed the group, which included several African Americans. By that afternoon the local newspaper carried the news that the Neals served Black customers. A crowd grew, and anonymous telephone calls started coming in. The FBI, having been contacted by Mrs. Neal, interviewed the local police chief, W. S. Rhodes, who said his men would keep an eye out for anyone trying to vandalize the Neals' establishments.[35]

Aggressive legislative and extralegal tactics were the result of both successful lawsuits and of everyday African American resistance to White pressure, including a boycott in reaction to the 1956 law. Perhaps discouraged by the lack of tangible victories after winning the fight, and probably to an extent afraid of both economic and physical reprisals, Black South Carolinians carefully chose their legal moves in the late 1950s, largely avoiding targeting schools for desegregation. However, the ranks of openly vocal supporters swelled in the face of the General Assembly's open hostility to the NAACP. Following the model of Montgomery, economic boycotts became a weapon of both supporters of the NAACP and of its foes. After Black South Carolinians began petition drives, citizens' councils demonstrated adeptness at exerting economic pressure on Black South Carolinians. When the opportunity presented itself, Black citizens retaliated with boycotts of their own. Orangeburg County seemed a hotbed of revolution given the boycotts and counter-boycotts in Elloree and protests at South Carolina State College. The Elloree Citizens' Council's purpose, members declared, was to exert "economic pressure on all persons connected with the NAACP."[36] Their primary targets were parents who had signed the school desegregation petition. Although some parents withdrew their names, the boycott expanded to include everyone associated with the NAACP. Black merchants found themselves without goods to sell, and credit dried up. Due to their relatively large portion of the population (about 50 percent), African

Americans in Orangeburg were able to mount an effective retaliation. Black leaders targeted twenty-three White businesses, at least one of which was reported to have failed. Meanwhile the Victory Savings Bank channeled money from the NAACP and other donors from across the county to Black citizens. In April 1956 students and some faculty at South Carolina State College staged a strike and boycotted classes to protest the state legislature's proposal to crack down on the organization.[37] By spring 1956 White citizens were willing to compromise, and the mutual boycott began to ease. In June 1956 Governor Timmerman and Lieutenant Governor Ernest F. Hollings appointed six members of a committee to investigate the activities of the NAACP.[38] At South Carolina State College, one of the targets of the anti-NAACP investigation, several students were asked not to return, and several faculty members' contracts were not renewed.[39] Other faculty members had not asked for contract renewals.

Economic boycotts and legislative reprisals represented new tactics in the struggle against the NAACP. Before pursing these tactics of "respectability," violence had been used in the attempt to deter Black civil rights activism and would be again. One of the most widely publicized incidents of violence involved Rev. J. A. De Laine of the *Briggs* case. De Laine had received a letter threatening his life early in October 1955. His church in Lake City was destroyed by fire a couple of days earlier, and his home was repeatedly bombarded with rocks or other projectiles. His home in Summerton, where De Laine lived when the fight to end school segregation in South Carolina began, had been destroyed by fire years earlier. Of course, he had lost his job as principal of a segregated school. Finally, on the night of October 10, De Laine retaliated when Leroy Moore and some others in a passing car fired shots at his home. De Laine fired back, ostensibly to mark the car for a subsequent investigation. Apparently he hit two of the car's occupants, Harry Gause and Donald Graham. Fearing for his life and facing charges of assault, De Laine left South Carolina for New York. He let the FBI know his whereabouts, claiming that he was not in New York "to dodge justice but to evade INJUSTICE." Like Judge Waring, he became an exile. Governor Timmerman accused the Justice Department of "discriminating in the administration of justice."[40]

Violence was a tactic for many average White people to express their frustration with the social elevation of Black South Carolinians, who in many instances were their economic equals or betters. In predominantly White Greenville County, a financially well-off Black man, Claude Cruell, found that it was a mistake to associate with White people. Sherwood Turner, a poor, illiterate White man, rented a house from Cruell, and occasionally Cruell would give Turner rides to the bean fields where Turner and his family scraped out a livelihood. On July 21, 1957, a group of "independent" Klansmen viciously

Elloree Training School Teachers (courtesy of Cecil Williams)

beat Cruell for associating with White people. The Turners had left their children with the Cruells at the time because Turner had to take his anemic wife to the hospital. After the beating Cruell's wife was forced into one of the Klansmen's cars, driven about five miles away, and, after being forced to remove her shoes, made to walk back home. Four of the Klansmen involved received jail terms, but the rest went free, the charges dismissed by state judge James M. Brailsford.[41] Cruell apparently had nothing to do with the civil rights movement. However, what his association with Turner represented was clearly a threat to the social hierarchy that most White South Carolinians believed was the appropriate one.

Teacher firings gave the NAACP an opportunity to challenge the anti-NAACP laws the General Assembly had passed in the spring. In the fall of 1956, officials fired twenty-four teachers at Elloree Training School in Orangeburg County when they refused to sign statements concerning their membership in the NAACP. Eighteen of those teachers, represented by Columbia lawyer Lincoln C. Jenkins and Thurgood Marshall, sued in federal court.

M. G. Austin, the district superintendent of Orangeburg County District 7, had distributed disclosure forms that the teachers had to fill out before their employment could continue to one the plaintiffs, Charles E. Davis. The form included the questions "Do you belong to the NAACP?" "Does any member of your immediate family belong to the NAACP?" "Do you support the NAACP in any way (money or attendance at meetings)?" "Do you favor integration of races in school?" and other similar questions. The plaintiffs refused to fill them out "for the reason that these questions inquired concerning matters constitutionally beyond the competence of the state to inquire into and infringed upon their rights as a citizen of the United States . . . to freely associate with others for the purpose of securing rights conferred by the Constitution."[42]

A subsequent interview on May 15 between Austin and twelve of the plaintiffs led to the same results. He immediately required them to sign a resignation form. Other plaintiffs answered some of the questions when confronted by Austin but refused to answer the most inflammatory questions, which included:

Are you satisfied with your work and the schools as they are now maintained? Yes _____ No_____ If yes, comment on back

Do you feel that you would be happy in an integrated school system, knowing that parents and students do not favor this system? Yes_____ No_____ (Check one and give reason for answer).

Do you feel that an integrated school system would better fit the colored race in their life's work? Yes_____ No_____ (Check one and give reason for answer).

Do you think that you are qualified to teach an integrated class in a satisfactory manner? Yes_____ No_____ (Check one and give reason for answer).

Do you feel that the parents of your school know that no public schools will be operated if they are integrated? Yes_____ No_____

Do you believe in the aims of the NAACP? Yes_____ No_____

If you should join the NAACP while employed in this school, please notify the Superintendent and Chairman of the Board of Trustees. Yes_____ No_____.[43]

Other plaintiffs refused both to answer the questions and to sign the resignation form. Although they told Austin that they wished to keep working, all were summarily fired.

The defendants responded to the complaint by alleging that none of the plaintiffs ever claimed that constitutional questions had concerned them when they refused to sign the application form. They also said that only one of the plaintiffs—Luther Lucas—ever stated a desire to remain in his position. None asked to be reinstated through official channels, and since the act of refusing to sign the NAACP questionnaire amounted to asking not to be rehired for the next academic year, the school board was under no obligation to rehire them. The plaintiffs had also failed to use the remedies that were properly available to them, such as a review by the school district trustees, the county board of education, and the state Circuit Court for the First Circuit—steps that were required in salary reviews as well.[44]

The defense ultimately argued that "the maintenance of a system of public schools in South Carolina has been made extremely difficult by the holding of the United States Supreme Court in *Briggs v. Elliott*," and the NAACP had not helped the situation any since that decision. Alluding to Judge Parker's 1955 *Briggs* decision, the defendants claimed that the decision "does not prohibit the school officials from operating racially segregated schools so long as they do not deny to any qualified applicant the right to admittance to any school because of race."[45]

"Nonracial" means of maintaining segregation were already being deployed as subterfuges. The defense's answer, written by Robert Figg, state senator Marshall Williams, and Gressette Committee attorney P. H. McEachin, among others, amounted to little more than an extended diatribe against the NAACP. They claimed that "the parents of [238,000 Black pupils and 550,000 White pupils] were and are satisfied with the education of their children on this [segregated] basis, and there has been no effort by any parent to have his child transferred from a school operated for one race to that operated for the other." It was the NAACP, they claimed, that bore responsibility for "causing serious deterioration of the friendly relations between the races, causing tension and unrest, . . . disturbing the peace, tranquility and progress of the State, . . . seriously interfering with the duties of school trustees to elucidate, assess, and solve their respective problems, [and] jeopardizing the very existence to public education in this State and violat[ing] the public policy of the State." The defense also raised *Clark v. Flory*, which had resulted in the closure of the Edisto Beach State Park, as a warning of the dire circumstances that were bound to follow any order to desegregate the schools. It was the NAACP's fault for "stirring up and encouraging litigation" that required the General Assembly to restrict employment for members of the organization.[46]

Marshall responded by arguing that "public servants have a constitutional right not to be deprived of their jobs arbitrarily." Recent cases supported Marshall. In *Wieman v. Updegraff*, the Supreme Court struck down an Oklahoma statute that required firing "teachers who failed to take an expurgatory oath which did not meet due process requirements." *Slochower v. Board of Higher Education* held that New York City could not automatically dismiss a municipal college teacher simply because he pleaded the Fifth Amendment before a congressional committee. Quoting the decision in *Slochower*, Marshall continued: "To state that a person does not have a constitutional right to Government employment is only to say that he must comply with *reasonable, lawful,* and *nondiscriminatory* terms laid down by the proper authorities." South Carolina's requirement of the relinquishment of a constitutional right as a prerequisite to employment was a violation of the "well-established principle" that "a regulation which would violate the Constitution if directly imposed will violate it if sought to be imposed indirectly as a condition to the grant of a privilege." Marshall continued the parallel, making it clear that he believed that the law requiring teachers to relinquish their membership in the NAACP to keep their jobs was tantamount to making membership in the organization itself illegal, which of course was the point.[47]

Marshall built his argument on questioning the reasonableness of the anti-NAACP law. A substantial body of law established the precedent that any state law that violated the rights of free speech "must show some paramount public interest which the exercise of these rights gravely endangers." Quoting Supreme Court Justice Felix Frankfurter's concurring opinion in *Wieman v. Updegraff*, Marshall strongly argued for the rights even of state employees—teachers were the subjects of the *Wieman* case as well—to assemble peaceably. Restrictions like the prohibition on NAACP membership have "an unmistakable tendency to chill that free play of the spirit which all teachers ought especially to cultivate; it makes for caution and timidity in their associations by potential teachers." "Contention and controversy" may indeed result from teachers' joining the NAACP, but that did not justify the anti-NAACP legislation. No "paramount public interest" had been "gravely endangered" to justify the law, and there was no valid legislative purpose behind it. "The aim of preservation of the peace—or, as in this case preservation of quiet on the question of racial segregation—does not justify laws which deny rights protected by the Constitution."[48]

Marshall argued that state law also violated the Equal Protection Clause of the Fourteenth Amendment, because the law depended on an arbitrary racial classification. Additionally the law allowed classifications based on political beliefs, which the Supreme Court from the earliest years of the Fourteenth Amendment had implied was suspect.[49] Since the law covered only members of the NAACP and not those who were members of any political organization, the law failed on equal protection grounds. For example, the law did not apply to White teachers who were members of citizens' councils. Someone who therefore believed in White supremacy could teach, while someone who believed in equal justice could not.

Marshall's final point was that since the anti-NAACP law punished people for acts that were legal when they took place, the law amounted to a bill of attainder. The Supreme Court had ruled on several occasions that government could not impose oaths under the threat of being prevented from practicing one's profession.[50] In *United States v. Lovett*, the Court held that Congress could not command the executive branch to withhold salaries of employees simply because of alleged subversive activities. The Court said "that legislative

Judge George Bell Timmerman Sr. and Robert M. Cooper (courtesy of Richland Library, Columbia, South Carolina)

acts . . . that apply either to named individuals or to easily ascertainable members of a group in such a way as to inflict punishment on them without a judicial trial are bills of attainder prohibited by the Constitution."[51] Members of the NAACP were indeed "easily ascertainable members of a group" who were being punished by having their jobs taken from them because of their membership in a legal organization.

A three-judge panel made up of Parker, Timmerman, and Williams heard the case on October 22. NAACP attorney Jack Greenberg argued that the plaintiffs' right of freedom of association had been violated. Defense attorneys David Robinson and Robert Figg argued that the case was not properly before the district court. Their decision was mixed: Parker and Williams both agreed that the federal courts should have jurisdiction but could not agree on when. Williams and Timmerman argued that the state courts should have first crack at the case. Ola Bryan and her coplaintiffs were forced to exhaust their state remedies before the case would be revived on the federal docket. Parker noted during the hearing that "South Carolina has passed a law affecting these rights [of speech and association]. These are the basis of our constitutional liberties."[52] He saw the law as "clearly unconstitutional . . . : The fact that organizations may render themselves unpopular with the majority in a community is no reason why the majority may use its power to enact legislation denying to their members the fundamental rights of constitutional liberty." Timmerman, predictably, saw things differently: the statute did not, he argued, outlaw membership in the NAACP; it merely "prevent[ed] its members from carrying their programs into the classrooms of public schools where it is deemed against the public interest to have them do so." Timmerman believed the state had not only the interest but also the right "to protect young minds from the poisonous effects of NAACP propaganda."[53] When the case was appealed to the Supreme Court, the state legislature repealed the law, replacing it with a more innocuous one. The new law required individuals only to list the organizations to which they belonged and did not carry a dismissal clause. As a result Black teachers still could be dismissed for their membership in the NAACP but would be unable to prove it.[54]

Despite violence and intimidation, however, Black South Carolinians refused to back down. The drive for desegregation continued and even intensified as the 1960s approached. In Greenville, just months after the beating of Cruell, rumors of a lawsuit to be filed by Black litigants to integrate the county's schools circulated. Unrest had already boiled over. Although the school system remained segregated, Greenville's high school buses were desegregated, and tensions on at least one bus ran high soon after school started in September 1957. Black students apparently moved to the front of one of the buses. One of the Black students, Peggy Ann Rose, sat next to George Clardy, a White student. On September 24 they got into a fight (she and two other Black female students allegedly took to yelling at the White students, Clardy among them); Rose hit Clardy with her shoe, and he hit back with one of his books. The next day, after the White students exited the bus, nearly one hundred White students crowded the bus while the Black riders remained inside. No violence took place, and the next day officials at both schools took measures to make sure that nothing unfortunate happened.[55] The county branch of the NAACP threatened legal action if the county did not respond to a year-old petition to comply with the Supreme Court's decision by mid-October 1957. However, no suit had been filed by the end of the month. The NAACP's local attorney, Donald James Sampson, stated that he was "not in any grand hurry" to bring a desegregation suit.[56]

During the 1959 legislative session, bills calling for the state to sell its school property and to make "fathering an illegitimate child"—something to which White officials apparently believed Black men were more prone—a crime that would prevent one from voting made it to the legislature's agenda.[57] Their actions reflected a pattern common throughout the region. State laws effectively reduced or restricted NAACP membership or the ability of the organization to function effectively. In Alabama the organization was virtually shut down from 1956 to 1964. Using a variety of state laws requiring organizations doing business in their states to register, Arkansas, Louisiana, and Alabama all tried to force the NAACP to pay taxes, to register as a corporation, and most important, to provide access to membership lists. Alabama's efforts to thwart the NAACP were the most successful, requiring four trips to the Supreme Court between 1956 and 1964. In South Carolina, however, less successful attempts to undermine the organization still had a negative impact on the organization.[58]

Southern leaders, including several from South Carolina, took their fight north to Washington in the spring of 1959 when they testified before the House Judiciary Committee regarding impending civil rights legislation. Edgar Brown testified to the wonderful race relations between White and Black South Carolinians. L. Marion Gressette; Robert McNair, a member of the state House of Representatives who became governor in 1965; and Thomas Pope, also a member of the state House of Representatives who had been speaker in 1949–50, joined in a statement reiterating the legislature's joint resolution of February 1956: that "the fundamentals of the Constitution of the United States" required "the States to order as they see fit their own internal affairs." "Destroy that," they argued, "and you invite anarchy or, even worse, the absolute tyranny of the demagog [sic]."[59]

State government officials; the General Assembly; county, municipal, and school officers; and the White public generally formed a phalanx to blunt the potential of desegregation. The federal bench in South Carolina consisted of three judges who believed in segregation and were able to delay progress of cases by resorting to procedure and precedent to limit remedies.[60] While they could not overthrow the US Supreme Court, these judges and state officials were firmly in control of the instruments of statecraft, and through them they effectively delayed any transformative intent of *Brown*. Through laws, judicial decisions, reprisals, and resistance, these officials made it clear that South Carolina in the late 1950s was preparing for an onslaught.

5

"WE DON'T ALLOW COLORED PEOPLE IN HERE"

Segregation to "Integration with Dignity," 1959–63

In November 1958 Air Force civil service employee Richard Henry, whose job required him to fly throughout the country, was forced to use the segregated waiting room at the Greenville Airport (now the Greenville Downtown Airport). Henry had come to Greenville from his station at Selfridge Air Force Base in Michigan to assist with a troop carrier exercise at the Donaldson Air Force Base in south Greenville, arriving and leaving through Greenville's airport. He arrived at the airport forty-five minutes before his flight was scheduled to depart and sat in the terminal's waiting room. After a few minutes, airport manager O. L. Andrews told Henry, "We don't allow colored people in here." Henry responded that he was an interstate traveler, and after being "put out" of the waiting room, he called the local Air Force base and his home base. He then waited outside for his plane to board, which it soon did. In January, after writing the NAACP, the secretary of the Air Force, and a "Senator Hare" (probably newly elected US senator for Michigan Philip Hart), Henry decided to sue.[1]

One of the key instruments of White obstruction in South Carolina was the judges on the federal bench. Doubtless the most obstructionist was George Bell Timmerman Sr. When Henry's suit came before Judge Timmerman, he almost immediately began to undermine Henry's case. In the hearing for a preliminary injunction, Timmerman consistently placed obstacles in the path of Jack Greenberg, who had come from the national office of the NAACP's Legal Defense Fund in New York to assist with the case. Timmerman refused to hear the motion for the preliminary injunction, even though Greenberg pointed out that he could hear evidence from witnesses in support of such a motion. Timmerman refused to allow additional affidavits or testimony at the hearing because they had just been introduced and the defense had not seen them. Forced to pursue the preliminary injunction with only the sole affidavit of the plaintiff for support, Greenberg started out at a disadvantage. Timmerman claimed that "it could aid one side or another to get an advantage that they are not entitled to. I don't intend being a party to that." He finally told Greenberg that he would proceed with the hearing, though it would be based solely on Henry's affidavit.[2]

A reluctant Greenberg argued that "it is now rather late in the day for anyone to argue that a governmental body may maintain racial segregation in any of its facilities. . . . It is perhaps one of the fundamental principles of our jurisprudence that this is something that a governmental body can not [sic] do." Abandoning any hint of judicial impartiality, Timmerman countered that most of the complaint was "made up of references to statutes and constitutional provisions. There is a very small part of it that deals with the factual issues. . . . It looks like somebody had picked up a digest of cases or a digest of the constitution and just at random picked out a whole lot of provisions to plead."[3] A member of the three-judge panel in the rehearing of *Briggs* in 1955 that resulted in the Parker dictum, Timmerman applied it to the Henry case. As had Parker, Timmerman echoed the opinion of the Supreme Court in *Plessy v. Ferguson* that "social equality" must be based on "voluntary consent" by both parties.[4] "This argument," Timmerman wrote, "fails to observe the important distinction between activities that are required by the state and those which are carried out by voluntary choice and without compulsion by the people of the state in accordance with their own desires and social practices."[5]

Following Greenberg's presentation, Thomas Wofford, the attorney for the Greenville Airport Commission, replied with a long (twenty-six-and-a-half pages in the trial record) oration on everything from the jurisdiction of the court (it should be denied because Henry never alleged damages of more than ten thousand dollars) to the state of Michigan ("why he wants to go back God Almighty in all of his own infinite wisdom only knows"). Wofford also offered several recent cases in which federal courts had allowed the doctrine of separate but equal to stand.[6] Greenberg said nothing after Wofford was finally finished. He probably thought better of even trying to justify the preliminary injunction after the speech by Wofford, preferring instead to wait until the trial and the actual admission of evidence from witnesses. Timmerman quickly rejected the motion for an injunction.[7] In doing so, he argued that keeping Henry out of the White waiting room was not the result of state action, because the legislation that incorporated the Greenville Airport Commission did not include the power to create waiting rooms. "The customs of the people of a state," he wrote, "do not constitute state action within the prohibition of the Fourteenth Amendment." He further implied that it was Henry who should be a target for injunction, given that it was he who was "deliberately mak[ing] a nuisance of himself to the annoyance of others. . . . The right to equality before the law, to be free from discrimination, invests no one with authority to require others to accept him as a companion or social equal."[8] Custom, to Timmerman and like-minded White South Carolinians, was more important than law. Despite the lack of equality, *Plessy* was still the controlling precedent. This mindset—that White people had the "right" to subordinate African Americans—was a key element of White resistance to desegregation.

In April 1960 the appellate court reversed Timmerman's decision and sent the case back. In July 1960 Timmerman wrote Lincoln Jenkins, who along with Matthew Perry had joined Greenberg in representing Henry, telling him that he would be taking a vacation in August.[9] After the delay the second hearing in Henry's case was finally held on September 14, 1960, at the federal courthouse in Greenville. Over Wofford's objections, Timmerman this time admitted supporting affidavits and allowed testimony from Henry and from Rev. J. S. Hall of Greenville, who also presented an affidavit. After establishing the basic facts with Henry on the stand, Greenberg turned Henry over to the defense for a lengthy cross-examination.

Henry testified that he had gone into the main waiting room to read a magazine and see the aircraft on the runway. However, Wofford quizzed him as to his knowledge of the existence of the segregated waiting room. While it is not clear whether Henry saw the sign for the "Colored Lounge," he did offer that if he had seen the sign, he would not have gone in. Wofford also argued with the witness as to the exact words in his original deposition. He was trying to get Henry to admit that Andrews never said that Black people were not allowed in the main waiting room. Interestingly, while on his way to Columbia for the initial hearing in July 1959, Henry had taken a side trip to Greenville from Charlotte and back before heading down to Columbia for the hearing. He had come to Greenville for just a few minutes "to see whether or not this practice was still being carried out." Andrews again ordered Henry from the main waiting room, and Henry left to get back on the plane that would return him to Charlotte.[10]

Following a familiar pattern, Wofford implied that the NAACP's involvement was somehow illicit, or at least suspicious. Wofford established, over Greenberg's objections, that Henry was not paying, or at least had not yet paid, Lincoln Jenkins and that the NAACP had recommended his services. As in many other South Carolina cases, the defense tried to paint the NAACP as the ultimate plaintiff, arguing that it was that organization, not ordinary Black people, which was trying to undermine the comfortable segregation that all South Carolinians supposedly enjoyed. As he had in the previous hearing, Judge Timmerman participated in the state's defense. When Wofford questioned the validity of Henry's affidavit and then alleged possible collusion between the

NAACP and Henry in bringing the case, Timmerman badgered Henry about when and where—and whether—he had actually signed the affidavit. When Greenberg objected to questioning about whether Henry had paid Jenkins a fee, Timmerman overruled him and directed Henry to answer the questions. Henry admitted that Jenkins had been recommended to him by the NAACP after the organization had been apprised of the incident in Greenville. Wofford asked if the NAACP was financing the Henry suit. Henry answered that he understood that to be the case. Timmerman interjected to ask if Henry ever expected to pay anything on the case and whether he had known Jenkins prior to the case.

> THE COURT: Did you correspond with him before you came to Greenville with reference to taking this case that you were going to set up?
>
> THE WITNESS: Oh, I beg your pardon. May I correct that? You asked me did I know Mr. Jenkins before I came to Greenville.
>
> THE COURT: Yes.
>
> THE WITNESS: Well, you are assuming . . .
>
> THE COURT: No, I am not assuming anything; I am asking you questions.
>
> THE WITNESS: Well, no, I didn't know Mr. Jenkins, and I hadn't corresponded with him before I came to Greenville for the Air Force.
>
> THE COURT: You did correspond with him before you came down to Greenville the first time?
>
> THE WITNESS: No, it was before I came to Greenville for the case today, and I suppose I came to Columbia . . .
>
> THE COURT: Well, suppose you listen to the questions and we'll get along better.
>
> THE WITNESS: All right, sir. I'm sorry.
>
> THE COURT: And let's answer the question I ask instead of another one.[11]

Reverend Hall testified that on several occasions he had been forced to use the segregated waiting room, though not on every occasion that he had to use the airport. Once in 1958 he had accompanied Clarence Mitchell, former director of the NAACP's Washington office and current chief lobbyist for the national organization, to the airport and sat undisturbed in the main waiting room. In October 1959 he had gone to the airport to see off Jackie Robinson along with several other people. Andrews had told them to move. Then on July 7, 1960, he and A. J. Whittenberg flew to Charlotte from the Greenville Airport, and Greenville NAACP vice president Mark Tolbert accompanied them to the airport. On that occasion the three men were asked, again by airport manager Andrews, to leave the main waiting room.[12]

Timmerman's decision, issued in mid-October, predictably supported the defense's position. He ruled that even "giving [Henry's] affidavit the most

favorable consideration it falls short of indicating any necessity for a preliminary injunction to protect any *legitimate* right the plaintiff has."[13] Ignoring the
fact that Andrews put Henry out of the waiting room, Timmerman interpreted
the words of the manager of the airport, who said that "we have a waiting
room for colored folks over there," differently than had Henry. To Timmerman
the words hardly constituted an order to leave the White waiting room, merely
a suggestion that Henry might be more comfortable elsewhere. Timmerman
invoked the spirit of *Plessy v. Ferguson* well:

> From whom was he segregated? . . . Was he segregated from his friends,
> acquaintances or associates, from those who desired his company and he
> theirs? There is nothing in the affidavit to indicate such is true. Was he seg-
> regated from people whom he did not know and who did not care to know
> him? . . . Suppose he was segregated from people who did not care for his
> company or association, What civil right of his was thereby invaded? If he
> was trying to invade the civil rights of others, an injunction might be more
> properly invoked against him to protect their civil rights. I know of no civil
> or uncivil right that anyone has, be he white or colored, to deliberately
> make a nuisance of himself to the annoyance of others, even in an effort to
> create or stir up litigation. The right to equality before the law, to be free
> from discrimination, invests no one with authority to require others to ac-
> cept him as a companion or social equal. The Fourteenth Amendment does
> not reach that low level. Even whites, as yet, still have the right to choose
> their own companions and associates, and to preserve the integrity of the
> race with which God Almighty has endowed them.[14]

Timmerman accepted the defense's motion to strike key jurisdictional ele-
ments of the complaint and to grant their motion to dismiss the complaint.
Segregation at the Greenville Airport, despite state sanctioning of the Airport
Commission, was not something that took place under color of state law.
Furthermore, Henry "did not go to the waiting room in quest of waiting room
facilities, but solely as a volunteer for the purpose of instigating litigation.
. . . The Court does not and should not look with favor on volunteer trouble
makers or volunteer instigators of strife or litigation."[15] Timmerman's opinion reveals his biases: as a southerner who came of age during the height of
Plessy-era Jim Crow, his segregationist ideas are unsurprising. His language,
though, illustrates the fundamentalism of White supremacy—the rights of
Richard Henry as a "negro" were secondary to the rights of those "whom he
did not know and who did not come to know him." This refusal to understand
or acknowledge that African American rights are not equal if their exercise is

conditional on White comfort appears over and over in White rationales—both political and legal—for ignoring or delaying meaningful desegregation.

The Fourth Circuit quickly directed Timmerman to rehear the case and to grant an injunction against the Airport Commission, reversing his patently incorrect decision. Defensively Timmerman wrote that the Fourth Circuit had created a "new rule of deductive evidence" by deciding that "from the *allegation* that [Henry] was directed to a separate waiting room maintained for colored people, it is fairly inferable that other negroes had been similarly treated." The circuit court's decision, as far as Timmerman was concerned, had "the appearance of a groping after a plausible excuse for according preferential treatment to some class." Indeed, in his original ruling Timmerman declared that Henry's suit was an effort to seek rights and privileges "superior" to those of White citizens by disrupting racial harmony and was not constitutionally protected. Reluctantly he issued the injunction.[16]

Grassroots activity suggests that many Black South Carolinians were tired of waiting for the "deliberate speed" mandated by the Court in *Brown II*. When Jackie Robinson was ejected from the same waiting room at the Greenville Airport in October 1959, two months after Timmerman's *Henry* decision, the Congress of Racial Equality organized a protest for January 1 (the day the Emancipation Proclamation went into effect in 1863), that was attended by at least 250 people.[17] Rising protests led the NAACP's lawyers, especially Thurgood Marshall, to reevaluate their role. Increasingly the LDF was called upon to defend clients who had broken segregation laws intentionally when trying to accelerate the pace of racial change. As a result the role of LDF lawyers in developing the strategy for dismantling segregation seemed to diminish. However, anyone who thought that the legal aspects of the civil rights movement were over or even declining would find out how wrong they were in the years to come. There was still a real and pressing need for active litigation.

In the early 1960s, mounting frustration among Black college and high school students began to overwhelm the voices of moderation. Continued resistance from White leaders contributed to a mindset that justified angry or violent responses by White people when African Americans attempted to get a seat at the table. Rather than following Martin Luther King's path of nonviolent resistance to White supremacy, some in the younger generation decided to fight back. For example, in Columbia several Black students from Allen University and Benedict College were arrested following a club-wielding attack on cars in a White drive-in. The attack was spurred by rumors of a cross-burning on one of the schools' grounds. Newspaper accounts vary as to whether the cross was burned on Benedict's or Allen's campus, as well as on the exact date of the

J. Arthur Brown,
Matthew J. Perry,
Lincoln Jenkins,
and Hemphill
Pride II, March 15,
1960 (courtesy of
Richland Library,
Columbia, South
Carolina)

occurrence. The judge in the case, John I. Rice (of *Elmore v. Rice*), told the defendants that "such violence would not be tolerated."[18] Ordinary crimes were also reported in ways to discredit the civil rights movement and paint Black South Carolinians as uncivilized. In Charleston three young African Americans were arrested for attacking, robbing, and allegedly attempting to carve KKK into the back of a twenty-four-year-old White man (though the relationship of the attack to the demonstrations was unproven). The sit-in movement that began in Greensboro, North Carolina, in February 1960 rapidly spread to Rock Hill and other South Carolina cities as well. By March crowds of marchers swelled. The police stepped in as tensions rose, arresting students who refused to disperse. Already there had been demonstrations that led to tear gas attacks by police and wide-scale arrests of Black students at South Carolina State in March 1960 as well as threatened marches on the state capital, threats that were actualized a year later when 187 high school and college students were arrested during a protest march.[19] In Orangeburg police used tear gas to quell a demonstration of about 1,000 people after they refused to disperse. Across the state African Americans were beginning to assert their rights: in Greenville two African Americans tried to use the library. There were lunch-counter demonstrations in Sumter, Florence, and Denmark. These incidents of violence provided an opportunity for South Carolina officials to criminalize all protest.

Students from Allen and Benedict in Columbia joined the sit-in movement when they sat in at the lunch counter at the F. W. Woolworth store. They received no service but were not otherwise disturbed. They followed the Woolworth sit-in by moving down to the S. H. Kress store, where all the seats were either occupied or roped off. The following day around two hundred students participated in sit-ins at ten different downtown stores and restaurants, again with no major incidents. After the city manager issued a statement saying that sit-ins would not be tolerated, the students retired to their campuses and homes, releasing a statement to the effect that their point had been made. Governor Ernest Hollings made no distinction between violent and nonviolent civil disobedience. He alleged that demonstrators "were intent on being jailed and promoting violence." Therefore, these threats overrode the First Amendment. Members of the legislature responded with several bills designed to curb the sit-in movement, ranging from redefining trespass to symbolically revoking the state's ratification of the Fourteenth Amendment.[20] Responding to threats of a march on the State House, Hollings warned that further demonstrations would not be tolerated. Students backed down when Hollings threatened mass arrests if they proceeded with the march. Later in March small groups of Black students started sit-ins at an Eckerd Drug store and a local pharmacy, and two students, Simon Bouie and Talmadge Neal, were arrested.[21] For the most part Columbia's Black population, despite the presence of two independent colleges and a small cadre of vocal Black leaders such as Modjeska Simkins, was more circumspect in its dealings with White South Carolina than were black people in Orangeburg, where 425 protestors were arrested.

In July 1960 a group of African American students that came to be known as the Greenville Eight, including Jesse Jackson, attempted to use that city's public library and were refused. Shortly thereafter seven of the eight (not including Jackson) filed suit in federal district court. A hearing before Judge Cecil C. Wyche in Spartanburg was made moot when the library was closed.[22] Only a public outcry led to the reopening of the library on a desegregated basis (though this was not publicized) later that year.[23] This was a rare occurrence prior to the passage of the Civil Rights Act of 1964. Other attempts at desegregating public facilities met with much less success, usually because the facility was closed.

Sit-ins began in upstate South Carolina in August 1960. Ten Black students told the Kress store in Greenville that they would attempt to get service at the lunch counter in the store on August 9. Kress had already made some concessions in other parts of the store, and one of the students, Doris Wright, believed that it might be possible to get further concessions if the Black community maintained pressure. The store manager had told them that he would not press charges. However, a Greenville city ordinance and a recently passed state law, which amended the state statute on trespassing to allow for fines and jail sentences for refusing to leave a business, allowed him to go no further. The city ordinance forbade restaurants from serving White and Black patrons in the same room, unless they provided separate eating utensils and tables and kept thirty-five feet of "display counters and merchandise" between White and Black customers. Separate cleaning facilities had to be provided as well.

The Greenville city recorder presided over the trial without a jury in recorder's court. An appeal to the county court was dismissed in March 1961. In November the state supreme court affirmed the lower courts' judgments and rulings. The students were convicted under the innocuous state trespass law rather than the city ordinance, a point they tried to challenge on appeal. However, neither the county court nor the state supreme court accepted the contention that the more explicitly segregationist city law was controlling. The state supreme court relied on the state law, which, the justices argued, merely upheld common law principles by which one could refuse service to anyone. Burke Marshall, head of the Civil Rights Division of the Department of Justice, contended, however, that the local ordinance could still be challenged and the convictions overturned before the US Supreme Court.[24] None of these cases made it into the federal courts, but they illustrate the restiveness of South Carolina's Black population as obstruction by White people continued. Despite the crackdown, Black South Carolinians continued to engage in civil disobedience.

Despite the value of direct action, litigation remained an essential component of eliminating state-sanctioned segregation. With the exception of the admission of Andre Toth at Allen University, which resulted in an intense backlash, segregation remained in place in the state's colleges and universities. Black South Carolinians routinely attended out-of-state colleges, with the tuition difference picked up by the state, for programs at both the undergraduate and graduate level that were not available at home. A US Civil Rights Commission 1960 report on college integration divided the South into four blocs: the pre-*Brown* states (Delaware, Kentucky, Maryland, Missouri, Oklahoma, and West Virginia, in which desegregation was largely accomplished by 1955); the token compliance states (Arkansas, North Carolina, and Virginia); the limited compliance states of Tennessee and Texas; and the resistant states: Alabama, Florida, Georgia, Louisiana, Mississippi, and, of course, South Carolina. These last states had no integration at all. By June 1962 the South, the border states, and the District of Columbia had 142 desegregated public colleges out of a total of 234 formerly all-White institutions. With the exception of the University of Georgia and the University of Mississippi, all the integrated schools were outside the Deep South.[25] This demonstrated that the legal strategies that had been adopted were successful. Although several African Americans had applied for admission to South Carolina public colleges, all had been turned down.

Despite the Fourth Circuit's repeated remand of cases to the federal district courts, neither White South Carolinians nor the federal district judges' resistance to desegregation softened. Neither did the resolve of the Black South Carolina plaintiffs who demanded institutional change. In January 1961 a young African American from Charleston, Harvey Gantt, applied for admission to Clemson Agricultural College—now Clemson University—as a transfer student. The application form Gantt filled out asked for the race of the student, and Gantt wrote an "N" in the blank. The application was returned to him on the grounds that the South Carolina Regional Education Board was paying the difference between his in-state tuition and the out-of-state tuition at Iowa State University, where he had completed two years toward an architecture degree. Gantt resubmitted his application in February and was joined in his attempt by Cornelius Fludd, also from Charleston, who had attended Morehouse College for a year.[26]

Sometime after receiving Gantt's second application, Clemson president Robert C. Edwards wrote Governor Hollings to request that the State Law Enforcement Division do criminal background checks on Gantt and Fludd. Both had been charged with trespassing at the Charleston Kress store in early 1960 during the sit-in movement. Gantt was also charged with interfering with a police officer in connection with the sit-in.[27]

University lawyers contended all along that Gantt had not completed an application, but Gantt argued that he and other Black applicants had been subjected to requirements that White applicants did not have to meet, including tests and interviews. He argued that the college had not informed him of his status until after the fall 1961 term began and that he had in fact complied with all the requirements of Clemson's admissions process. Gantt alleged that applications from potential Black students were not being acted upon quickly enough and that Clemson's administration was dragging its feet. Gantt's complaint detailed over a year of delaying tactics by Clemson. While he had reapplied in February 1961, the application remained unprocessed until June. In June, Clemson registrar Kenneth Vickery wrote Gantt that there were additional requirements that he had to meet. Despite Gantt's attempts to meet the requirements, at the end of August Vickery wrote him that his transfer application was incomplete and that therefore he could not enter Clemson in September. In fact the only requirements still to be met were Gantt's college entrance test scores, which Vickery said had arrived too late to be considered, and a personal interview, which Clemson officials had never attempted to schedule.[28]

Judge Cecil C. Wyche
(from Cecil Wyche
Papers, South Carolina
Political Collections,
University of South
Carolina Libraries)

Vickery also told Gantt that he would have to file another application to be considered in the future. Gantt did so in December 1961, but by June 1962 he was still being told that his application was incomplete.[29]

Because of the continued delays, Gantt, through his father, sued. President Edwards immediately called Sen. Edgar Brown, a member of the board of trustees, and board chairman R. M. Cooper to inform them of the suit and followed up with a memorandum to the board outlining all that had gone on up to July 11. State attorney general Daniel McLeod was notified, and he in turn was to notify David Robinson and Robert Figg. A meeting of the full board was then tentatively scheduled for July 19 in Columbia.[30] The dean of Clemson's School of Architecture wrote Gantt to request a portfolio of his work in architectural design from Iowa State, ostensibly because the conversion of his work in Iowa would be difficult for Clemson to accomplish. Although Gantt wrote Dean McClure to say that he would furnish any information he could, the lawsuit led Clemson's attorney to cut off communications.[31]

In August 1962 the details of Gantt's application became centrally important. Since Gantt had been told that his application was incomplete partially because of the lack of an interview that Clemson had never scheduled nor told him would be necessary, President Edwards would be caught in a vicious circle. Edwards defended the notice at the hearing on the grounds that the lack of interview was marked on the form as a matter of course.[32]

At the hearing in August 1962, Judge Wyche displayed annoyance when Matthew Perry wanted to bring Edwards to the stand. Accusing Perry of deliberately delaying the proceedings, Wyche argued with Perry and LDF attorney Constance Baker Motley over allowing the defense the opportunity to offer a rebuttal witness. Motley argued that the defense knew that the hearing would be held and should have brought any witnesses with them, but Wyche allowed them the opportunity to submit any witnesses they wanted later.[33]

Edwards testified that Clemson's board of trustees had never discussed the admission of Black students to Clemson—a claim that directly contradicts the historical record. Trustee minutes from 1948 clearly indicate that the board took up the issue with Edwards's predecessor, Robert F. Poole. When asked what Clemson's policy was, Edwards responded that Clemson "had never had a completed application from a Negro student," which was also not true. While the application may not have been complete, Poole had written Spencer Bracey, then a student at South Carolina State, that it was "the well-established policy of this state to furnish separate and comparable facilities" for Black and White students.[34] When pressed, Edwards insisted that the situation of having to decide whether to admit a Black applicant had never come up; therefore Clemson had no policy on the issue. Perhaps because it would protect Clemson from penalties under the 1960 Civil Rights Act, Wyche denied the motion for a preliminary injunction on September 6, 1962, the same day that Clemson's fall term began. Shortly thereafter Edgar Brown wrote to Charles F. Young, a New York attorney who had sent him some clippings concerning Constance Motley and Jack Greenberg. Brown promised Young that, should Gantt be admitted to Clemson (and Brown expected that he inevitably would) there would not be "a situation like Little Rock or Oxford at Clemson. We think we have too much sense for that. . . . The student will be allowed to find his own way to Clemson . . . with the students which are now there, and take his chances on how he will get along."[35]

It was not the incompleteness of Gantt's application that prevented his enrollment at Clemson. His race and associations made his desire to be admitted suspect. President Edwards wrote representatives of the Olin Foundation on October 15 that "there is no question that Harvey Gantt is being used by the NAACP to force integration upon this institution." Edwards expressed confidence that the two main points of the defense—Gantt's incomplete application and the "fact" that his application received the same treatment as all the other incomplete applications—had been accepted by Wyche. He went on:

> All of us in South Carolina are extremely conscious of the very difficult position we are in. Somehow, by the grace of God, we are determined to find a way to resolve this problem in a manner that will reflect favorably to the credit of Clemson College, the State of South Carolina, and, I hope, the United States of America. We are not going to allow a Mississippi situation to develop in South Carolina.

Edwards expressed dismay at "what the NAACP attorneys have been able to get away with in their pleadings and in their arguments in the courtroom," as well as "the terrible predicament we are in with the every-increasing [*sic*] centralization of power in Washington. At the same time, we must recognize that orders of the Courts must be obeyed and that we must maintain law and order."[36] Like most White officials in the state, Edwards felt he had to use the very court system he criticized to delay the college's desegregation as long as possible.

Following two hearings before the Fourth Circuit Court of Appeals, during the first of which the court refused to grant a temporary injunction that would have allowed Gantt to enter Clemson in the fall, the case was remanded to Judge Wyche and was reheard in November. Wyche, under pressure from the court of appeals for a speedy trial so that an appeal could be heard in January, accelerated the pace to accommodate the appellate court. Before an overflowing courtroom in which more than half the crowd was Black, an often-irritated Wyche snapped at the crowd when they laughed at a comment by one of the witnesses. "This is no theater. This is no place for curiosity seekers." Constance Baker Motley, referred to by the *Columbia State* newspaper as "the Negro woman attorney," took the lead in the questioning of registrar Vickery. Using the correspondence between Gantt and Clemson, Motley tried to establish a foundation for arguing that the state was engaged in a systematic attempt to keep Black students out of Clemson. Reiterating the importance of the statute that would close Clemson if it admitted Black students, Motley also noted that blind copies of all the correspondence between Gantt and Vickery went not only to Rebecca Connelly, the administrative assistant for the State Regional Education Board, but also to Senator Brown and David Robinson. When Motley asked Vickery if he would agree that the Gressette Committee was "established to maintain segregation in South Carolina," the judge ruled that it was up to him to decide upon the nature of the committee.[37]

Gantt testified the next day. Implying that Black students were incapable of keeping up with White schools' standards, Clemson attorney William L. Watkins asked him if his attorney, Matthew Perry, had told him that it would be easier to get a court order than to meet Clemson's entrance requirements. This was a common tactic in primary and secondary school cases, but since

Gantt had been accepted at Iowa State and excelled there, it seemed a desperate measure in this case.

The two-day trial also included testimony from President Edwards, who insisted that Clemson had treated Gantt just as it had every other applicant. He also noted that he assumed he had the power to admit Black students to Clemson if they were qualified. Edgar Brown testified that segregation was "just a way of life down here." Yet Brown was mystified as to why Gantt went to Iowa State—at taxpayers' expense through the Regional Education Board—if he truly wanted a quality education in architecture that was not available at any in-state Black college. He thought Gantt was happy at Iowa State "because we never heard anything from him."[38]

Court inaction also played a role in maintaining segregation in the state's parks. Although Edisto Beach State Park remained closed, the state park system reemerged as a target for desegregation. In September 1960 J. Herbert Nelson, the chair of the state NAACP's veterans committee, wrote Matthew Perry to request his services if he "should decide to bring charges against the State Forestry Commission." Nelson and a group of friends had attempted to enter the Myrtle Beach State Park at the end of August. Police officers, led by J. P. Strom, the head of the State Law Enforcement Division (the state equivalent of the FBI), met the group at the park and refused to admit them. Nelson heard on the radio on his drive back to Sumter that the park had been closed early because Strom knew of the attempt to enter the park beforehand.

Nothing further happened until the following summer, when J. Arthur Brown, who along with Etta Clark led the futile effort to desegregate Edisto Park, led a second group of African Americans from across the state in an attempt to enter Sesquicentennial State Park, located near Columbia. Following a state meeting of the NAACP at New Ebenezer Baptist Church, where Medgar Evers served as keynote speaker, a group of people including I. DeQuincey Newman, the national field secretary of the NAACP for South Carolina, discussed the prospect of going to Sesquicentennial Park the following day. The state park superintendent, an aide to the governor, the sheriff of Richland County, and, again, J. P. Strom prevented them from entering.[39] These actions suggest that the state had infiltrated the NAACP and used their inside knowledge to thwart actions that could lead to court cases.

After being refused entry to the park, the activists returned to the NAACP offices in Columbia, where eight of them signed a document authorizing Perry to take the case to court. In addition to Brown and Nelson, six other African Americans were named as plaintiffs in the suit. Harold White, a recent high school graduate with no plans for college, was a clerk at an A&P store in Columbia. Nurse's aide Mary Nesbitt, who had been told of the meeting in

Columbia through her local NAACP branch in Spartanburg, went down to Columbia for the meeting along with two other members of the Spartanburg branch. She related that she, Murray Canty, and Edith Davis had gone to Columbia to hear Evers; after leaving the church, she and the others were told that they were going to a park the following morning, and she went along.[40]

Jerrivoch Jefferson of Belton installed underground cable for the telephone company but happened to be on vacation when the call came from his local chapter in Anderson for three volunteers to go to Columbia. Jefferson remembered that he had been invited on a picnic following Evers's speech but recalled no mention of trying to enter the park. However, after being refused entry, he asked separately to be represented by Jenkins and Perry in "any legal action which was fit to take."[41] Sam Leverette was a student at South Carolina Area Trade School in Denmark and a member of the Anderson branch of the NAACP. Leverette, along with Jefferson and Gladys Porter, had already been involved in an attempt to desegregate a waiting room in Greenwood while on their way to Columbia for the Evers speech. Unlike Jefferson, Leverette decided to join the suit.[42]

The class action suit Perry filed on July 8, 1961, subsumed both the Myrtle Beach and Sesquicentennial Park groups and was the first case to challenge segregation in an entire park system. Perry asked for a three-judge court to hear the case as well as temporary and permanent injunctions. Circuit Judge Simon Sobeloff decided against appointing a three-judge panel, and the case assumed its place on the regular docket of Judge Timmerman.[43]

As usual, attorneys for the state immediately attacked the NAACP membership of the principal plaintiffs. At the time of the attempt to enter Myrtle Beach Park, H. P. Sharper of Florence had been president of the state convention, a role that Arthur Brown now held. Herbert Nelson, the veterans committee chair, was also with the group. State Attorney General Daniel McLeod and Gressette Committee attorney David W. Robinson argued that the national NAACP was the true plaintiff in the case. It was the goal, they said, of the NAACP and the Legal Defense Fund "to destroy the park system of South Carolina pursuant to their purposes to require all persons to integrate regardless of the wishes of the peoples." At depositions taken in August 1961, Robinson asked Brown numerous questions concerning the role of the NAACP in the case, even going so far as to demand "a list of all the NAACP employees or agents or attorneys that are employed by either the State Branch or the National Branch or by . . . the Legal Defense Group [sic], and what their compensation is."[44]

Timmerman stepped down from regular duties in October 1962 to become a senior judge. The state park case languished until the summer of 1963. That spring, the US Supreme Court ruled in a Tennessee case, *Watson v. City of Memphis,* that the continuation of segregated public facilities under the rubric of separate but equal was unconstitutional. Because of the decision in *Watson,* Judge Martin had no choice but to grant the plaintiffs' motion for a summary judgment. He issued his decision after the July Fourth holiday and delayed implementation for sixty days, making sure that the parks would not be open on an integrated basis until after Labor Day. The transition period was necessary, he argued, because of the safety concerns that had been brought up at trial— specifically the effect of having members of both races in close proximity without police protection.[45]

National parks and some municipal facilities throughout the state had voluntarily opened their facilities to African Americans by 1963. However, following Martin's decision, the State Forestry Commission, acting on the advice of the state attorney general and following through on the threat it made when the Edisto case was initially filed in the mid-1950s, closed all twenty-six state parks. South Carolina thus became the only state to shut down its recreational facilities in response to a court order to desegregate. In fact, of four instances in which facilities were closed, three were in South Carolina.[46] Closures had the benefit of rendering the factual bases for plaintiffs' filings irrelevant.

Officials preferred closures over allowing African Americans to exercise their rights, as a second Greenville closure demonstrates. In February 1961 several Black youths in Greenville tried to use the skating rink at the city's Cleveland Park and were refused entry. A regional convention of the NAACP was in progress, and a group of eleven young men and women met on February 18, a Saturday, at Springfield Baptist Church and decided to go to the park. When they arrived, the attendant told them that they had to have a permit to skate, which they did not. Nor did they need one, according to the testimony of J. Roy Gibson, the supervisor who was on duty that day. Only the purchase of a ticket was required for entry into the rink. After about ten minutes, a voice over the loudspeaker announced that the rink was closed and that everyone had to leave. (The rink reopened later that evening at around 7:15.) The police arrived a few minutes later and ordered the would-be skaters to leave. Since it was raining, they decided to stay on the porch, but the police told them they were violating a city code against loitering. When one of the activists, Mary Elizabeth Norris, demanded to see the code, the police said they would have to go downtown to see it. They rode down to police headquarters, were read the ordinance, and were promptly booked. They had never been informed that they were under arrest before that point. James Carter testified that he had tried to change his mind about getting in the police cars to go downtown and was told, "No, you can't turn back now, get in the car." When they arrived at the station, the officer read "something . . . kind of fast," and when Carter asked to see the code, the officer "flashed it in [his] face and shut the book; then he said, 'book 'em.'"[47]

In June the would-be skaters filed suit in federal court asking for temporary and permanent injunctions against the skating rink and the city for operating a segregated institution. The defendants, who included the city manager, the director of parks and recreation for the city, the chief of police, and the chief of detectives, countered that rather than being "clean, orderly [and] dignified," as the plaintiffs stated in their complaint, they were engaged "in an effort to stir up strife and trouble and not truly seeking recreation."[48] In preparing his defense for the civil trial, Greenville city attorney W. H. Arnold deposed four of the seven plaintiffs. All of them had been active in protests before, either in Greenville or in Columbia. Classie Rae Walker had been involved in a march on the State House grounds; James Carter, Mary Norris, and Horace Nash had participated in protests in Columbia and Greenville, including sit-ins at the Greenville Kress store. All were members of the NAACP.

Arnold's desire to place this information in the record followed the typical strategy of attorneys for the state and localities involved in suits in which the NAACP or its members were a party. Each deponent in the case, as usual, was asked whether they were paying for their representation (they were not). While not clearly relevant to the issues, the information that Arnold and his counterparts in other cases managed to get into the record established the involvement of the NAACP in prosecuting desegregation suits. Donald Sampson, the Greenville-based lead attorney for the plaintiffs, mocked Arnold's strategy during his cross-examination of Mary Norris in this exchange with the witness:

Q. Are you proud to be a member of the NAACP?
A. I am.
Q. You intend to stay a member?
A. Yes.
Q. You're not a member of the John Birch Society, are you?
A. No.[49]

The trial, held on August 20 before Judge Wyche, consisted of the testimony of city manager Gerald W. Shaw, director of parks and recreation Carl Hust, and James Gibson, the manager of the skating rink and swimming pool at Cleveland Park. As in locations throughout the Jim Crow South, there was not a city ordinance requiring segregation in the city's parks. Rather Cleveland Park and other parks in the city were segregated by custom. Gibson therefore had the discretion, at least technically, as to whom he would sell tickets. There were only a few rules, none of them specifically designed to segregate the rink.

He testified that he would not sell a ticket to a Black skater on the day of the trial, just as he had not sold any on February 18. In this as in many other cases, however, the city would soon act to make the case moot.

Before Judge Wyche could rule on the Greenville skating rink case, the city closed both rinks. As both rinks had been "abandoned and permanently closed," Wyche had no alternative but to dismiss the case, but not before noting that the city had the right "to preserve the peace and assure a peaceful enjoyment of skating rinks to all races, regardless of which group of citizens, Negro or White, causes disturbances. The plaintiffs' constitutional rights to use and enjoy the skating rinks on an equal basis with White citizens in the community does not encompass a right to cause a disturbance."[50] Citing *Clark v. Flory,* the judge noted the right of the plaintiffs to the injunction, if the situation that warranted the injunction still existed. Sampson and Perry tried to reopen the case with a new trial, arguing that the controversy was still alive. Since the city continued to operate a segregated park system, closing the skating rinks had not solved the problem of desegregation in the city's parks and recreation facilities.

Attempts to force desegregation took place across the state. In Orangeburg teacher and activist Gloria Rackley played a significant role in the movement by desegregating the city hospital. In early 1962 her daughter Jamelle had been taken to the local hospital because of an accident that dislocated her finger.[51] The Orangeburg hospital, which had been built with matching funds from the Hospital Survey and Construction Act of 1946 (commonly known as the Hill-Burton Act), required segregated waiting areas while also requiring that Black patients receive equal care. Hospitals in Greenville and Aiken that received Hill-Burton money were nearly equal in treatment of White and Black patients, and the Aiken hospital had an integrated staff, like several other Hill-Burton hospitals in the South. As early as 1956, 25 percent of southern hospitals had Black professionals on staff, and the level of staff integration was almost at northern levels. Many of the hospitals that admitted Black patients were under no compulsion to do so, however, as many did not receive Hill-Burton money. In Columbia, for example, Black patients were put in a separate wing that had no X-ray equipment and had to be carried outside to the White wing for X-rays. By contrast none of the hospitals in the Medical College of Virginia system allowed Black doctors to practice, and Black patients routinely were housed in very unequal rooms in separate buildings.[52]

Orangeburg Regional Hospital, though built with Hill-Burton money, continued to practice segregation. Gloria Rackley's experience there meshed with her activism in other civil rights concerns. While her daughter was being cared for, Rackley sat down in what was supposed to be an all-White waiting area. When asked to leave, she refused and had to be forcibly removed. Soon thereafter she filed suit in federal court. The case went to Judge Timmerman, who ruled against Rackley. However, on appeal the case was sent back to be retried in November 1962 because Timmerman rejected the class-action issues connected with the case.

Segregated public accommodations were also under attack in communities less known for civil rights agitation. Sumter County operated two public libraries: the Carnegie Public Library and its Lincoln branch. The former was for White patrons, the latter for Black, though all the books were theoretically available for patrons of either race. In late 1962 three men—Rev. F. C. James, Rev. E. M. Miller, and Dr. B. T. Williams—applied for membership in the Carnegie Library and were refused. Instead they were "assigned membership in the Lincoln Branch of the Library."[53] They consulted Matthew Perry and Lincoln Jenkins, who brought suit on their behalf on June 4, 1963.

Unlike in Greenville in 1960, where the libraries were closed for a time, the defendants relented. Soon thereafter the trustees of the library met and "adopted a resolution authorizing acceptance of membership of all persons otherwise eligible for membership in Carnegie Public Library, regardless of race or color." The three plaintiffs had already been admitted to membership. The defense accordingly moved to have the case dismissed, given that the defendants had "in good faith complied with all the demands set forth in the complaint." By the time the case was wrapped up, the passage of the Civil Rights Act of 1964 had rendered most of the issues moot. Charles E. Simons, district judge for the Eastern District, struck down the state statute but obviously felt no need to issue an injunction in the case.[54]

Sumter was not the only community that began to move slowly toward change. Columbia mayor Lester L. Bates had entered secret talks with Black leaders, and by spring 1963 the talks began to grow into action. Despite criticism of the mayor's move from both sides, Columbia businessmen began to realize that ending segregation made sense, especially given the alternative of litigation, which Lincoln Jenkins made clear was a possibility. Thus by the end of summer 1963, most White businesses in Columbia were desegregated. The city was rewarded the following year by being chosen an All-American City by Look magazine, an award that the city had won before and that Mayor Bates coveted.[55]

Bates exemplified a new attitude among some of South Carolina's White leaders, who began to call for desegregation. He formed a Community Relations Council to develop plans for gradual integration. In Greenville, too, new efforts began to bring about gradual integration by 1964. The business community was particularly involved. Charles Daniel in 1961 gave what came to be called the "Watermelon Speech," in which he equated recognition of civil rights with economic development. Robert Toomey, a hospital administrator, was "delighted" that "the Black leadership was working with" the White leadership of the city but was equally convinced that the NAACP had no presence in Greenville and was not involved in the move to desegregate the city.[56] If the state's political and economic elite were beginning to recognize the inevitable, they wanted to be seen as acting under their own authority rather than under duress.

While there was a decrease in resistance to desegregation of public accommodations, schools remained another matter. In Clarendon County, where the initial assault on segregation began, schools remained segregated. In the spring and early summer of 1959, ten parents in Clarendon County District 2 filed petitions for the transfer of their children from the all-Black schools they attended to the all-White schools still forbidden to them. Some parents had petitioned as early as July 1958. On September 1, 1959, David W. Robinson sent school district attorney Joseph O. Rogers, Marion Gressette, and Charles Plowden a draft letter that would inform the parents that their applications came "after school assignments for the current year were made." Robinson and Robert Figg were both "of the opinion that the less the local authorities say about this situation the better it will be."[57]

When Jenkins, representing the plaintiffs, asked the school board to comply with the *Brown* decisions and start desegregating District 2, his letter offering to meet with the school board was sent to Rogers, who forwarded it to Robinson in Columbia. Someone, probably Robinson, sent back a template for a letter to Jenkins in which the school board would say that "since it believes that no useful purpose would be served by conferring with you, or with the organization [not plaintiffs] which you represent, they have not set up any conference." Gressette, who received copies of the correspondence, thought that Jenkins was "trying to build up a record and [his letter] should be ignored."[58]

On April 13, 1960, forty-two Black children from Clarendon County School District 1, which encompassed the original district in the *Briggs* case, petitioned the federal court alleging that the district continued to operate a segregated school system. The students, some of whom had been involved in the original *Briggs* case decided by the Supreme Court as part of *Brown* in 1954 and by the district court in 1955, requested that district officials comply with the courts' directives and put an end to segregation in the school system. W. C. Sprott, the chairman of the school district's board of trustees, responded that the deadline had passed. However, according to the complaint, the deadline was never announced or published.[59]

Robinson moved to strike all parties except fourteen-year-old Bobby Brunson, whose name was first on the list of plaintiffs, and to make sure that the case could not be heard as a class action. The case languished for two years. In May 1962 Judge Wyche agreed with Robinson's interpretation: since state law required that each child individually request a transfer, there was no "common question of fact" justifying a class action. State law allowed any student to attend any school other than the one he or she was assigned to, provided they jumped through a series of administrative hoops. The law also required "that the case of each child shall be considered individually." Wyche's conclusion was foregone: since only a relatively few students had actually requested transfers, he could not assume that there was a class of individuals whose interests could be represented by Brunson and the others. Lincoln Jenkins called the ruling "one of the most asinine" he had experienced, adding that he "really [did not] think that judge expects his ruling to be upheld." It was a delaying tactic from a judge who "apparently put state law over federal law."[60]

In Marion County, African Americans sued to open the schools on an integrated basis in September 1960. The school board had divided one school district into two. White children were allegedly allowed to transfer across districts, while Black children were not. What was unusual in the case was that Black students were petitioning for the right to transfer to another Black school rather than to a White school.[61] White officials may very well have feared establishing a precedent by allowing Black students any type of transfer.

By the summer of 1960, the Charleston city schools were 70 percent African American. Total Black enrollment at Burke High School, the school for Black Charlestonians, was 1,783, while 1,528 White students were divided among three different high schools.[62] In September a group of Black parents submitted a list of demands to relieve some of the inadequacies of the district, including overcrowding in the Black schools. In October, after the school board rejected the demands on financial grounds, Black students staged a one-day boycott of the city's schools. Over 8,300 students, 94 percent of the total Black enrollment, refused to attend school on October 12.[63]

Following the boycott, parents of fifteen Black students ranging in age from six to sixteen requested transfers to White schools in the city under new rules in effect since the summer of 1959. Four White schools would be affected if the transfers were approved, with as few as one and as many as six Black students enrolling in the White schools of the city. The requests were denied, in one case at least because the request had been submitted after the deadline. The school board also rejected their requests "on the ground that the best interests of each of the respective children would best be served by the child remaining in his former educational environment, where the school personnel were familiar with his background, prior performance and capabilities." Of course, since all the Black students who might apply were better known by his or her Black teachers in the "former educational environment," it seemed unlikely that the board would ever approve an application for transfer. One of the parents, state NAACP president J. Arthur Brown, petitioned the board on behalf of his daughter Minerva later in October, but no action was taken. In the spring of 1961, some of the parents tried again. This time, Brown's younger daughter, Millicent, was one of the applicants for transfer.[64]

The school board met in July 1961 after conducting "thorough investigations . . . to ascertain . . . each child's record, each child's background and each child's personality." The board interviewed the students' principals and teachers before advising the parents to be present at the hearing with their children. One child, Lydia Glover, was visiting relatives in Tennessee and unavailable; although her father was there, the board took her absence "as silent evidence that the parent was not altogether anxious to press the Petition." Regardless, the Special Committee of the Board of Trustees of School District No. 20 allowed for delay in Glover's case and made no determination at the hearing. Thomas Seabrook was not a model student: his record, according to the committee, was "atrocious." The committee was reluctant even to let him attend school at all and rejected his request for transfer. Millicent Brown was another story: she was "above average" intellectually, though "she ha[d] never quite realized her full capabilities." The only reason Arthur Brown could give for desiring a transfer was that he "felt he had a right to have the child attend any school of his selection." However, since Millicent lived closer to her current school, the committee denied her application. Other students did not fare any better. Ralph Dawson was classified a "moron" on his intelligence tests. Delores Wright was a rising senior. Finally Clarice Hines was a "timid introverted child," and transferring her would "expose [her] to psychological difficulties."[65]

The committee concluded that the children, with the exception of Millicent Brown, were uncooperative—even unwilling to participate in the transfer. "In no instance did it appear that welfare of the child was a factor in the action taken by the parent." The committee emphasized that the only consideration was the best interests of the children. Brown threatened a federal lawsuit if positive action on the requests was not taken, but at a hearing in November, the county board of education refused to grant the transfers.[66]

The end of the 1961–62 school year marked the first time since 1954 that any public schools in the nation had successfully desegregated without accompanying violence, but South Carolina, Alabama, and Mississippi continued to segregate all schools despite indications that the South and the nation were beginning—however gradually—to accept desegregated schools.[67] Still, December 1961 brought with it hints of change among some of South Carolina's White political figures. A few weeks earlier, state senator Francis B. Nicholson of Greenwood County suggested the possibility of pursuing a "local option" program of desegregation. State representative Robert E. McNair, who was running for lieutenant governor in the next year's election, said that "people in the areas affected will have to determine their own course of action. . . . Some might prefer to leave the schools closed. Others might want other solutions." Governor Hollings noted later that there were no laws against voluntary desegregation and said the state had "a firm policy of flexibility" in the issue.[68] Despite occasional minor hints that the segregationist wall was beginning to crack, the majority of White people, including legislators, remained adamantly in favor of segregation.

In March 1962 US Secretary of Health, Education, and Welfare Abraham Ribicoff ruled that segregated schools attended by children residing on military bases would no longer receive federal funding as of February 1963. Nine South Carolina counties were affected by the ruling, which state politicians unanimously lambasted. Hollings recalled his opposition to the federal aid to education bill as he excoriated the Ribicoff move as "an unconstitutional attempt to control the state public education systems." Senator Gressette, implying that desegregation would yield only further segregation, commented that "South Carolina is relatively free of agitation and disorder in the field of education."[69]

Black parents in Darlington County brought suit in May 1962 to force the school district to present a desegregation plan by giving the court only two options for remedies: enjoining the district from maintaining its dual-system policy immediately or requiring the district to submit a desegregation plan "within a period of time to be determined by [the] court."[70] Meanwhile, in the years since the case was originally filed, Bobby Brunson had graduated, but the case bearing his name continued into the appeal phase. The defense in the 1962 appeal in *Brunson v. Board of Trustees* turned *Brown v. Board of Education* on its head. Taking the argument from *Brown* that forcing members of a minority to attend a separate school creates in them "an inferiority complex" and completely reversing it, Robinson argued that since Black people outnumbered White people eight to one in Clarendon County, forcing White children to go to integrated schools would violate their rights to equal protection.[71] In effect, attending integrated schools in which they were the minority would create in White children the same kind of inferiority complex that Black children suffered in segregated schools. This argument foreshadowed the "reverse-racism" arguments that the Gressette Committee and other White defendants would attempt to hammer home later in the 1960s.

Since the Parker dictum held that *Brown* had not required desegregation but had only outlawed government-imposed segregation, Robinson argued that the school board was correct in continuing to operate as it had before. Parker's dictum theoretically allowed segregation to continue forever. Besides, argued Robinson, the segregation that existed in Clarendon County was voluntary. District parents continued to send their children to the same schools they had always attended or would have attended prior to *Brown*.[72] Transfer applications were convoluted and often denied. Since economic or violent reprisals could not have been the reason that Black parents continued to send their children to Black schools, their satisfaction with the status quo must have been the reason.

In December 1962 the Fourth Circuit struck down Wyche's May 1962 ruling prohibiting class action in the *Brunson* case, thereby allowing all the "persons similarly situated" to take part in the case, which was remanded to the district court for a full trial. By May 1963 the case began to make its way back through the system. Matthew Perry argued that the record clearly indicated that relief was due the plaintiffs, since, as in Charleston, the district had "not given . . . any attention to their duty to initiate desegregation of the Clarendon school system."[73]

In November 1963 Black parents in Orangeburg officially requested transfers for their children. One of the Orangeburg parents was Gloria Rackley, recently elected state vice president for the NAACP, who stated vehemently, "We want the transfers immediately. We don't want to wait until the next school year. . . . [We don't want our children] to be hampered and handicapped by the evils of school segregation."[74] In March 1964 the promised desegregation suit against Orangeburg District 5 was filed by Rudolph, Brenda, and Theodore Adams and twenty-three other Black students, including Rackley's daughter. The district became the sixth in the state to be sued in federal court for school discrimination.[75]

The backlash to Black South Carolinians' "pressing the victory" to exercise their rights after "winning the fight" for their rights included legal, bureaucratic, and, when necessary, legislative strategies that effectively stalled Black efforts to desegregate South Carolina institutions. Legislation to bring about economic and other kinds of pressure is but one example of South Carolina's "peaceful" strategy. Legal arguments invoked recently passed laws to defend segregation in the courts. Federal judges admitted and ruled favorably on these arguments, which necessitated appeal. Similarly, laws outlawing the NAACP, the refusal of school districts to develop desegregation plans, and the bureaucratic paper blockades of the transfer process were met by lawsuits from African Americans that demonstrated their commitment to securing their rights.

6

"WE HAVE NOT YET RUN OUT OF COURTS"

Desegregation in the mid-1960s

Black South Carolinians were keenly aware that not all levels of the federal court system were on their side. South Carolina in the early 1960s may not have been Mississippi or Alabama, but White South Carolinians' commitment to resistance was as unquestionable. The fact that their chosen means did not include violence should not divert observers from the realization that the legislature, state and local bureaucracies, and the federal courts were all used to discourage African Americans from seeking desegregation and to prevent its implementation. Defending segregation and maintaining White supremacy were the only ends in mind. The tide began to turn against White South Carolina's resistance in late 1962 when the appellate court compressed the time it took to review their cases and the Supreme Court rebuffed the state's appeals. That did not, however, prevent the state's lawyers from trying to find a legal path to maintaining segregation.

Judge Cecil C. Wyche dismissed Harvey Gantt's case in December, technically because he had still not met all the requirements for admission. Gantt's team immediately appealed to the Fourth Circuit, which reversed the lower court and ordered Wyche to issue an injunction admitting Gantt. With only eleven days left before registration for the spring 1963 term, it seemed that Clemson did not have many alternatives. Robert C. Edwards kept the board of trustees up to date with daily memoranda outlining their strategy to petition the court of appeals for a stay of the injunction order and failing that, to petition the Supreme Court.[1]

Following the appellate court's refusal to issue the stay that Clemson lawyers had requested, there was not enough time to appeal to the Supreme Court. Other than overt defiance, Clemson had no choice left but to admit Gantt to classes on January 28, 1963. The reaction to Gantt's victory among those associated with Clemson was magnanimous, but only on the surface. L. Marion Gressette, the chairman of the South Carolina School Committee, issued a statement on January 23 advising Clemson's trustees "to perfect their appeal to the United States Supreme Court for what it may be worth" while acknowledging that "the Trustees have made the only choice possible under the circumstances." Gressette continued:

> For more than a decade South Carolina has successfully defended its public schools from ill-conceived and ill-fated sociological experiments which have produced only discord and disaster for both races and retrogression of scholastic standards and individual educational opportunity.
>
> We have not yet run out of Courts.
>
> We recommend to the Governor and the General Assembly continued resistance by every lawful means to further encroachment of the Federal Government upon the right and duty of the State to operate its schools in the best interest of education. In short, we intend to retain control of education in the hands of [White] South Carolinians.

The next day the Clemson board adopted the recommendation of the administration to admit Gantt and "employ all of the means at [the college's] disposal to preserve the orderly operation of the total educational program of the college and to preserve law and order upon the Campus and the peace and dignity of the institution."[2]

Clemson had already begun preparing for Gantt's enrollment. "Outsiders" would not be welcomed on the campus when it opened for spring semester registration. Clemson had learned from events at the University of Mississippi, where four White nonstudents had been indicted for rioting. Clemson's public relations director, Joe Sherman, issued a press release in which he attempted to make clear the school's policy: to treat Gantt "as any other student at Clemson College" as long as "he, in turn, conduct[s] himself in compliance with the rules of conduct for Clemson students."[3]

Meanwhile Clemson's lawyers tried to make their case that Gantt's entry to Clemson should be delayed. Expecting rejection from Judge Simon Sobeloff at the appellate level, the lawyers arranged to see Chief Justice Earl Warren in his chambers. However, they still had little chance: no delay had been granted by the Court in the Meredith case in Mississippi, and the full Court had denied an appeal in that case. Although they had no realistic options, Clemson officials kept going through the motions, if for no other reason than to maintain the facade of resistance.

The Fourth Circuit's opinion led Clemson officials to determine what Gantt's matriculation meant regarding the operation of the institution. Robert C. Edwards wrote to William Watkins for an explanation of the injunction. Watkins replied that Clemson would have to treat Gantt like any other transfer student but that Clemson was not responsible for attempting to shape the attitudes of other students. Although Clemson now had to treat applications from prospective Black students without discrimination, officials did not have to change school policy in any other way. For example, Gantt would be entitled to bring a friend to any school function, but that would not "remove from the College the right to exclude other Negroes from the general public from attending the same or a similar function."[4] Desegregation of the student body did not require desegregation of the campus.

The election of Ernest F. Hollings as governor in 1958 has been assessed as "probably the most decisive factor in South Carolina's change in attitude." That assessment is too favorable when it comes to race. As mentioned earlier, Hollings was not averse to using force to quell unrest when it accompanied civil disobedience. As late as October 1962, Hollings stated, without any evidence, that the Black community agreed that South Carolinians were "100 per cent in sympathy with the people of Mississippi,"[5] which had just experienced rioting associated with the admission of James Meredith to the University of Mississippi. Hollings had a reputation as a moderate New Southern Democrat who represented economic progress as governor despite supporting anti-integration laws while serving in the state legislature. He was a segregationist at a time when more vigorous enforcement of desegregation would have been not only impractical but also politically suicidal. As such he was not an effective leader of the desegregation movement. When confronted with the reality of Clemson's impending integration, Hollings called for calm, but he did little to assuage the more virulent anti-integrationists in the state. Rather than take a definite stand, he reasserted that South Carolina's official position would be one of "firm flexibility."[6] One could read his statement to mean South Carolina's firm commitment to segregation required flexibility in the strategies used by the state to preserve the institution.

Opposition from state politicians leading up to the Gantt ruling varied in intensity, but all were opposed to the court's actions. When Sen. John Long of Union called for the closing of Clemson, Gressette himself rose to defend the state's actions in the Gantt case. "We may lose a battle but we are engaged in a war," he stated to rousing applause, which was followed by a vote of confidence in his committee. James F. Byrnes, like Edgar Brown a life trustee of Clemson, was "confident there will be no acts of violence [at Clemson]. . . . But like any other man who forces himself where he is not wanted, [Gantt] will not be embraced by all. Thank goodness, not even the Supreme Court has ordered that be done—as yet!"[7]

Reflecting the success of historical misremembering, South Carolina has been referred to as a moderate state regarding its resistance to integration. In their attempts first to postpone and then to minimize integration, White South Carolinians' reputation for moderation led to greater success than other White southerners enjoyed, particularly those whose policies leaned toward defiant massive resistance.[8] "Moderates" successfully avoided federal intervention. When the inevitable happened and Harvey Gantt matriculated at Clemson, the lessons of moderation were vindicated. By complying in a token way with the directives of the federal judiciary, South Carolina's White leadership ultimately won. Having seen the violence associated with the University of Mississippi's integration in 1962, South Carolina's leaders, wanting to avoid federal interference, realized that complying with the law, even minimally, would serve their ends better. Of course, this compliance took place within a context of continued resistance. Clemson continued to prepare its appeal of the circuit court's decision ordering Gantt's admission.

Colleges that did not admit Black applicants faced the prospect of lawsuits. In addition to Gantt's lawsuit, which was filed in July 1962, Henrie Monteith (niece of Columbia activist Modjeska Simkins) and her parents were reportedly considering whether to sue to gain her admission to the University of South Carolina, which had rejected her the previous spring. Three months later, in October 1962, Monteith filed suit. Rather than accept the Gantt ruling as controlling, University of South Carolina officials went to trial in June 1963. In a rare demonstration of frankness, university officials acknowledged that they had refused Monteith's admission because of her race. The university decided not to appeal Judge J. Robert Martin's order to admit her, and by July Robert Anderson had also been accepted and James Solomon was in the process of applying. By August those two Black students had been accepted, but the university reconsidered its decision not to appeal, since an appeal would put the school on solid ground if Clemson's appeal were successful. Both schools challenged the class-action components of the adverse decisions, most likely to increase the cost and limit the number of admissions of Black students. Registration for the university was set to begin on September 10. Henrie Monteith affirmed her decision to attend the university the next day. After attending the College of Notre Dame in Baltimore the previous year, Monteith became one of the first three Black students to attend the university since Reconstruction.[9] At the same time, Robert Figg, now dean of the University of South Carolina Law School, announced that its first Black student, Paul Cash, had been accepted for classes in the fall of 1964. Figg had been one of the lead attorneys in the original *Briggs* case and had been a staff attorney for the Gressette Committee before his appointment as dean of the law school.[10]

After Gantt's and Montieth's successful lawsuits, desegregation occurred in a few other public colleges without litigation. When Winthrop College

Matthew Perry and Henrie Monteith (courtesy of Richland Library, Columbia, South Carolina)

students were reported as being ready and able to "face integration if it came"[11] in February 1963, college president Charles S. Davis reinstituted an old rule requiring any reporters wishing to contact students to get permission from the president's office. This brought about cries of censorship from the *Rock Hill Evening Herald,* which had polled some of the college's students in the first place. Davis further argued that the newspaper's report was inaccurate, since it was based on the opinions of only a few students. In July 1963 Winthrop College, an all-female, state-supported school, admitted its first Black student in the summer session term "routinely and without incident." Cynthia Plair Roddey, already a graduate of Johnson C. Smith University and a teacher in Rock Hill, enrolled in graduate courses. News reporters missed her arrival on campus but were on hand later, along with South Carolina Law Enforcement Division agents and local police, who also guarded gates at the school. That fall, two Black women, Arnetta Gladden and Delores Johnson, enrolled as freshmen, and a third Black woman was admitted, though she did not appear for registration. Winthrop students stated that they were ready to support integration.[12]

Private colleges began to make similar moves. In June 1963 the South Carolina Conference of the Methodist Church met and decided on a policy to place "no restraints" on college officials regarding whom to admit. The decision affected Wofford, Columbia College, and Spartanburg Junior College.

In October, Furman University, operated by the Southern Baptists, decided to consider "all qualified" applicants, opening the door for African Americans to attend. Despite the actions of the Methodist Conference, no affiliated school moved toward integration. Therefore Furman was actually the first private school to establish such a policy. The State Baptist Convention's general board requested a delay in implementation of the new rules so they could analyze the effect on other Baptist-controlled institutions. Two members of Furman's board, both from the lowcountry, resigned just before the vote on the change. Meanwhile Wofford was considering a desegregation policy, as was Newberry College, which was affiliated with the Lutheran Church.[13]

In May 1964, two months before the passage of the Civil Rights Act of 1964, Lander College, which at the time was supported by Greenwood County, received its first application from a Black student and announced that the application would be handled like any other. Alice Brown told reporters for the *Greenwood Index-Journal* that she had "always wanted to go to college and [she] would not be able to attend any other way."[14]

After Wofford decided to admit a Black applicant for the 1964 fall semester, state Methodists attempted to censure the school, but the two measures were defeated in close voting. Several Methodist churches in the state voted to withdraw funding from the school, but textile magnate and Wofford trustee Roger Milliken offered to cover any shortfall. Nevertheless the admissions went ahead as planned that fall. In November the State Baptist Convention met at the First Baptist Church of Columbia—the site of the Secession Convention in 1860—and voted 905 to 575 to continue segregation at its schools. The state's Baptist Student Union, however, voted to end segregated activity in December, 121 to 57.[15]

By contrast the state's system of technical education, which began its existence with the segregated opening of the Technical Education Center in Greenville in 1962, almost immediately began to desegregate. This was especially beneficial to African American students, for there was only one technical school for them in the entire state, Denmark Trade School. Students had to attend residentially rather than commute. By the fall of 1963, twenty African Americans attended three of the centers around the state, including nine at Greenville.[16]

The public display of Gantt's peaceful matriculation and his strength of character as a student certainly paved the way for desegregating other colleges and even gained a positive review in the press. As desegregation proceeded—however slowly—the *Columbia State* newspaper, edited by *Southern School News* correspondent William D. Workman, established a stance on the desegregation of higher education favoring the slow progress that was taking place.

The paper worried about what it called "marginal mixing": "In the area of extra-curricular activities . . . integration is moving faster than the public and many parents realize. . . . More and more student local gatherings . . . are serving as vehicles for racial admixture."[17]

Left untold were the details of lawyers' efforts to prevent Gantt's admission, to turn him out legally before he graduated, and to challenge the basis of class-action law to force other Black applicants to sue individually, making lawsuits so costly that plaintiffs would become discouraged. Until October 1963 Clemson officials expected to win their appeal. They remained critical of judicial decision-making even as Gantt's enrollment caused no significant upheavals. The Supreme Court ruled that the Gantt case had properly been brought as a class action, effectively ending the efforts to roll back desegregation of higher education. But even knowing the Gantt case was not going well for Clemson did not stop the University of South Carolina from filing a suit or the Citadel from rejecting an applicant. South Carolina in 1963 was a state at the beginning of what some thought would be a relatively quick transition. The year has been called the "year of decision." However, events over the next seven years—including the continued resistance of White South Carolinians to public school desegregation beyond the tokenism used by the few districts that did "desegregate"—reveal the continuing devotion of South Carolina's White leadership to segregation and their inability or unwillingness to lead White South Carolinians toward racial equality with their Black compatriots.

In their use of the legal system, South Carolina's White establishment was not merely trying to delay the inevitable; they were attempting to undo it. Ultimately compliance begrudgingly became the policy of the state, but compliance on such a limited scale that it failed to stem litigation.[18] Compliance did not mean acquiescence. Here, as in other cases, White people believed that the law was on their side as federal judges who were products of their community considered judicial arguments that were no longer generally accepted. This not only delayed desegregation but also encouraged White litigants to continue to use arguments that inevitably were rejected at higher levels of appeal. The objective was always victory, not to put off surrender for as long as possible. Only after the appeals court rejected and remanded cases—sometimes multiple times—did White South Carolinians accept, begrudgingly, a new reality. The *Brown* decision, theoretically applicable across the spectrum of segregation, laid the foundation for modern civil rights litigation. All that was required was for the lower courts to implement the Supreme Court's decision. South Carolina's federal district judges disagreed with the Supreme Court's mandate and therefore applied it as narrowly as possible. As J. Waties Waring predicted, the state did everything possible to fracture litigation to make gains piecemeal.

More than one historian has marked 1963 as a watershed date in the civil rights struggle in South Carolina.[19] In the year that Martin Luther King Jr. delivered his "I Have a Dream" speech, South Carolina finally began desegregating educational institutions, making it the last state to do so. However, if 1963 was indeed the year of decision for South Carolina, it was not immediately clear what that decision was. Despite moving forward with college desegregation, efforts to desegregate schools continued to face stiff White resistance even after Charleston schools were desegregated in 1963. In districts throughout the state, Black parents filed lawsuits, usually after being denied transfers for spurious reasons. Because each district could withstand desegregation until defeated in court, and because the state was willing to assist recalcitrant districts, including supporting appeals, through Gressette Committee lawyers, most districts put up a defense when faced with lawsuits well into the 1960s. New strategies were tried when old ones failed, including White parents' bringing lawsuits on behalf of their children, arguing that *their* rights were at risk should segregation end. Outcomes varied from district to district. Some desegregated, at least on a token level, relatively quickly. Other districts, typically those in majority-Black counties, remained defiant until the end of the decade. Although Black South Carolinians continued to pursue justice in the courts, pressing old cases and filing new ones, in 1963 and afterward, few cases were heard. Some were never decided and continued under court jurisdiction for decades.

Judicial vacancies slowed the pace of adjudication. Ashton Williams died in 1962, and eighty-one-year-old George Bell Timmerman Sr., who became a senior judge in 1962, was often ill and unable to preside, though he remained on the bench until his death in 1966. In June 1963 the two replacements for Timmerman and Williams, Robert W. Hemphill and Charles E. Simons Jr., began their tenures. Hemphill had represented the state's Fifth Congressional District and had voted against the 1957 Civil Rights Act, arguing that civil rights bills did nothing but "keep the pot boiling, stir up feeling, give vent or opportunity to people to express hatred or feelings which might be lived down." A new civil rights bill would "not improve race relations."[20] Simons's political career was not as distinguished. He had served in the South Carolina House in the 1940s, was elected again in 1960, and was serving there when nominated to the judiciary by President Lyndon Johnson. While no supporters of integration, these jurists were less fire-breathing than predecessors such as Timmerman had been.

The state was hailed for achieving "integration with dignity" as Harvey Gantt became the first Black student at Clemson College, but he could still not enjoy his lunch at Oconee State Park near the college.[21] When the state reopened the parks in June 1964, it was on a limited basis. No swimming was allowed. Only in 1966, well after the passage of the 1964 Civil Rights Act, did the state legislature pass a law requiring the Department of Parks, Recreation, and Tourism to "open any State park to public use for . . . normal recreational, educational and forestry purposes and uses."[22] As White South Carolina grudgingly began to allow African Americans into parks, restaurants, and even colleges, it was not indicative of a recognition of the futility of their cause. It should be seen for what it was—a strategic retreat to protect the metaphorical hill they were willing to die on: the prevention of legitimately desegregated schools for children. In colleges, parks, and restaurants, White adults could control the extent of interracial interaction but had little ability to do so in the schools. Integration of impressionable White children with Black children was a threat to White supremacy.

South Carolina's White leadership was among the most obstinate in asserting and defending their "constitutional" interpretations of civil rights. Attorneys and politicians often used military metaphors as they continued to push back against the progress of the civil rights movement. Staying on the field of battle while others gave way reflects the state's characteristic resistance to authority that dates to the colonial era. Officials acted strategically— giving ground only when necessary—and building new lines of defense along the path of retreat. White officials made Black Carolinians who had allegedly come under the sway of the NAACP—the ultimate enemy—pay for every inch of ground gained. While ground had been given in public accommodations, in the field of education there was still substantial resistance that continued to be refined in the courts and through bureaucratic measures designed to subvert *Brown*. Outside state institutions, some private businesses continued to resist equal access to accommodations that served the public.

Every victory that Black South Carolinians won in their struggle for equal citizenship came with sacrifice. White South Carolinians could not control the US Supreme Court, and by the mid- to late-1960s, even the South Carolina natives who sat on the state's federal courts cooled to the effort to forestall the advance of civil rights, since they could not look like judicial outlaws and maintain their credibility. Therefore supporters of segregation relied on White political and institutional control within the state to deter African Americans' pursuit of equality. When that failed, White South Carolinians were not above using that same power punitively—termination of public employees, first used in 1956, remained a potent tactic—and often to such a degree that some activists decided to leave the state. Indeed, provoking self-exile may have been the intent of the retaliation that occurred. Cases involving two teachers from South Carolina illustrate both the changes in the nature of the civil rights movement and the necessity of continuing the struggle in the courts. Gloria Rackley and Irene Williams were dismissed from their jobs as teachers in Orangeburg and

Lurma Rackley (left) and her mother, Dr. Gloria Rackley Blackwell, Orangeburg, South Carolina (from Isaiah DeQuincey Newman Papers, South Carolina Political Collections, University of South Carolina, Columbia)

Sumter, respectively, for engaging in civil rights demonstrations despite the fact that civil disobedience was a cornerstone American value. The activities of both women were in line with Project C, which was occurring in Birmingham at the same time.[23] Following their dismissals, they sued in federal court.

Gloria Rackley started working in the schools of Orangeburg District 5 in 1959. She had a bachelor's degree from Claflin College (1953) and a master's degree from South Carolina State College (1956), both in Orangeburg. During her first year of employment, she worked as a substitute and began full-time work the following year teaching underachieving third graders, usually much older than traditional third graders. Her short career in the Orangeburg schools was spent in that assignment. Her conduct in class was always exemplary, and in the events that followed, her classroom skills and behavior were never questioned. She even took some of her students to church with her if they were unable to go, which was relatively often, given the disadvantages suffered by many of her charges.[24]

Rackley, who had been active as a recruiter for the NAACP in Dillon County in the 1950s, was also a member of the Orangeburg chapter, at first working to increase membership and then working specifically to undermine the "pattern of segregation" in Orangeburg. She also served as first vice president of the state chapter. She worked to desegregate lunch counters and restaurants and to get some of the city's White-owned businesses to hire Black clerks. She was repeatedly arrested for challenging segregation policies in the city. Her lawsuit to desegregate the Orangeburg Hospital, which was filed in 1962, however, was still pending and would not be resolved for three years. Rackley and others also encouraged Orangeburg's Black community to engage in a selective buying campaign, which included picketing local establishments that continued to discriminate. Eventually there were even mass demonstrations. Rackley acted as one of the directors of the pickets, and among the picketers were some of her students from Whittaker Elementary, although she denied any attempt to recruit students directly out of her classes.[25]

The desegregation of Clemson College in January, the University of South Carolina in September, and public schools in Charleston in August 1963 represents the first tangible successes for African Americans seeking an end to Jim Crow since the 1940s. Like NAACP activists across the state following these victories, Rackley and the Orangeburg NAACP redoubled their efforts to end segregation in the city. Although clearly an activist, Rackley never missed a day of class unexcused. She and other members of the Orangeburg NAACP did not stop their activities despite the possibility of arrest or jail. In summer 1963 Rackley was scheduled to speak at a mass meeting in Charleston. She and other members of the state NAACP, including state chair I. DeQuincey Newman, tried to have lunch at the Fort Sumter Hotel, where they were not only refused service but also arrested for trespassing, for which they were later found guilty. In August she was arrested in the Orangeburg County courthouse for going to the White bathroom while there for a court appearance. On September 7, 1963, she was arrested again for distributing announcements of a mass meeting in violation of a city ordinance. (White people who were nearby distributing religious materials were not arrested.) On September 28 a mass meeting that began at Rackley's church, Trinity Methodist ("the headquarters for the movement in Orangeburg"),[26] became an impromptu march that wound its way through town with the intent of returning to the church. As the approximately two hundred marchers moved through the city, however, police officers split them into smaller groups and finally began to arrest them. Rackley was arrested when a group across the street from hers was threatened with fire hoses from city trucks and she ran across the street to ask why such a thing had to be done. The marchers, faced with the choice of giving up their march or going to jail, chose the latter. Some of them were later tried for trespass and convicted. Their decision to go to jail followed a philosophy developed in 1961 by Tom Gaither, who had attended Claflin, located next to South Carolina State College. Gaither was a field secretary for the Congress of Racial Equality when he developed the "jail-no-bail" approach to civil disobedience that was used in sit-ins in Rock Hill, South Carolina.[27]

On October 7, 1963, District 5 superintendent Harris Marshall gave Rackley a letter of dismissal. While formal action still had to be taken by the school board, Marshall's letter effectively ended Rackley's teaching career in South Carolina. The letter outlined reasons for her dismissal, including her leadership of the mass demonstration a week earlier. Her "conduct was such that it encouraged juveniles to break the law, jeer at policemen, promote violence, and disturb good order and public tranquility."[28]

The school district's representatives, William Clark and Superintendent Marshall (who once told the Orangeburg Rotary Club that he would rather see the schools closed than see them desegregated), insisted that Rackley was fired because her numerous arrests were "a demoralizing factor in our school system, that one of our teachers would go to these great extremes . . . and creat[e] a disturbance that would bring a bad image . . . to our profession." Marshall apparently felt vindicated in his allegations against Rackley because of boycotts of the school itself that began after his initial letter to her. Attendance at the Black schools in the district dropped by almost two-thirds, which Marshall regarded as disruptive. In addition, the following February (1964), after Rackley had been fired for four months, students at Wilkinson High School again boycotted the school following the arrest of several of their classmates in downtown Orangeburg. To Marshall this was evidence of how "the influence of this type of leadership extended itself over into other activities, affecting our schools."[29]

Defining her acts as crimes rather than as principled stances against segregation, Marshall cited Rackley's arrests for trespassing in Orangeburg and Charleston and her arrest in Orangeburg for distributing handbills as reasons for her firing. Marshall questioned the legitimacy of her cause and charged that she had "become so *rabid in your desire for social reform* that you are advocating breaking the law as a means of calling attention to what you consider your grievances. A teacher in the public schools cannot advocate lawlessness without destroying her usefulness in teaching young people."[30]

Rackley, represented by Matthew Perry, sued the district for wrongful termination based on her civil rights activity. For a year she lived in Orangeburg with no job save a brief stint working with the NAACP in memberships as the third vice president, a newly created position. During that period she brought the fight for civil rights directly to the door of the namesake of the Gressette Committee.[31] On July 21, 1964, nearly three weeks after the passage of the Civil Rights Act of 1964, which included a prohibition against discrimination in public accommodations among its provisions, several African Americans in

Orangeburg, Rackley among them, attempted to buy tickets (for the ground floor rather than the customarily reserved balcony) at the Edisto Theater and the Carolina Theater. The Orangeburg Theater Corporation, which was primarily owned by James H. Gressette and John H. Rembert, owned and operated both theaters. Gressette was the brother of L. Marion Gressette, the head of the Gressette Committee. In the first weeks after the suit, the Edisto Theater tried to convert to a private club, with no membership fee other than the price of admission to a picture. In August, however, the theaters' board of directors met and adopted a resolution to comply with the Civil Rights Act. Henceforth no restrictions would be made as to who could sit where in either theater.[32] Rackley's time in South Carolina ended on this high note. In September 1964 she moved to Norfolk, Virginia, to teach English at Virginia State College. Despite the higher salary in Virginia, Rackley expressed her desire to return to Orangeburg to teach: "South Carolina is my State, Orangeburg is my home, my work is here, and I want to work here."[33]

At Rackley's trial in September 1965, local attorney and former state and US congressman Hugo Sims asked her whether she thought she had been discriminated against because of her race. She argued that she had sued because she had been denied a chance to teach. Sims then asked her if she thought a White teacher would have been dismissed for similar actions. Rackley said she had never thought about it. Throughout, the issue of segregation lurked in the background, but Rackley handled Sims's attempts to bring that issue into the trial. Sims asked, incredulously, "The only way that the School District is discriminating against you is because they won't allow you to teach?" Rackley replied: "My salary has been held up and I am not allowed to teach. That is what this is all about. Of course while I was working, I was segregated to Negro schools. I feel this is discrimination, but I guess we will talk about that after I am back in the school system." Unfortunately her answer allowed Sims the opening for which he was looking. Attempting to separate her civil rights activism from the laws she broke (trespassing and handing out bills without a permit), Sims argued that Rackley had been active in the NAACP for several years, and clearly the school district authorities knew of her opinions. It was only after a number of arrests that she was fired. Rackley was well aware of the part that race played in her dismissal, as well as the surrounding events. She responded with an eloquent defense of her actions:

> I don't know that anything has been said about color other than it was my race certainly that relegated me to the school in which I taught, to the particular type of pupil I taught, made me, as no one else, particularly attuned and sensitive to their problems and sensitive to the community

in which I lived, that denied these students the future that I felt should be theirs. Now this was because I was a Negro, I suppose. I have never been anything else, so I don't know.[34]

Matthew Perry later recalled Rackley to the stand to ask her impressions of a 1962 meeting between herself and Harris Marshall during which he intimated that her actions—specifically her penchant for getting arrested—could prove embarrassing. Rackley had replied that "these arrests were peculiar to the racial issue and the system in which I worked and the system under which Negroes in this community lived and that I was in direct opposition to these customs, and I felt it was imperative . . . that this system be changed." After that meeting Rackley was reappointed for the 1963–64 school year. She, therefore, understood that to mean that her arrests for protesting the racial situation were "not the same as a drunk teacher being arrested in the street, or if I was arrested for beating my wife, or something. . . . I was arrested simply because I was a Negro in the community, that these arrests would not have been in any other situation or at any other time." She interpreted her renewal for that year, if not as board approval of her activities, as an indication that she was not being asked to stop.[35]

Judge Simons ruled that Rackley's dismissal grew directly out of her participation in civil rights activities in Orangeburg. While school boards were justified in considering "a broad range of factors other than classroom conduct" in deciding whether to keep or fire teachers, "such discretionary power must not be exercised in an arbitrary, capricious, or discriminatory manner. . . . The discretion exercised by the school boards must be within reasonable limits, so as not to curtail, impinge or infringe upon the freedom of political expression or association, or any other constitutionally protected rights." Citing *Johnson v. Branch*, Simons ordered that Rackley was entitled to back pay from the time of her dismissal through May 1964, plus interest. In addition she was "entitled to be reemployed as a teacher in defendant school system in the same teaching position which she formerly held, or in a position of equal status and pay range as she enjoyed at the time of her discharge." If she accepted, which she did not, "such employment . . . shall be continued by defendants without regard to plaintiff's exercise of constitutionally protected activities in the civil rights field."[36]

Gloria Rackley was not the only teacher to be fired for her civil rights activity. In the course of her work with the Sumter Movement for Equal Rights, Irene Williams picketed and engaged in peaceful demonstrations.[37] Despite the nonviolent nature of those protests, she was arrested for breach of the peace. Other incidents mounted up over the years. Finally, in May 1964, without informing her of the reasons, Hugh Stoddard, the superintendent of Sumter School District 2, told Williams that her contract would not be renewed for the 1964–65 school year. Subsequent meetings between Williams and the district board of trustees failed to reveal any reason for the dismissal. Even when Williams appealed to the County Board of Education, her dismissal remained unexplained.[38] Her principal, Benjamin Robinson, said in his deposition that in his experience the school board had rehired every teacher whose rehiring had been recommended. He gave Williams his highest accolade, calling her "the best [teacher] that we had." Further, Robinson had not been told himself of any reason for Williams's dismissal. Williams, he said, was well respected by her students and colleagues.[39] Williams, a ten-year veteran teacher at Sumter County's Manchester School who had received an "A" grade on the National Teacher Exam, faced the prospect of losing her professional career.[40]

By not providing a reason for her termination, the school district made it harder for Williams to get justice. She believed Stoddard had removed her from her position because of her attempt to have her students participate in the American Woolen Contest, which would have required them to attend the contest at the segregated Wade Hampton Hotel in Columbia, a problematic prospect at best. The contest itself was innocuous: a "Make It Yourself with Wool" contest designed for home economics classes and sponsored by the Women's Auxiliary to the National Wool Growers Association, the American Wool Council, and the Southern States Sheep Council in South Carolina. Williams worked with members of her classes on the projects for several weeks, only to be informed by Superintendent Stoddard in early November that "in the 'Make It Yourself With Wool' contest . . . there will not be participants from Manchester High School of this School District."[41]

Although it came after Williams's insistence on her students' participation in the wool contest, school authorities never offered Williams a reason for not renewing her contract. The school board's defense rested on the fact that she missed the first teachers' meeting of the year without receiving permission from her principal. Relying heavily on what they perceived as distortions of the facts, the defense contended that the issue of the wool contest was moot, since Williams had not followed the correct procedure in entering her students. Only one student from each county was eligible, and Williams had six contestants, with no time remaining to have an elimination round. Given the logistics of how the competition operated, which involved each state being able to send a junior and senior winner to the national competition, the explanation was suspect.

When the school board's attorneys finally offered a justification for her firing, it was clear that her civil rights activism was the root of the issue. They contended that Williams's leadership role in the Sumter Movement, especially her activities associated with the selective buying campaign and the arrests of local schoolchildren for various offenses connected with the movement, made her an unfit role model, even though White teachers had engaged in similar boycotts to suppress Black civil rights activism themselves. "As a member of the governing body of the Sumter Movement, we suggest she was responsible for the mis-direction of these children and for their arrest and being placed on probation." A total of 112 children ranging in age from ten to sixteen had been taken before juvenile court for various offenses ranging from parading without a permit to "conducting themselves in a manner . . . dangerous to their welfare and the welfare of those around them."[42]

Defense attorney Shepard K. Nash argued that the courts should stay out of the question of Williams's employment. Unfortunately for the defense, one of the cases he cited to support his argument, *Sarratt v. Cash,* did not help much. That case held only that courts could not interfere with school boards if their interference was arbitrary or unreasonable. Williams's case depended on the contention that her dismissal was arbitrary. Ultimately, however, the defense argued that Williams was not unlawfully dismissed, because she had simply not been renewed as a teacher for the state. Since her job was based on a year-to-year contract, failure to renew did not amount to a dismissal or firing.[43]

During the trial Superintendent Stoddard addressed several factors that Williams said led to her not being renewed for 1964. The wool contest, which the defense had not given much weight in their brief, reflected "on her mature and professional judgment." Her picketing of stores in Sumter "reflected poor professional judgment and did not dignify the position which she held in the schools and in the eyes of the community." Stoddard admitted that Williams in fact had permission from the principal of her school to miss the first meeting of teachers "but not permission from the office of the superintendent or other personnel." He also admitted that in the aftermath of her arrest in September 1963, he did nothing in the way of disciplining Williams. Her record as a teacher was never questioned. She had never been reprimanded for in-class or personal conduct, had never mishandled school funds, and had never been questioned about her teaching. In short, Irene Williams was an exemplary teacher in all respects except in the exercise of her First Amendment rights.[44]

After agreeing with the defense on several points, including the power of local school boards, Judge Hemphill declared that "this court *is* prepared to protect, interpret, insist upon the securing to plaintiff of all of her constitutional rights." Citing the North Carolina case of *Johnson v. Branch,* a case bearing some remarkable similarities to the *Williams* case, Hemphill declared that "'however wide the discretion of the School Boards, it cannot be exercised so as to arbitrarily deprive persons of their constitutional rights.' The action

Judge Robert W. Hemphill
(from Robert Hemphill
Papers, South Carolina
Political Collections,
University of South
Carolina Libraries, CC
BY-SA 4.0, https://commons
.wikimedia.org/w/index
.php?curid=56488201)

of the Sumter Board was, is, arbitrary, capricious, without constitutional foundation, and beyond constitutional authority. . . . The refusal of the Board to specify [a reason for not renewing Williams' contract] is silent witness to the discrimination."[45]

Unlike many of his colleagues in positions of authority in South Carolina, Hemphill acknowledged the existence of the civil rights movement and its influence on the modern South: "In the revolutionary processes now in and about our great country seeking definition, preservation of men's rights, their civil rights, color is the key, the causa sine qua non of a trouble[d] society." Since the school board did not have "objective standards for the employment and retention of teachers" that were applied "to all teachers alike in a manner compatible with the requirements of the Due Process and Equal Protection Clauses of the Constitution," Williams was entitled to a writ of mandamus.[46] She was reinstated and continued to teach until her retirement.

White efforts to prevent elementary and secondary school desegregation continued. The influence of teachers such as Rackley and Williams as activist role models was a clear threat to White supremacy, to school segregation, and to social hierarchy.[47] A study of cases dealing with public education, already the main battleground of contested constitutional interpretation since the *Briggs* case, reveals the distances South Carolina officials were willing to go to preserve segregation. After Wyche's ruling in *Brunson* and the subsequent appeal, decided in December 1962, it was not until the following August, as schools were getting ready to open, that a hearing in a school desegregation case took place, although cases had been filed.[48] For months only two judges out of four for the state were available for work on the docket. As a result cases were substantially delayed. While the Fourth Circuit's demands for a speedy trial had accelerated the *Gantt* case that integrated Clemson earlier in the year, only school cases from Charleston, which was initially filed in 1960, and Darlington, which had been filed in May 1962, had a hearing in 1963.[49] Charleston was the only one decided that year. Two more cases were filed in 1963. Days before Charleston's school case was decided in August, students in Greenville, after having been rejected for transfers, filed suit in federal court on August 19, 1963. The first to sue was service station owner A. J. Whittenberg on behalf of his daughter Elaine. The next month, airmen at Shaw Airfield in Sumter County filed suit on behalf of their 30 children to desegregate the Sumter County District 2 schools—essentially all the county schools outside the city limits of Sumter proper. Still, some steps toward desegregation were taken in the state's parochial schools while public school cases languished. In June 1963 the bishop of South Carolina's Catholic Diocese announced that by September 1964 all the parochial schools in the state would be open to all children regardless of race. St. Anne's School in Rock Hill had been desegregated since the fall of 1954. Of 105 students in the spring of 1963, 14 were Black.[50]

On January 9, 1963, as Harvey Gantt prepared to enter Clemson, Governor Hollings gave his state of the state address, attesting that

> We have all argued that the Supreme Court decision of May 1954 is not the law of the land. But everyone must agree that it is the fact of the land. Interposition, sovereignty, legal motions, personal defiance have all been applied to constitutionalize the law of the land. And all attempts have failed. As we meet, South Carolina is running out of courts. If and when every legal remedy has been exhausted, this General Assembly must make clear South Carolina's choice, a government of laws rather than a government of men.[51]

While Hollings was not capitulating, and his recognition of the reality of *Brown* may seem statesmanlike, he knew that the legal fight was far from over. He may have given lip service to the concept of "government of laws," but South Carolina's government encouraged maintaining legal resistance until the last appeal was denied. The fact that Black parents in South Carolina repeatedly had to resort to the courts to gain enforcement of federal decisions suggests that most White South Carolinians agreed that "every legal remedy" had not been exhausted. In the 1963 legislative session, state senator John D. Long, one of the state's most outspoken defenders of segregation, proposed an amendment to the annual appropriations bill that would have required segregation by sex rather than by race in the state's public schools. In order to "take the heart out of the integration crowd, because the ultimate goal is to conglomerate the races," Long proposed to "place a barrier between our white women and colored men." Senator Gressette noted that his committee had taken a look at the possibility but that the members did not "think we have reached the point where it is necessary," although "there may be a day in the not too distant future when it becomes necessary."[52]

Long's proposal and the Charleston school case, when it finally came to trial, revealed several issues that would continue to arouse controversy. Legal motions and personal defiance continued. To these, new strategies were added. The core of these new strategies relied on inverting *Brown*, creating a White victimhood in which compliance would do irreparable damage to White children. They would lose the privileges of their race, including the (segregated) schools that were part of the mechanism of supporting that privilege. Most of these arguments combined historically racist tropes, including a belief that African Americans had inherent intellectual deficiencies while possessing advanced physiological and sexual development. The defense in *Brown v. Charleston* offered its own sociological evidence in the hope of undermining the weight of the similar evidence that had been offered by the plaintiffs in the original *Briggs* case back in the early 1950s. S. Emory Rogers, the attorney for the Clarendon district in *Briggs,* believed that White South Carolinians had to use "the same psychological and sociological warfare that has been used so successfully against us."[53]

School district attorneys consulted George S. Leonard, who was working with White parents in Savannah, Georgia, as well, to take advantage of his collection of "evidence" of innate Black intellectual inferiority to justify segregation based on intelligence. A body of literature in the field of "scientific racism," a field of intellectual endeavor that was increasingly out of favor among academic psychologists, sociologists, and others since the 1930s, experienced a resurgence during the mid-1950s that continued through the mid-1960s.[54] A handful of respectable, if not exactly revered, social scientists adhered to notions of Black inferiority and expressed those views in a series of predominantly self-referential works appearing during the period. In the September 21, 1956, issue of *U.S. News and World Report,* Frank C. J. McGurk published "A Scientist's Report on Race Differences," which was "apparently the first systematic effort by a social scientist to dispute the social science incorporated in the

Brown decision." Indeed *U.S. News* and other magazines as well as individuals and organizations such as James J. Kilpatrick and the citizens' councils were responsible for the dissemination of the ideas of scientific racism.[55] Much of the scientific racism evidence had been admitted in a case in Savannah, Georgia. *Stell v. Savannah Chatham County Board of Education* became a model for the suit in South Carolina. In the *Stell* case, a group of White parents petitioned to intervene in the case because the school board was doing an inadequate job in defending their interests. Their petition was based primarily on the tenets of scientific racism.[56] Their intent was no less than to destroy the underpinnings of *Brown* and therefore the foundation of desegregation.

State officials began to realize that the constitutional arguments underpinning their defense of segregation were no longer going to be accepted by the courts. By winning suits on public accommodations and transportation, every category of *Plessy* that had been untouched in the original *Brown* decision had now been explicitly overturned. South Carolina officials understood as well that *Brown* could not be overturned by appealing to the Tenth Amendment—they had tried that argument in the late 1950s, to no avail. Two new strategies emerged. The first required undermining the sociological basis of *Brown: Brown* was bad law, went the argument, because it was based on flawed science—not on a flawed reading of the Constitution's equal protection provisions. The other strategy that emerged, one that in the long run would be more successful as a delaying tactic, was used by White parents to argue that their children would be harmed by desegregation. While arguments to that effect were common throughout the desegregation movement, an argument relying on harm to White children set the stage for more vigorous challenges by White people to a wide variety of civil rights initiatives, particularly affirmative action.

The argument from the Savannah case had been somewhat successful. On May 13, 1963, Judge Francis Muir Scarlett accepted the arguments of the intervenors and denied injunctive relief to the Black plaintiffs. Although the Fifth Circuit Court of Appeals ruled just ten days later that Scarlett had overstepped his discretion and ordered him to grant the injunction a little more than three months later, on August 22, 1963, a group of White students and their parents in Charleston intervened in the case using much of the *Stell* material. Their motion to intervene directly challenged the findings of noted authorities such as Kenneth Clark, who had testified in the *Briggs* case and who was criticized by name sixteen times in Scarlett's *Stell* decision. The "self-devaluation and identification with Caucasian values and standards of beauty" were "not the consequences of legally sanctioned racial segregation *per se*, but rather of the total social situation." In short Black people should be expected to have bought into White standards of beauty because "the 'ideal of beauty' of a particular society or culture is an idealization of the physical features of the dominant racial type." Further they argued that Black children who went to segregated schools actually had stronger self-images and greater "race pride and solidarity" rather than less. Had "impartial" authorities testified at the earlier trials that had resulted in integration decrees, they were convinced, those decrees would never have been issued.[57]

District lawyers used this spurious "science" to argue that there were "such [immutable] differences and disparities between the ethnic group allegedly represented by Plaintiffs and that represented by Defendants as to form a rational basis for separating such ethnic groups in the schools of Charleston." The defense then claimed that Black children in the district were intellectually deficient. "The mean mental age of White School children in the . . . District ranges from two to four years ahead of the mean mental age of Negro school children." They could not in good conscience combine children of disparate real ages, but if they combined children of similar real ages, then "existing academic standards in the now all-White schools cannot be maintained and the system of education *for the White children* will be virtually destroyed."[58]

The "socio-moral and behavioral standards" of the Black students were also cast as lacking as well. "Rates of emotional instability, behavioral delinquency, illegitimacy and venereal diseases among Negro children and their parents are vastly greater than among White children and their parents." These "racial differences in physical, mental and behavioral traits" were "to a large extent genetically determined," and such differences, having been genetically determined over millennia, constituted "a rational basis for segregation of races in schools."[59]

After continuing the sociological analysis of the problem of race formation and the connections between "ethnic group identity" and "optimum growth and maturity," the defense concluded that integration would inevitably lead to "sex problems, . . . disciplinary problems" due to several stereotypically deviant behaviors, and a "severe strain on the time and talents of the [White] teachers."[60] Charleston School District superintendent Thomas A. Carrere testified that standards would suffer if Black students were allowed into classrooms of White students. In a variety of achievement tests, Black students consistently scored below their White counterparts. Echoing the defense's psychosocial arguments, Carrere argued that putting students in classes of the same age group would result in students of vastly different achievement and that matching achievement levels would lead to classes with students of different ages. Under cross-examination by Constance Baker Motley, Carrere admitted that he believed that genetics largely determined the differences in the achievement levels of different students. Carrere also admitted that Black teachers were accepted with a lower score on the National Teacher Examination.[61]

Psychologist Henry Garrett and economist Ernest van den Haag were called in to support the defense arguments that Black students were inferior.[62] Van den Haag was a conservative commentator on a broad range of issues who circulated his racial views in popular publications such as the *National Review*. Garrett contended that Black people lagged behind in "the realm of . . . abstract intelligence . . . , those things which made European Civilization and never have made a civilization in Africa in five thousand years." Van den Haag testified to the inadequacies of Kenneth Clark's science in the *Briggs* case and argued that prejudice would increase if integration took place. Even if smart Black students were placed in classes with smart White students, the result would still be undesirable, since the Black elite would no longer have their leadership position and most Black students would consequently suffer. Judge Martin admitted the intelligence evidence to "develop the record" while emphasizing that it was "not the issue" and could have no bearing on his decision, since the Supreme Court had already ruled on the matter of school segregation.[63] While the objectivity and quality of their science were rejected in the professional sphere, it was clear that White people who opposed desegregation found Garrett's and van den Haag's ideas useful in support of their cause. In "The Equalitarian Dogma," Garrett identified "the man in the street" as the only faction that was skeptical of the shift in opinion regarding the equality of the races.[64]

Lawyers for the Gressette Committee used the intelligence test data to develop a plan to "integrate" the state's schools. Calling for the creation of a system of educational classification, which would admittedly not result in "absolute segregation," Columbia lawyer and former journalist Augustus Graydon noted that a system based in some way on educational qualification would "allow the public educational system to continue without educational chaos and complete frustration." Graydon considered a variety of alternatives: classification by sex appealed to him primarily because "sexual problems [would] be accentuated by the introduction of the racial factor," but classification by intelligence, by chronological age, or by "behavioral or psychological criteria" also made the list of possible means of dividing up the student population.[65]

Such a system would result, Graydon thought, in a "predominantly white" high classification (IQ of 100 or more), a more-or-less equal grouping of Black and White children in the middle range (IQ of 85–100), and a "predominantly Negro" class of those at the bottom (IQ below 85). The bottom group "(predominantly negroid at the outset) would become more negroid as the chronologically older Negroes who failed were continued in this group." This system, designed for primary grades, would be "accentuated in the secondary (8–12) grades." The system would lead to a deepening level of segregation: vocational and manual education would be for those who could not pass the primary grades; the higher grades and upper-level tracks would be predominantly White; and Black students would increasingly disappear from high schools altogether, as "the majority of Negroes would not be able to attain any standard of academic achievement based on national levels in the secondary grades."[66] This plan had the added benefit of being similar to the state's teacher salary scheme, which was based on scores on the National Teacher Exam. An ostensibly objective measure could and would be used to perpetuate discrimination.

The end was so desirable that Graydon called for implementation of a testing plan for the upcoming school year. Upgraded academic standards "would result in chaos in the Negro schools but demonstrate the necessity for a realistic educational reappraisal of the *de facto* situation." The new educational standards would reveal conclusively "that separate schools are advantageous from the standpoint of each racial group" and that using achievement tests as a means of pupil assignments was a reasonable idea.[67]

Graydon and John S. Wilson, who along with his law partner Shepard K. Nash represented Sumter schools in their efforts to thwart desegregation in the 1960s, embarked on a plan to prove the uses of "achievement tests in classifying pupils to obtain some measure of *de facto* segregation." W. B. Royster, the coordinator of testing and guidance services for the South Carolina Education Department, noted that African Americans generally did not test as well, though there were always some who classified in the middle and higher ranges. Royster believed that social acceptance would ultimately be a stronger factor in keeping schools segregated. Graydon ultimately and reluctantly agreed: in his report he lamented that lower-achieving White students would inevitably end up in classes with Black students. There was no reason, therefore, to increase the level of testing in the state "at this time as a force to meet the integration situation in various school districts."[68]

Judge Martin issued his order in *Brown v. Charleston* on August 22, 1963, sixteen days after a two-day trial in Columbia. Bound by *stare decisis* to reject the arguments of the defense, especially given the Supreme Court's ruling in *Watson v. City of Memphis* criticizing the continued delays that states in the South routinely engaged in, Martin ruled that the school district was "completely segregated" due to the practice of having dual attendance zones, in which White and Black students were assigned separately based on geography. Freedom of choice, first proposed by George Timmerman Jr. during his campaign for governor in 1954, was created ostensibly to lead to desegregation by giving students a choice on what schools they attended, but Martin found that it did not really exist in the district: no rules were spelled out at any time for initial assignments or transfers. The district had never "taken [any] action . . . towards carrying out the mandate of the United States Supreme Court" to end school segregation.[69]

Martin ordered the district to admit the plaintiffs "at the white school, where a white child would normally attend, if he resided in the same school zone that each of plaintiffs respectively resides in, subject to the same terms and conditions of other students enrolled there." He stopped short of ordering the immediate integration of the entire district, citing a variety of administrative headaches and the shortness of time before the start of school in the fall. That would have to wait until the following school year, when the district would have to "freely and readily grant" requests for transfers. Martin also required the district to provide a notice to all the parents of the district that they could choose the schools their children would attend.[70] Charleston thus became the first city in the state with any level of integration in its public elementary and secondary schools.

Continued delay met every order from Judge Martin as the defendants built a record to undermine *Brown*. Following his original ruling, the district petitioned to vacate the order. Martin summarily denied the petition, leading the district and the intervenors to appeal the case to the Fourth Circuit. The *Stell* intervenors had already filed for a rehearing, which was denied, and then appealed to the Supreme Court. South Carolina's attorney general, Daniel McLeod, filed an amicus brief on behalf of the state, along with six attorneys general from other southern states. The Charleston intervenors asked the appeals court to consider the sociological evidence they had submitted at trial—evidence that Judge Martin said he had no authority to consider but nevertheless allowed into the record. Their brief dramatically argued that mixing the two races, when it had been proven that Black children were inadequately educated, would "cost this country its leadership and endanger its constitutional system. . . . The compulsory congregation of classes requested by the plaintiffs would seriously diminish, and could ultimately destroy, the education of thousands of Charleston children, both white and negro."[71]

Pleading that they were concerned only with the "educational benefit and psychological health" of children, the White parents argued that the state must be allowed to discriminate on the basis of ability while not discriminating on any basis of race or color. This shift in the nature of the argument put forward by White lawyers did not alter the underlying goal—maintaining segregation. The brief then discussed the importance of test results that supposedly revealed significant differences in aptitude between Black and White children. These differences, they argued, were "innate, related both quantitatively and qualitatively not to color or race but to certain common physical variances in the relative size, proportion and structure of the brain and neural system."[72]

The new evidence of psychological harm being done to children in the mixed-race classroom, went the argument, required no less than a reconsideration of *Brown v. Board of Education*. *Brown* had been decided on the basis of inferior, now-discredited (at least by their own experts) testimony, and the new evidence clearly indicated that Black children would be more harmed by being in class with White children rather than segregated from them. "Hence, the continued operation of a dual school system in Charleston . . . constitute[d] a reasonable and constitutionally permissible classification." Nowhere was it acknowledged that Black children's inadequate education was a direct consequence of the state's historic underfunding of Black education for nearly three quarters of a century. In January 1964 the court of appeals ruled against Charleston District 20's, and the intervenors', attempt to use the spurious science that claimed segregation was beneficial to students of both races.[73]

Meanwhile, although working under the handicap of a double workload, Judge Martin unexpectedly called for the hearing of the Darlington case. On December 18, 1963, *Stanley v. Darlington County School District No. 1*, on the docket since May 1962, had its first pretrial hearing.[74] It was the first of several such hearings, and like most post-*Brown* cases in the state, there would be no trial. In May 1964 Martin met with the attorneys. Since all the evidence was in the briefs and exhibits, the attorneys agreed that no trial would be necessary, Martin took the case under advisement, issuing his order in July. He ordered the district to enroll the Black students that fall. He also issued an injunction preventing the district from denying admission to other students on a racial basis.[75]

Lawyers for the school districts continued to seed cases with arguments of harm to White children should desegregation go forward. Defendants in Orangeburg School District 5, like the Charleston district, alleged that segregation existed not by law but because of the voluntary decisions of parents in the county, White and Black. The defense added what appeared to be a crucial argument: the case was filed in March, but the statute on pupil transfers required all requests be made no later than one hundred days before the next school year started. Consequently the district could wait until at least mid-May before considering transfers. They argued that it was district policy to wait until all requests for transfer were in hand before making any decisions.[76] Finally the district raised similar arguments regarding the disparities between White and Black students that the Charleston defense had used, including arguments about the differences in "mean mental age" as well as "emotional instability, behavioral delinquency, illegitimacy and venereal diseases."[77] The fact that the

Stell case remained alive to this point gave White South Carolinians another opportunity to try to garner a favorable ruling. There was also a brief from a group of White students as intervenors in the case. Their arguments read almost verbatim like that of the White Charlestonians.[78]

Matthew Perry argued that the plea for intervention should be denied. The Supreme Court had foreclosed the claimed defense, and the plea for intervention would create a whole area of discussion in the case that had been rendered irrelevant. Perry argued to strike the similar paragraph in the defendants' answer on the same grounds. David Robinson, representing the school board, argued that the ethnological evidence was indeed relevant. "The school board feels that those differences are important to it in the management of the schools. It may be that the Negro has certain natural tendencies that should be reflected in the curriculum which would capitalize, for instance, in the field of coordination." He went on to marvel at the strength and agility of "those defensive halfbacks, most of whom are Negroes," as evidence "that in that field of coordination, the Negro race is very superior." This argument led almost inexorably to the conclusion that "over a period of the last years that the disadvantage to the Negro children has been attempting to put them into a white pupil's curriculum. It may be that we ought to have different courses."[79]

Since the Charleston school case was still active (it had been heard and affirmed by the circuit court in January), Judge Simons felt that his decision in the Orangeburg case would be bound by the decision of Judge Martin in the Charleston case, which had allowed such evidence to be admitted only to establish a record for future appeals. Simons also allowed the intervenors into the case. He went on to ask school district attorney Hugo Sims whether the requests for transfer had yet been acted on; they had not. The one-hundred-day deadline was only to make sure that no one could apply for transfer within one hundred days of the start of school, and it would be appropriate for the school board to act on the requests at any time. Sims told the judge that the next monthly meeting would probably take care of the issue, though Simons noted that if the next meeting were postponed, then no action would be taken before the start of the school year.[80]

Simons was determined to have the case decided before the start of the school year. Some people in Orangeburg were already worried that the judge was planning to wait until the last minute to undermine any decisions that could be made on opening private schools in the county. Simons made it clear that he wanted to allow plenty of time for compliance following any order he issued. After agreeing to accept the record from the Charleston case, meaning that there would be no additional testimony in the case, the sides repaired to write their briefs.

Even as attorneys were preparing for the pretrial conference in the *Adams* case in Orangeburg, the US Justice Department was busy filing a suit against Sumter County District 2, which had announced that it would no longer educate children from nearby Shaw Air Force Base effective on July 1, 1964. The district had offered to rent a school to the Air Force for use by the base's children. The district had also offered to accept children into the district schools provided they accept assignment according to the district's segregation guidelines. The district had already been sued by some of the base's Black airmen on behalf of their children. The government argued that most of the money used to construct Shaw Heights Elementary in 1953 had come from the government under a plan that would require the district to educate all the children in the district.[81] In addition the government alleged that it had spent nearly a million dollars for various school construction projects in the district between 1950 and 1960, compared to less than seven thousand dollars spent by the district in the same period.[82]

While *Brown v. Charleston* was being appealed, two Charleston County districts, one of them District 20, told the state Department of Education of their intention to participate in the new tuition grants program that had passed the state legislature earlier in the year. The South Carolina plan would give students money equal to the state's annual per-pupil expenditure, to which would be added the amount usually spent by the district as long as students attended a private school that was not religiously affiliated. The money would be awarded regardless of race. School officials from the piedmont, where the Black population was a minority, vigorously opposed the plan. Officials from the lowcountry and Black belt, however, were firmly behind the bill, which ultimately passed both houses of the state legislature with decisive majorities. Governor Donald Russell, a proponent of the bill, floated the possibility of calling a special session of the legislature to get money flowing into the program. Of sixteen White children whose parents responded positively to the program in Charleston County, fifteen were already attending private schools.[83]

The chair of Orangeburg's fifth school district also said it would participate in the state's fledgling tuition grants program. T. Elliot Wannamaker, the leader of the private school fight in Orangeburg, if not the state, said that "we know Orangeburg's schools will be integrated by September." Wannamaker, a chemical manufacturer, headed the plan to develop a private school system for Orangeburg County and spoke of developing private schools "that can handle every white child in the community. . . . We are planning to offer a freedom of choice to every white child whether the child is able to pay the tuition or not." According to the *Columbia State*, about 60 percent of the area's White parents had expressed some level of interest in the private school program, which seemed to grow in popularity with every setback suffered in the courts. Other districts in Charleston and Clarendon Counties had already started planning for private schools. The state had approved a quarter of a million dollars for tuition grants for private schools, but the state board of education had yet to receive any formal applications.[84]

Hugo Sims and David Robinson, meanwhile, in the Orangeburg case, urged Judge Simons to acknowledge the proposed racial differences even though he could not issue an order based on them, since the court of appeals had already affirmed Judge Martin's ruling to that effect in the *Brown v. Charleston* appeal. If Simons acknowledged the evidence of racial differences, the "appellate courts [would] have a basis for determining whether such factual findings require a holding that the ruling in *Brown v. Board . . .* is not *stare decisis* here." Judge Sidney Mize of Mississippi had just recently done so in approving school de-segregation plans in that state.[85] On August 12 Simons issued an order similar to the one that Martin issued in Charleston, recognizing *Brown* as *stare decisis* and ignoring the defense's pleas to consider the intelligence data. As in other cases, Matthew Perry and his partners objected to the plan's use of Martin's criteria for transfer, because it remained too subjective.

The plan that Martin approved for desegregation in Charleston, mean-while, came under attack from Black plaintiffs. Martin had approved a plan based on five basic criteria: the student's preference, whether his educational program could be met by the school transferred to, the capacity of the school to be transferred to, the availability of space in schools other than the ones being transferred from and to, and the distance the student lived from those other schools. Black plaintiffs in Charleston and Greenville, even though they had been admitted, realized that under the class-action rules, other African Americans would be affected by the transfer rules approved by Martin, and clearly they were designed to disadvantage Black students in those districts.[86]

In Greenville, Martin ordered the school district to act by April 6, 1964, on the transfer applications it had. He also added to the list of plaintiffs the names of students who had recently applied and been rejected. The trustees of Greenville's unitary district agreed to desegregate that fall. Martin issued the official order on April 27. The Gressette Committee, meanwhile, hoped that the Supreme Court's decision in *Brown v. Board* would soon be modified under the weight of mounting decisions that recognized the possibility of racial dif-ferences and the White public's unwillingness to comply with integration.[87]

The argument that the public was unwilling to comply with integration was losing credibility. On June 10 the schools of North Charleston became the first in the state to desegregate without court action, announcing that four Black children would begin attending White schools that fall. School districts in Beaufort County (District 1) and York County (District 3, the city of Rock Hill) voluntarily desegregated in July, and Greenville, where the Whittenberg suit was ongoing, announced the acceptance of fifty-five more applications for transfer. Pickens County was reported to be close to an announcement of voluntary integration.[88] Beaufort's schools were in heavily military areas and faced the cutoff of more than a million dollars in federal funds, a move Strom Thurmond called "economic blackmail in its rawest form."[89] In the government's case on behalf of Shaw Air Base, Judge Hemphill in July enjoined the district from refusing to educate Black children of parents stationed at the base. North Charleston, like Beaufort, also had a significant military presence. The North Charleston school board's statement noted that they had "been advised that, . . . from a legal standpoint, no useful purpose would be served by going to court. . . . [Therefore,] upon advice of counsel, the board determined to admit these four Negro students, all of whom had made timely application." There was also limited progress in the districts that were being sued or had been placed under court order. Two weeks later Charleston's District 20 announced that seventy-seven Black children would be transferring that fall. Greenville was considering seventy-five transfer applications, and James Island was voluntarily considering three. Around the same time, Black parents in Richland County's first school district submitted a list of demands that did not include immediate integration. Instead most of the demands were intended to gain improvements in the Black schools of the district.[90]

The passage of the Civil Rights Act certainly contributed to this change, if not in attitude then certainly in behavior in many South Carolina school districts. Title IV of the 1964 Civil Rights Act, signed on July 2, 1964, by President Lyndon Johnson, expanded significantly the role of the federal government in trying to achieve school integration. The Office of Education in the Department of Health, Education, and Welfare now had the power to give assistance to local school districts and was required to make a report to Congress on the progress of integration within two years. Title IV also gave the attorney general the power to initiate lawsuits against school districts and colleges if he received a meritorious complaint. Putting the resources of the federal government behind desegregation suits made it easier for plaintiffs, who would no longer have to drain their resources. It also relieved the NAACP, which could devote its resources to other areas. Title VI gave the federal government the power to withhold federal dollars from school districts (as well as any other agency or organization receiving federal money) if they did not desegregate.[91]

On July 11, 1964, in a limited ruling, Judge Martin ruled that White schools in Darlington County must be opened to five Black children who had filed suit previously. Martin also forbade the district from making admission or transfer decisions based on race and mandated that applications for transfer be made available. Until July 1962 the assignment criteria were determined by racial designations. However, when the school board dropped the use of "White" and "Negro," they did not bother to tell the public of the decision. The school district's three area superintendents had almost absolute authority to determine which schools a child would attend, and consequently the schools remained totally segregated. The appeals procedure for pupil assignments or transfers required written applications be submitted four months before school started. Martin ordered the further desegregation of the schools that fall. He ordered the district to announce publicly the policy that transfers could no longer be based on race. Martin used the same five criteria for transfer that he had set down in the Charleston case and, continuing the practice of not recognizing class-action status, he also required students to attend the same school they had attended (outside of promotions, of course) unless they applied for transfer.[92] This came to be known as the Darlington plan and would govern integration in the state until the end of the decade. Perry objected to Martin's order, as he had in other cases. "A biracial school system is not saved from unconstitutionality by superimposing on it procedures by which pupils who have been initially assigned by race may escape from segregated schools only by making formal application and submitting to administrative procedures."[93] The Darlington plan was criticized for vagueness, because it still allowed for excessive discretion by the school board in assigning pupils. The board still had the authority to deny transfers based on space availability, the educational program offered by the school, and the distance the child lived from the school.[94] Like other court-imposed plans, it also did not account for desegregation of faculties or extracurricular activities.

On August 18 Columbia city schools (Richland County District 1) decided to approve the requests for transfer of "qualified" Black applicants. Citing recent decisions in the US Supreme Court and the Fourth Circuit Court of Appeals and under pressure from Black parents, the board decided that litigation would serve no useful purpose. Already by August the number of school districts expected to be integrated in the fall of 1964 had risen to twelve. The next day, schools in Oconee County also decided to accept applications from four Black students to Northside Elementary and Seneca Junior High. This followed an earlier vote in which the applications were denied.[95]

As school began that fall, sixteen districts opened their doors to Black children, fifteen of those for the first time, and only four under federal court orders. Although these sixteen districts represented less than 15 percent of the state's total, they were in major population areas where industry and the military were modernizing forces. Charleston County was the state's most populous;

Greenville's unitary district was the state's largest geographically. The largest high school in the state, in Spartanburg, desegregated in the fall, as did the schools of the capital city, Columbia. Horry County schools announced that they would desegregate in January 1965. Schools in Aiken County, under threat of a suit, announced desegregation would begin in the1965–66 year. In two of the newly desegregated districts in Sumter and Orangeburg, recent court orders from Judge Hemphill and Judge Simons, respectively, prompted the move to integrate. Neither case ever went to trial. Very few Black students actually attended school with White students (261 throughout the state—0.1 percent of the total number of Black students—and 84 of those in Charleston alone). Although the great majority of the state's school districts remained segregated, a great many Black students—more than a third of the state's total student population—lived in desegregated districts. Therefore they had theoretical access to formerly all-White schools.[96]

Among the districts in the state that were still segregated, however, was Clarendon County's Summerton district (District 1), the site of the original *Pearson* and *Briggs* cases from 1947 and 1951. In addition Black parents of twenty-five students in Cheraw, after having been told that their applications for transfer on behalf of their children were filed too late, filed a new suit in federal court. Lawyers for various plaintiffs throughout the state also filed motions challenging the desegregation plans for Orangeburg and other areas, which had become a blueprint for other areas. The plans, based as they were on Judge Martin's five criteria, were "inadequate and unreasonable," according to the complaint in the Orangeburg case.[97]

In October 1964 *Brown v. Charleston* reached the Supreme Court on appeal from the White intervenors in the case. The Court refused to rule, upholding the appellate court's rejection of the spurious science undergirding the arguments of racial differences between White and Black people.[98] For hardliners the rejection of this science was not the end of the battle. The denial of certiorari led Robinson to reconsider the strategy the state should use in future cases. Since "innate differences between the two races" could not be used to justify segregated schools, Robinson thought that integration could be kept to a minimum. Achievement testing, a strategy that had been ruled out earlier, should be expanded to ensure that children of relatively similar abilities would be in the same classroom. In addition districts should add more vocational training in Black schools to discourage them from wanting to transfer to White schools, which presumably would be focused on a more academic curriculum.[99] In all likelihood the expectation was not that desegregation would be eliminated entirely but that it would be kept to an absolute minimum. Perhaps the parents of the few Black children who were expected to test well might withdraw their children if they faced social isolation. While the tide may have been turning against segregation, its acolytes continued to adhere to its tenets.

While some progress was made in breaking down state-sanctioned segregation, in public accommodations by 1964 not all South Carolinians were willing to abide by the new Civil Rights Act. In Columbia, following passage of the act in the summer of 1964, J. W. Mungin, a local Black minister, filed a complaint with the FBI against Maurice Bessinger, the owner of several local drive-in barbecue restaurants—and one eat-in establishment—and the president of the National Association for the Preservation of White People. On July 3 and August 12, 1964, Bessinger denied service to Anne P. Newman, wife of civil rights leader I. DeQuincey Newman, and two other African Americans at his Columbia restaurant. Bessinger denied that he served food to interstate travelers —in fact small signs were placed in the windows of the restaurants to that effect—but admitted that he did not serve Black customers for on-site dining. Bessinger said in a press conference backing George Wallace for president that he planned to continue his practice of requiring Black patrons to come to the back door and leave the premises with their orders. Forcing him to allow Black customers at the drive-in or inside the restaurants would violate not only his "constitutional right" but also his "divine right" to refuse service to anyone he pleased. Bessinger was confident that very little prosecution under the new law would take place before November's presidential election, when he hoped a new Republican administration would back off from rigorous enforcement of the act.[100]

Judge Simons disposed of most of Bessinger's arguments in short order. Bessinger relied on his own rights to due process and equal protection as well as protection under the Commerce Clause of the Constitution, but the Supreme Court had already ruled against similar arguments, particularly in *Heart of Atlanta Motel, Inc. v. United States*, decided two years earlier.[101] Simons also rejected Bessinger's argument that forcing him to serve African Americans would violate his right to freedom of religion under the First Amendment. Simons wrote that while "Bessinger has a constitutional right to espouse the religious beliefs of his own choosing . . . he does not have an absolute right to exercise and practice such beliefs in utter disregard of the clear constitutional rights of other citizens." Ultimately, though, Simons ruled that the drive-in restaurants did not constitute restaurants under the definitions in the 1964 Civil Rights Act; the plaintiffs were not entitled to relief as far as those restaurants were concerned. Bessinger's one eat-in restaurant, however, was ordered to serve Black customers as it would any other. In April 1966 the Fourth Circuit Court of Appeals reversed Simons's decision concerning the drive-ins, ruling that the Civil Rights Act was clearly meant to apply to those as well.[102]

Even as the Bessinger case worked its way through the legal process, the *Columbia State* reported that there was very little opposition to the new Civil Rights Act in the state. I. DeQuincey Newman reported that "100 of 121 formerly all-white establishments [in fourteen cities and towns throughout the state] had served Negroes since passage of the bill." While an incident in Charleston and the Bessinger incident were reported, the paper noted that most establishments either admitted Black customers following passage of the act or in some cases already had admitted black customers or clients. Newman also noted that Governor Russell had not publicly urged compliance with the law and that state officials were "not living up to expectations of leadership requirements." However, Newman was encouraged by Attorney General McLeod's plan to meet with law enforcement officials to discuss the law.[103]

Newman urged restraint rather than immediate action against those who did not comply. Places that did not serve Black customers at first would be given a second chance, then the NAACP would resort to the courts. Only then would demonstrations be undertaken. Throughout the civil rights struggle in South Carolina, Black citizens had been far more likely to try their hand at a victory in federal court following an incident. Even when demonstrations and boycotts were used, as in Orangeburg, South Carolina's Black population continued to regard the federal courts as their best friend in the struggle.

The lack of judges on the federal bench in South Carolina, the racial conservatism of the judges who did serve, and the tenacity of White officials and their lawyers combined to make 1963 something less than a year of decision. White citizens from Clemson, Charleston District 20, and the University of South Carolina appealed adverse decisions even as they began to desegregate. Rulings in 1964, which allowed officials to craft convoluted compliance measures, and the limited nature of those rulings made that year not much better than 1963. The brightest spot was the Civil Rights Act of 1964, which gave the executive branch a stronger footing. When reprisals made Black South Carolinians more circumspect about filing suits, the federal government was able to step in. Federal funds—or the threat of their withdrawal—also became a lever of power. However, even these were not sufficient to break the resistance of White South Carolina.

7

"WE'VE RUN OUT OF COURTS, AND WE'VE RUN OUT OF TIME"

Freedom of Choice and School Desegregation to 1970

Before 1963 *Brown II* established that desegregation was primarily a matter between plaintiffs, defendants, and federal district judges who were willing to rule narrowly and conservatively—much to the consternation of the Supreme Court, which noted that *Brown II* was not intended to engender "infinite delay." Consequently, by 1964 only a little more than 2 percent of Black children in the former Confederacy attended integrated schools. In exasperation the Court noted that remanding cases to the district courts "did not mean, however, that the discretion was even then unfettered or exercisable without restraint."[1]

By 1964 two basic approaches to achieve nominal desegregation had developed across the South. Geographical zoning plans were probably the most effective in minimizing large-scale integration because of residential segregation, particularly in urban areas. However, freedom of choice plans, which gave parents more control over the schools their children attended and which were more conducive to preventing all but token desegregation, became the preferred method in South Carolina. The presumption was that White parents would choose segregation. Given that the plaintiffs in the desegregation cases were Black, they would be most likely to choose to integrate a school; however, since judges limited relief in their rulings to plaintiffs, they would only do so in negligible numbers. Ultimately judges controlled the class-action status of a given case or approved district plans when developed, and they managed the pace of desegregation in the states. Denying class-action status limited the number of Black students affected by positive rulings. This strategy may have been the more effective.

As discussed in chapter 6, after the Civil Rights Act went into effect in July 1964, districts had to comply with Title IV of the act by desegregating public education or lose Title VI federal funds. To qualify for government funds, school districts were required to remove "all practices characteristic of . . . dual or segregated school systems." Compliance could come in one of three ways. Districts could submit HEW assurance form 441, which could only be submitted by those who were in immediate compliance with desegregation. The form affirmed that the school system—including buildings, transportation, activities, and placement of faculty students and staff—was not racially biased. Second, they could submit a desegregation plan that used freedom of choice, geographic attendance zones, or both in combination. These plans could not use race as a factor in any facet of school operation. The plans allowed for a less abrupt unwinding of segregation than would a court order—unless the order established a timetable. To demonstrate "good faith" effort, desegregation plans had to integrate at least four grades in 1965 and establish grade-by-grade timelines with an expectation for full school desegregation by fall 1967. Finally, a district could be subject to a court order that desegregated the entire system rather than grant relief to named plaintiffs, as many South Carolina district court decisions had. Officials who did not sign an assurance form could face a lawsuit, often with the United States as the plaintiff, resulting in a court order.[2] Two judicial tactics that had abetted delay were prohibited during the first year of implementation. A Supreme Court ruling made it more difficult to limit class action and to use protracted desegregation plans that resulted in plaintiffs aging out.[3] A ruling by Fifth Circuit judge John Minor Wisdom dispensed with the use of supposed racial intelligence differences as a legal justification for delay. Wisdom also criticized Parker's "over-simplified dictum," which had been cited forty times as a "misunderstanding of [the] principle" of *Brown*.[4]

Throughout the latter half of the 1960s, lawyers representing White officials in various South Carolina school districts engaged in a contest of legal wits with federal officials and were often abetted by the state's federal judges, whose rulings might contradict those of colleagues or of themselves in earlier cases. Local school districts, lawyers, and elected state officials engaged in a coordinated effort to postpone or limit the impact of desegregation rulings. The willingness of the state's federal courts continually to rehear old arguments, to limit relief only to named plaintiffs, and to remain skeptical of the legitimacy of the new powers the Office of Education claimed under the Civil Rights Act delayed meaningful progress toward integration for years.

Of South Carolina's 108 school districts, 42 filed desegregation plans by the March 4, 1965, deadline set by the Office of Education, although State Superintendent Jesse Anderson refused to divulge the names of the districts. Pressed by newspapers, Anderson said, "They're not public unless I make them public." Most of the districts that had sent plans admitted it, however. Nearly all (96.5 percent) of the submitted plans contained "freedom-of-choice" programs based on the five-point program set forth by Judge Martin in his decision in the Darlington case.[5] The number of submitted plans soon grew to 79, perhaps because federal dollars provided under the Elementary and Secondary Education Act of 1965 were at stake and failure to submit a plan could result in withholding of funds. HEW was not opposed to freedom-of-choice plans in principle. However, those plans were expected to achieve desegregation. Therefore several plans that did not appear to move toward that aim were sent back to the state for "more information." According to Fort Mill (York County) superintendent J. E. Thompson, "They're [the US Office of Education] encouraging us to forget 'freedom of choice' plans. . . . They want to push it all in geographic zoning." The federal Office of Education required notification of individual parents, rather than the public announcement that had become customary, and nondiscriminatory bus transportation. The office's letter to the Fort Mill district perceptively analyzed what many in the state left unsaid: "In theory, freedom of choice is unobjectionable. The practical difficulty is that the choice open to many may not be free."[6]

By May 1965 it seemed that almost all of South Carolina's districts would be at least nominally desegregated by that fall. Ninety-five districts had submitted assurance forms, though the Office of Education replied to seventy-two of those, noting their inadequacies.[7] Those districts would have to rework their plans. On May 8 York County District 1 became the first in the state to get a voluntary plan approved. Unlike the plans developed under court order, many of which were modeled on the Darlington plan, the York plan made no reference to Judge Martin's five criteria. The York District 1 plan gave priority in school assignment to children living closer to a given school. As a geographical plan, it ran counter to the trend across the state. York mailed the required notification to the parents of children who would enter junior high or high school that fall.

Clarendon County's three districts were among only ten in the state that defied the requirement to file forms or desegregation plans with the Office of Education.[8] L. B. McCord (who had been county superintendent since 1940) remained defiant. Only "some terrible force" would get him to sign a compliance form. McCord at one point forced cancellation of a football game between Manning and the desegregated St. John's High School. McCord said that "we've got a good bunch of colored people in this county. But the taxes the colored people pay in this county wouldn't hire a janitor." Another unnamed official from the Pee Dee region said he thought his district might sign the forms and then forget them. State Superintendent Anderson advised against signing the forms unless a school district was "fully integrated." Instead he suggested that local districts submit desegregation plans to HEW.[9]

While Judge Parker's *Briggs* dictum held that *Brown* meant that governments could not consider race as a factor in any way, lawyers and intellectuals confronting racism in later years began to argue that "to get beyond racism, we must first take account of race."[10] The necessity to take account of race was readily apparent in South Carolina. In the Clarendon 1 case, US Attorney Terrell Glenn prepared an amicus brief arguing that increasing numbers of Black students should attend formerly White schools each year.

As HEW became more involved in scrutinizing the progress of school desegregation, more school districts' assurance forms and desegregation plans were found wanting. The promised desegregation failed to materialize in meaningful ways. Technical compliance with Title VI grew rapidly. By the late summer and early autumn of 1965, more steps toward desegregation in the state's schools were taking place, at least on paper. The actual rate of desegregation remained extremely low. By August ninety-six districts had submitted desegregation plans; of those only eighteen had been accepted. In addition five districts were operating under court-ordered desegregation, so slightly more than 20 percent of the districts were no longer operating their schools on a segregated basis when school began in the fall. In the South overall, 71 percent of the districts were in compliance. By the beginning of the 1965–66 school year, the figure for the region was more than 98 percent.[11]

The district courts remained part of the oversight of desegregation, and these competing authorities explain why, despite the filing of plans, little progress was made. White South Carolinians continued to delay the onset of desegregation by keeping cases before the courts as long as possible. The district court judges had remained some of White citizens' most reliable allies in dragging out desegregation. Black parents, often joined by Justice Department attorneys, continued to press their cases. With the federal government on their side, Black Carolinians remained hopeful of ultimate victory.

In May 1965 a pretrial conference was finally held in the *Brunson* case from Clarendon's District 1. By that time only nine of the original forty-two plaintiffs were young enough to be in school the following fall. The state was winning its war of attrition as students who tried to transfer grew older and graduated before their cases came to trial. Finally in August, Judge Simons found for the plaintiffs. Like Judge Martin's limited remedy in the Charleston case, Simons's order applied only to the nine students remaining from the original case for the upcoming school year. In short the ruling allowed only Black students who were part of the case the right to apply for transfer, not the right to transfer in itself. Any other Black student wishing to transfer would have to wait until the following fall. Perhaps anticipating a situation similar to that in Charleston, Matthew Perry filed a motion to vacate the ruling, specifically the portion that allowed for significant discretion on the part of the school board in determining initial school assignments.[12]

In August 1965, after attempting to work within the system for a decade after *Brown II,* the parents of eleven children in Clarendon County District 2 filed a complaint and moved for an injunction to force the district to desegregate. The students had applied for transfers but, like many Black students before and after them, were denied for several different logic-defying reasons. The school district argued that "to grant the requested transfers on the grounds of the pupil's 'rights' to attend a particular school would have discarded every educational, humane, and moral criteria, and this the Defendants decline to do."[13] The school board argued that they were actually doing the students a favor by disallowing their requests.

In the meantime the federal government began to exert financial pressure on segregated districts in the South by using HEW's right to revoke grants of federal assistance to school districts that failed to comply with desegregation orders. In September 1965 US Commissioner of Education Francis Keppel sent school districts that had not complied with the Civil Rights Act a notice that hearings would be held in Washington in October. Two South Carolina school districts were on Keppel's list: Calhoun District 2 (the town of Cameron) and Clarendon District 1 (the town of Summerton and the target of *Briggs v. Elliot* and *Brunson*). The commissioner sent Cameron superintendent J. P. Dufford a letter in August urging compliance. When no evidence of a move toward compliance appeared, Keppel wrote again in September. The September letter was accompanied by a notice of the October hearings. "Fewer than two percent" of formerly segregated school districts had required such warnings, but Dufford continued to resist. He forwarded the letter to Senator Gressette, who asked David Robinson whether the school district could avoid filing a compliance document. The school board argued that because the district was 79 percent Black, "any plan which would be acceptable to HEW would totally disrupt the Public School system in that District." They preferred to run their schools under a court order rather than voluntarily submit a compliance plan.[14]

Voluntary compliance equaled capitulation and threatened the veneer of die-hard segregation. Court orders also had the advantage of taking additional time to implement, which many, if not most, of the state's federal judges were willing to accommodate. By November 8, 1965, only twenty-four of the state's districts (22.4 percent) were out of compliance, twenty-two of those because of unacceptable plans and two—Clarendon District 1 and Calhoun District 2 —because they had not submitted any plan at all. By December 80 percent of the districts of the state, covering 88 percent of the state's pupils, were in pro forma compliance. Yet only 1.46 percent (3,864) of the state's Black schoolchildren attended school with White children, trailing only Alabama (0.43 percent), Mississippi (0.59 percent), and Louisiana (0.69 percent).[15] An HEW report submitted to the Special Subcommittee on Civil Rights of the House Judiciary Committee in hearings on desegregation in the South contained an appendix showing that hundreds of districts across the South, including nineteen in South Carolina, had substantiated noncompliance, the first step in a three-part process that could lead to loss of funds. Some cases, including five in South Carolina, had advanced to the hearing stage. In some states districts had reached stage three, which resulted in loss of funds.[16]

Robinson informed Gressette of the federal government's options in the situation: it could terminate all federal assistance or, if a Black parent complained, bring a desegregation suit. Robinson advised the district to file a "Darlington type" desegregation plan, which HEW would find inadequate but which would give the district a stronger case in federal court. On October 1 the board decided simply not to appear at the scheduled hearing: "Having concluded that the educational interests of the pupils of the School District would be better served by declining to accept Federal financial assistance [on HEW's terms, the board] decided not to file a 441 compliance form."[17]

Although HEW officials believed that southern states would comply with the law, observation proved them wrong. Court orders by sympathetic judges allowed White southerners to impede meaningful desegregation. The Civil Rights Commission noted that "districts in which racial segregation and attitudes of racial superiority [were] deeply entrenched" automatically qualified for continuation of federal funds under final court orders merely by agreeing to comply with the order. The commission found this problematic because the final orders varied widely in character.[18]

The failure of their effort to enlist White southerners in transforming their region resulted in HEW and the Department of Justice exercising more stringent oversight over desegregation. Deputy Attorney General Ramsey Clark told members of Congress that school superintendents and school boards believed that Title VI applied to discrimination but not to desegregation. Therefore they continued to argue that segregated schools are proper so long as any Black student who requested a transfer to a White school was granted the transfer. They alleged that the HEW policies were a "usurpation of power" because they allowed no consideration for local conditions. Therefore implementation rules for 1966 were strengthened. Even then, resistance from southern administrators remained significant.[19] A 1966 US Commission on Civil Rights report affirmed what was evident in the case of desegregation in South

Carolina—that the latitude provided for in *Brown II* had failed to achieve substantial desegregation.[20]

The Southern Regional Council, along with numerous other organizations, was highly critical of the Office of Education's original policy. In December 1966 they published a scathing review of the first year of the HEW program titled "School Desegregation 1966—The Slow Undoing." They excoriated the "conservative approach" of HEW, calling the initial proposal "too weakly drawn and too timidly enforced." The Southern Regional Education Board (SREB) also lambasted HEW's trust of southern officials: "In view of the long history of attempted evasion of court orders since 1954 on the part of many of these same officials and on the part of governors and other public office holders, this assumption was questioned by many interested in obedience of the law." The US Commission on Civil Rights supported a "federal law to protect Negro students who attend white schools from intimidation and harassment." This was proposed in a 1966 Civil Rights Act that failed to pass Congress. The commission outlined the issues that led to failure of existing "freedom of choice" programs, including the burden placed on Black citizens to be responsible for desegregation, harassment, and intimidation.[21] The SREB called the new guidelines HEW implemented in 1966 the "End of Innocence," referring to the possibility that the White South would cooperate with desegregation.[22]

The year 1966 proved to be a pivotal one for school desegregation in South Carolina. While there were still relatively few Black students attending schools with White students, the courts were active starting in the late winter and through the late summer of the year. By February the Justice Department had become interested in the Clarendon 2 case and filed an application to intervene on the side of the plaintiffs. The department also sued Lexington School District 1 based on complaints from an unnamed Black parent.[23] Later that month, at the pretrial conference in the Clarendon 2 case, the district's lawyers stipulated that the school district was a dual, race-based system. At trial Superintendent Weldon did little to belie that sentiment, consistently referring to the White schools as "our" schools and the Black schools as "their" schools.[24]

Despite the school equalization program that was instituted in the early 1950s, Black schools in Clarendon 2 were valued at less than 40 percent of the White schools of the district. A building and improvement plan, while spending more on Black schools by a five-to-three margin, was still not enough to equalize the facilities. Thus, while the total value of the two separate systems was relatively equal in 1966, the greater number of Black students—68 percent of the county's population was African American—created a disparity in per-student spending on infrastructure in the district. An even worse disparity affected annual per-student instructional expenditures in the district: spending per White student was $305.91, while only $119.89 was spent per Black student. Removing teachers' salaries from the equation—they had been largely equalized through earlier litigation—reveals an even greater disparity: $18.60 for each Black student; $127.80 for each White student. White students enjoyed a language lab, newer and more typewriters, more sewing machines, greater choice in course selection, hot lunches instead of bag lunches for many more White students than Black students, special education classes for White children only, smaller classes, "better" teachers (based on scores on the National Teacher Exam), and more extracurricular activities. The end result was that twice as many White students entered college as Black students. Of those, only one of thirty-three White students entering college had to take a "subfreshman" course, while ten of fifteen Black students entering college had to take such courses.[25] The Justice Department's preferred relief at this stage was the relatively conservative freedom of choice plan based on HEW guidelines, but such plans were hardly effective at ending the realities or the effects of discrimination.

David Robinson asked the court to consider a freedom of choice plan, modeled on the Darlington plan that had been approved for other districts in the state, including preference, educational program, school capacity, availability of space in other schools, and distance from other schools.[26] Despite the rulings from several federal courts from 1963 onward, including *Brown v. Charleston*, that such considerations were off-limits, Robinson and his fellow attorneys continued to call attention to the educational deficits and poor academic records—which they interpreted as innate intellectual deficits—of the children wanting to transfer.

On April 21 Hemphill issued his order in the case. It was a scathing attack on the district questioning their "will" to change. The district's plan for desegregation was "at best . . . merely a contrived 'paper tiger'" that amounted to "a needless temptation for further delay." The district's lawyers (Joseph O. Rogers and David Robinson) argued that the facilities were in fact equal in spite of the figures offered by the government in its trial brief. For example, the White Spanish teacher's lab would be replicated at the Black school if the Black French teacher wanted one. There were fewer typewriters at the Black school because there were two typing teachers and therefore smaller classes. The lunch program was cost-prohibitive despite a higher federal subsidy for Black students ($0.15 compared to $0.05) because only one-quarter of Black students bought their lunches.[27]

Hemphill required the school board to submit a revised desegregation plan to the court by May 15, 1966. The board's original plan still left room for school authorities to avoid integration, as the plaintiffs were quick to point out, and as Hemphill noted in his ruling:

> There is no provision in the plan for the mandatory exercise of free choice by all pupils annually. The ills attending a voluntary choice plan are patent. This is particularly true in this case where a student who does not exercise a choice will be assigned to the school he previously attended. The possibilities presented for the perpetuation of the status quo by this combination are obvious. Viewed in the most benign light it is a needless temptation for further evasion.

Hemphill took notice of the revised HEW guidelines and encouraged the defendants to include some of its aspects, though he did not necessarily require "absolute adherence." Unlike the Darlington plan, which had outlined processes for implementation, Hemphill's process in this instance included a list of five items that can be boiled down to "do not discriminate on the basis of race in any of these aspects of school operation." Hemphill was silent on how his order was to be implemented. He required the district to develop a plan with "convenient speed" and required the plan to be ready for the upcoming school year. Hemphill acknowledged the "difficulties involved" and time wasted in the past. However, he expected good-faith effort and would not be sympathetic to delay. "Defendants through their able counsel have expressed to the court their good faith, their ready will to comply, the high purpose and endeavor with which they have faced the task; but the proposal put forward implies the standard of reasonableness was either too obscure or somehow repugnant to them. . . . Choice should be an exercise of the will—not a *successful stratagem of administrative chess.*"[28]

In Calhoun County the district's submission of a voluntary desegregation plan was off the table due to the district's recalcitrance, so in April 1966 HEW had moved to the second option: court-ordered compliance. An anonymous individual had complained of continuing segregation, and the department moved to rectify the problem. F. O. Hutto, the chair of Cameron's board of trustees, wrote to John Doar, assistant attorney general for civil rights, requesting the name of the complaining parent. Doar replied that under the Civil Rights Act he was unable to comply with Hutto's request. When apprised of the Doar letter, Robinson suggested a disingenuous reply. The school district should say they were seeking out the parent's name "to see whether we could correct any difficulty that might have arisen. . . . In this school district all pupils of school age are free to attend any school in the district which the parent wishes the child to attend."[29]

School districts often cited "administrative difficulties" as reasons to delay integration further, but Hemphill dismissed those as "non-specific," adding that "our purposes should not be limited or perverted by them."[30] Hemphill did allow for some leeway: whether the student's desired educational program could be met by the school to which he or she wished to transfer, one of the Darlington plan's criteria, could factor into the district's decision. It was not discrimination per se that was to be eradicated, but "'racial discrimination' in public education which must be excised here from the American culture." Hemphill believed that "certain training, perhaps vocational or preparatory, may be centered in one school or another due to economic or other pragmatic considerations. In the same manner the practice of separating study groups or classes into accelerated or slow sections is a matter for educators. 'Discrimination' bears no stigma in connotation." He denied the use of attendance zones and required the new plan to be implemented in all grades for the upcoming year, rather than for the initial grades of elementary, middle, and high school. He also required that remedial courses be made available to students who needed them.[31]

Hemphill required the school district to send letters offering the transfer option to parents of all children in the district. By the July 23 deadline, 2,275 of 3,818 letters had been returned. As expected, no White students requested transfers to previously Black schools, but fifty-five Black students requested transfers to White schools. Of those, fifty-four were granted. However, remedial education courses, which Hemphill said would be necessary to help those affected by segregation, would not be offered. The district supposedly lacked the funds and was not eligible for funds from the state. The district also pled poverty when it came to improving the physical facilities. Only token efforts were made to integrate the teaching staff: a White remedial reading teacher volunteered to teach in the Black schools, pending funding, and the White bandleader volunteered to organize a band in the Black high school.[32]

In December 1966 the US Office of Education refused to certify that Clarendon 2 met the requirements for receiving federal aid. The requirements included meeting the June order's directive eliminating the "educational program" and "space available in other schools" requirements that Hemphill had allowed, as well as other aspects of the desegregation plan. Hemphill confirmed that the district was attempting to comply, and the district applied for the federal funds later that month.[33]

As the Clarendon 2 and Calhoun 1 situations illustrate, expectations for desegregation remained unfulfilled in several areas of the state well after passage of the Civil Rights Act. In Charleston as well, the only real "progress" that had been made by June 1966 was that the district had decided to adopt an equal opportunity policy in employment, though "it recognize[d] that long-standing customs and traditions in the community may constitute obstacles to a wholesale reshuffling of negro and white teachers in the system." Even as the district made token efforts toward desegregation, the willingness of White people to change their positions was limited at best. The Charleston school board promised "to make a start in this direction for the 1966–67 school year." In the classrooms of the city, only one school had a White enrollment exceeding 25 percent. One other was 24.9 percent White, and the other eight elementary schools were all Black. This illustrates a central problem in districts where desegregation was fiercely opposed: a high percentage of Black students. Much of the ongoing litigation arose from districts with substantial, if not major-ity, African American populations. The problem was exacerbated by "White flight" to other districts or to private segregation academies specifically estab-lished to give White parents a refuge from integration. Only 432 of nearly 7,000 students in Charleston's elementary schools were White. In the high schools, a similar situation made desegregation difficult: of 3,623 students, only 382 stu-dents were White. Only one of the district's four high schools was more than 50 percent White. Two were all Black, and the fourth was more than 70 percent Black.[34] Also in June 1966, Orangeburg District 7 (Elloree) lost $55,000 and Calhoun District 1 (St. Matthews) lost $137,000 in federal funding for failure to comply with desegregation plans.[35]

By the 1966–67 school year, 89 of South Carolina's 107 districts were in compliance with the Office of Education's guidelines. Although the number of districts deemed in compliance increased slightly, South Carolina continued to have the fourth lowest rate—after Mississippi, Louisiana, and Alabama—of Black children attending integrated schools—5.6 percent, or 14,853 Black stu-dents out of a total enrollment of 642,477. For the same period in the South as a whole, 489,973 Black students out of a total Black school enrollment of slightly more than 3 million (about 16.5 percent) attended desegregated schools.[36] This was up from 4,308 out of more than 2.6 million (less than one-tenth of a per-cent) in 1960–61. In August 1966 Chief Judge Martin issued an order for the cases from Greenville, Charleston, and Darlington, and Judge Simons adopted that order for *Brunson*. The districts in question were to present desegregation plans within sixty days.[37]

Darlington's school board attorney, Benny Greer, objected to allowing the United States to participate as amicus in the case. The goal of the federal gov-ernment, he argued, was

> to put the local school boards under the full and complete domination of the "all-wise" and "all-knowing" so-called Education Department in

Washington. The idea is that Washington can then impose a "police state" system of rules designed to bring to heel even the most "recalcitrant or reluctant" school system. The imagination, wisdom and desire of all local boards should be shackled. All local school personnel should be treated as persons posing as educators but known to the "all-wise" and "all-knowing" Civil Service Operatives in Washington as the true enemy of the state.

More specifically, Greer objected to US Attorney Terrell Glenn's efforts to convince Judge Martin to accept the 1966 Office of Education guidelines for desegregation as his guide for deciding the fate of the district. The end result, argued Greer, would be greater federal domination of the school system, leading to disastrous consequences. Greer laid out thirteen points, most of which attacked the bureaucracy that would be required to implement the 1966 guidelines. In his final point, Greer argued that the guidelines "would—and may be worst of all—destroy the present good relations between the races as they have worked together to bring orderly and continued substantial progress in social reform and would substitute the creation of an atmosphere of bitterness and resentment." Once again White South Carolina had gotten caught up in its own misconception. White people such as Greer believed that the relative silence of the majority of Black South Carolinians implied their consent to the racial status quo rather than any fear of reprisal. Greer followed his brief with interrogatories to Glenn alleging that the government assisted the plaintiffs with their case, even accusing him of letting the plaintiffs use his office's typewriters and Xerox machine.[38] Given his belief that most African Americans were content in their subjugation, Greer apparently thought that the government attorneys were leading the Black plaintiffs where they did not want to go. By January 1967 the Darlington defendants still had not written plans, so Martin revised the order to command the Darlington, Greenville, and Charleston districts to develop plans by early February or have them written for them by the court. On March 10 Martin issued the required order, requiring freedom of choice and setting down the requirements for implementation, describing transportation requirements, desegregating faculty and staff positions, and requiring desegregation in activities, facilities, and programs.[39] Still, by February twenty-one districts were listed as probably in a state of noncompliance, and in March four more districts had their funds cut off. Districts throughout the state began to develop plans that would create unitary districts as expected in the assurance forms.[40]

The federal government continued to press, investigating the extent of student and faculty integration in Clarendon 2 for 1967–68. Of more than 4,100 students in the district, only 83 (2 percent) went to school with students of

another race. Faculty integration was similarly insignificant: a few White teachers worked in the Black schools, occasionally part-time; one African American
was made supervisor of instruction and another supervisor of audio-visual aids
for the district.[41]

By 1967 it was increasingly apparent that time was running out on segregation, but efforts at the state level extended its life. In January Judge Simons
rejected the federally proposed plan for Clarendon 1, demonstrating the obstruction that federal judges could engage in regarding desegregation attempts.
In February, Simons, while expressing sympathy for "the manifold problems
encountered by local school boards in administering their school systems today," pointed out that he was satisfied with the implementation of his previous
(1965) order but that new law from the Supreme Court and the court of appeals
made it necessary to make adjustments in desegregation efforts. The new plan
for Clarendon and the other districts allowed for complete freedom of choice
in schools, access to transportation for students choosing schools farther away
from their homes, equal access to all elements of the curriculum and school
activities, and desegregation of the faculty beginning with new hires.[42]

In March 1967 Judge Hemphill noted that Clarendon District 2 was in
compliance with his order of the previous June but that further relief was necessary under Martin's August 1966 order.[43] The new rules required any plan to
allow students to choose their own schools on an annual or otherwise periodic
basis. No reason for a change in schools had to be noted on the choice form.
All aspects of school life—facilities, faculties, and transportation, in addition
to students in classrooms—must be desegregated.

In Orangeburg, where Judge Simons had approved a freedom of choice
plan in 1966, the *Adams* case lumbered on. In August 1968 District 5 superintendent W. J. Clark sent a short form to parents inquiring whether they preferred geographical zoning or freedom of choice to accomplish desegregation.
With increasing federal pressure and growing impatience from the courts, this
was just another delaying tactic. Since most White parents could be expected
to prefer freedom of choice to a zoning plan, the results of the poll were likely
used for political purposes later or to identify Black parents to mark them for
future reprisals. In fact, almost all parents regardless of race chose a freedom
of choice plan, though the numbers indicated that about 10 percent more Black
parents than White parents preferred zoning.[44] Then again, Black parents who
preferred freedom of choice probably interpreted the idea more literally than
White parents did.

The Supreme Court's decision in *Green v. New Kent County* on May 27,
1968, signaled the end of practically all freedom of choice plans for the South.
Finding the New Kent County, Virginia, freedom of choice plan inadequate, the

Court determined that "where there are reasonably available other ways, such as zoning, promising speedier and more effective conversion to a unitary school system, 'freedom of choice' is not acceptable." Officials there, as in South Carolina, had made no significant effort to comply with *Brown II* for a decade. *Brown II* was a mandate for the dismantling of entrenched dual systems tempered by an awareness that complex and multifaceted problems would arise, which would require time and flexibility for a successful resolution. School boards operating dual systems were clearly charged with the affirmative duty to take whatever steps might be necessary to convert to a unitary system in which racial discrimination would be eliminated root and branch.

New Kent County bore similarities to Clarendon County, so South Carolinians took great interest in the outcome of the case. The main argument put forth by Jack Greenberg for the NAACP was that freedom of choice plans were not really free—there was no choice for most Black students. Faced with the prospect of economic reprisals or violence and still subject to the psychological effects of segregation, Black parents did not exercise, or were unwilling to exercise, the right of free choice in picking schools for their children. The Supreme Court, in an opinion by Justice William Brennan, agreed. The decision severely hobbled the doctrine of freedom of choice by putting the burden on school districts to prove it was effective.[45]

In South Carolina, school cases accelerated even before the Supreme Court's decision in *Green,* which was argued on April 13, 1968. That same month, the Darlington school district faced new questions regarding their ongoing delays, and the Justice Department added its weight in the case against the district. District officials had not submitted the compliance reports required by HEW and refused to allow HEW officials to look at the district's records or conduct inspections of its schools. HEW regulations required districts that received federal money to submit documents and allow inspections. Benny Greer considered the attempt to inspect the records of the district "improper and illegal," especially since Darlington was operating under court order. The HEW complaint against the board requested Judge Martin to issue an order forcing the district to submit compliance records.[46]

Greer answered the government's complaint predictably:

> The defendants deny that the School District must be so manipulated and controlled as to assign students to public schools "in order to overcome racial imbalance" . . . since the Congress . . . forbids any federal agency or department . . . from using the Civil Rights Act of 1964 for the purpose of promulgating Rules or practices designed to force the assignment of pupils to public schools in order to overcome racial imbalance.

HEW, he argued, had sought "to impose illegal conditions and requirements upon the defendants."[47]

Matthew Perry's appeal in the *Brunson* case gained strength following the *Green* decision. The district was clearly operating dual systems that were prohibited under HEW guidelines. The three Black students who attended the White junior high school in 1967–68 were graduating and would attend the White high school. The formerly all-White high school would have twenty-five White students and six Black students, while the Black high school remained all Black. Only ten Black students chose to move to White schools following the 1967–68 school year. New hires of teachers were racially segregated: of nine vacancies at the White schools, none was filled by Black teachers; of seven vacancies at Black schools, all were filled by Black hires. No teachers were transferred. Despite the defendants' assertion that "no choice was denied" for either White or Black students in the district, figures from the spring of 1968 indicated that the junior high schools in Clarendon 1 would remain totally segregated for the 1968–69 school year. Following *Green*, Judge Simons had little choice but to modify his 1965 ruling and require the development of a totally new desegregation plan. While the school board argued that it would be impossible to achieve integration with a White school population of only 12 percent, Perry correctly pointed out that their argument did not matter. The fact that White students might leave the schools in droves also had no bearing on any decision the court might issue. What mattered legally was the fact that segregation continued and was supported by the school board.[48]

South Carolina's district judges issued a joint order in September 1968 requiring school district defendants to modify their desegregation plans to comply with the *Green* decision or submit their reviews to HEW if they believed that their plan did not require any modification.[49] Intransigent White people remained steadfastly committed to segregation in the four districts (all at least 60 percent African American) that had come under federal sanction even though eleven districts had funding terminated for submitting unacceptable plans.[50] School boards in Cameron (Calhoun 2) and Elloree (Orangeburg 7) districts refused to move to a unitary school system, which would eliminate any White majority districts. If a unitary system was all that HEW would accept, it would have to be done through a court order, giving the districts time to appeal. Augustus Graydon, like others in the state, hoped that, with a new administration arriving in Washington with the new year (1969), "a change in attitude . . . may be in the offing." Although his hopes were misplaced, Graydon pressed on, noting in January that "none of the attorneys in the Civil Rights Division is under Civil Service and that if the administration has any desire to change the 'attitude' of the Civil Rights Division, all of the present personnel can be replaced." Sen. Strom Thurmond advised school districts to hold out and await the new administration's policy, guaranteed to be more amenable to White southerners. The proposed plan Graydon devised for Elloree was "frankly a 'stall,' as [he hoped] that there [would] be some change in the attitude of the Department of Justice after January 20." Despite assuring his fellow segregationists that he was just stalling, Graydon insisted to US Attorney Klyde Robinson in November that "we are doing what we can in those two districts [Cameron and Elloree] to obtain meaningful desegregation."[51]

The Elloree plan was a simple one. The school board promised not to discriminate in enrollment, pupil assignments, or any number of other institutional matters. But it was also very general: there were no specific steps to desegregate the schools in any way—merely assurances that the school district would not discriminate. Essentially it amounted to a continuation of a now unconstitutional free-choice plan. Not surprisingly HEW attorneys objected to it. Freedom of choice had led to only nine Black students in White schools in 1967–68 (1 percent) and only 16 the following year (1.8 percent). Only one Black teacher worked at Elloree Public School, and only one White teacher taught at Elloree Training School.[52]

Under a court-approved freedom of choice plan, nine Black students attended Cameron High School in Calhoun District 2 in the fall of 1966 but left after the Christmas break. No Black students attended the school the following year. When the Supreme Court struck down freedom of choice plans in 1968, Cameron was forced to devise a new system. The new plan called for teacher transfers as well as for moving eighty Black students to the Cameron school, but when the superintendent met with parents and faculty, only two White teachers volunteered to teach in the Black schools. Thirteen others resigned rather than risk being assigned to the Black schools. Ultimately no White teachers appeared in the Black schools when school opened that fall. The two Black schools in the district remained open, though no White teachers taught there.[53]

After all the White teachers either retired or resigned after being reassigned in 1968 and no White students showed up for school in the 1968–69 school year, the district was left with only two schools to operate. St. John's went from first through twelfth grade, and Cedar Grove went through the seventh grade. White students were either going to Wade Hampton Academy, a private segregation academy, or transferring out of the district, which the superintendent made quite easy. Cameron High School considered leasing its gymnasium to Wade Hampton but was advised against it given the federal suit.[54]

Clarendon County officials also believed that, despite its prohibition, freedom of choice was the best plan for them and filed their response in December 1968. The board also sent a note to parents asking them whether they preferred zoning or a freedom of choice plan. Eighty-five percent of the responding parents chose freedom of choice, though of course the poll was meaningless given the possibility for reprisals. Desegregation of faculty and staff was minimal at best: six individuals, four of whom were White, worked at schools of the other race. The two Black staff members worked with both Black and White schools.[55] Officials argued that switching to a zoning plan would not lead to an appreciable level of integration, but it is important to note that under a zoning plan, twenty-five White children would have attended the district's Black schools. (Fifty Black students would go to White schools; it would have reduced segregation in any case.) Those twenty-five White children, the board expected, would probably switch to the private school. The board also noted, predictably, that the Black students lagged behind their White peers, meaning that the "educational opportunities" of White students would be threatened by integration of that sort.[56] In February 1969 Matthew Perry attacked the rationalizations of the Clarendon 1 school board as "legally irrelevant." He argued that the reasons the school board gave for continuing a freedom of choice plan—White flight, parental preference, Black student achievement, and the disproportionate number of Black students—simply should not matter.[57]

In March 1969 the state Department of Education noted that thirty-four districts had received federal approval of their plans and just fourteen districts had not yet received approval. Six districts, threatened with subpoenas from the Justice Department, submitted briefs to defend their plans. Of those, two districts had had their federal funds terminated. Several districts were in various phases of hearings before a Department of Education reviewing board. Twelve were operating under court orders to desegregate.[58] Most continued to impede desegregation through court appeals. However, by this time South Carolina's federal judges, with their latitude increasingly foreclosed, became more proactive in the case of recalcitrant defendants, especially since the judges were under the close eye of the Fourth Circuit Court of Appeals. Years of complicity with the delaying tactics of White officials gave way as the higher courts now were making it clear that delay was no longer acceptable. The power of the appellate judiciary; the authority and willingness of HEW to ally itself with Black plaintiffs, which magnified the litigating power of the NAACP; and the increasing dependence of the state on federal education dollars began to have a significant impact on White officials' behavior. The threat of punitive sanctions rather than respect for the rule of law governed the state's response. White South Carolinians, despite facing mounting pressure and the force of law, still managed to delay any real desegregation. Their defiance did not go unnoticed.

Even so, Judge Martin's March 31, 1969, order in the consolidated cases met opposition again from Darlington school board attorney Benny Greer. In addition to more mundane objections, Greer, sounding more like an armchair philosopher than a legal professional, contended that the order was

> in direct contradiction to the established system of separation of powers of the various departments of the United States Government. . . . The cooperation of the Judicial and Executive Branches of the Government to impose any plan of operation or any decree upon a party litigant is an effective denial of the due process of law since it deprives the parties in litigation of a source of independent determination of justiciable issues.

Greer, of course, was wrong. The Civil Rights Act maintained judicial control even though it gave the executive branch the authority to intervene as a plaintiff.

Still, White stubbornness continued as the start of the 1969–70 school year approached. In Elloree the new plan, which was to go into effect for that school year, met with the usual dismayed wringing of hands from White officials: Augustus Graydon, in a letter to David Robinson regarding the proposed plan for Elloree, said that "the thing that we cannot live with is assigning white children to the Negro school," which Graydon apparently feared might result if HEW had its way. In a letter to Leon Panetta, Graydon noted that the implementation of full integration would lead to "a monolithic Negro system of public education" in the county, as it already had in an adjoining district.[59]

The sticking point in Clarendon 2 continued to be the use of any sort of freedom of choice plan. The federal government's lawyers called for any alternative, such as pairing or zoning, which could achieve the objective of a unitary system more rapidly. School board attorney Marion S. Riggs and David Robinson responded by arguing that the changes that had taken place—they were not specific as to what those changes were but were likely referring to the minuscule progress in desegregation—in Clarendon 2 met with "high community acceptance," without which "no public institution can render an acceptable service." School board attorney Joseph O. Rogers remained hopeful that "the new administration will not press this theory"—that *Green* "require[d] the abandonment of freedom of choice."[60] Matthew Perry attacked the school district's response, arguing that the court should issue a decree calling for immediate implementation of a genuine desegregation plan for the 1969–70 year. The plan would be based on the report of the Office of Education, which called for the establishment of attendance zones, reassigning of teachers, and integration of all the other "services, facilities, activities and programs of the district."[61] As late as May 30, the Darlington school board was still holding out against any desegregation plan for 1969–70 designed by HEW. Orangeburg 5 and all three Clarendon districts also refused to adopt plans developed for them by the department.[62]

In Clarendon County, especially, delay built on delay. In June 1969 Robinson asked the court for a hearing on the matter, and in October he requested an extension to December for developing a desegregation plan. The board feared an "exodus" of White students from the schools if the HEW plan was used. Perry countered Robinson's request and submitted a proposed decree that would end any delays and force Clarendon 1 to desegregate its schools immediately based on recommendations of the US Office of Education, to integrate faculty and staff through reassignment, and to require annual reports of the progress toward desegregation.[63]

On July 23, 1969, Hemphill issued yet another order in the Clarendon 2 case, in this instance discussing the notion of freedom of choice at some length and indicating that it was an unacceptable remedy. His sympathies lay clearly with district officials, as it was they who had to deal with the federal government:

> "Freedom-of-choice" as a process of obtaining equal (in quality) education has every connotation of justice. It gives the individual the right to choose his course. It preserves the American ideal that every individual is consequential and important, and his desires are to be respected. . . .
>
> If freedom-of-choice had produced results here, this court would be quick to endorse a continuation of such a plan and practice. Not only has it miserably failed to accomplish, but the record has every appearance of deliberate effort to deny the Negro children of the school district equal education. . . .
>
> This is not to say that the trustees have not pursued [desegregation] in good faith. . . . It is to be remembered that they live in the communities involved. Their chief *tormentors* come from Washington and New York, or other distant places, and can escape from the problems at pleasure. The "school board" has to live with the problems, in the racial climate of the district, seven days a week. It would indeed be fortunate if the community gave the board the cooperation and direction necessary to accomplish that which, in the absence of voluntary response, the court must direct.[64]

The success of freedom of choice plans as a delaying tactic had had an adverse effect on the school districts' cases. Districts never granted any meaningful freedom of choice, but after *Green* judges could no longer be expected to approve what had never been a good-faith approach by White South Carolinians. Despite ruling that freedom of choice plans were farcical, Hemphill further displayed his sympathy for the defendants by delaying immediate implementation for 1969–70. He did order the district to begin desegregating the staff, including

ordering extensive in-service training, which the HEW guidelines suggested as
a means of attaining community buy-in, during the upcoming school year. Part
of this program included the establishment of biracial teams of teachers to assist in the implementation of the program. Teachers would ultimately spend a
total of four weeks teaching in the schools of the other race. (The district objected to this on the grounds that the greater number of Black teachers would
result in White teachers in Black schools for more than one four-week period
and students ultimately having as many as three teachers in one year.) Hemphill also ordered that students should also participate by spending some time
in schools for the other race, with activities scheduled by the professional staff.
During the school year, student organizations would meet with their counterparts from the other schools. Buses would pick up all the students on a given
route regardless of what school they attended.[65]

Hemphill's order required Clarendon 2 to desegregate fully in 1970. Going
further than the district would have if it had voluntarily desegregated, Hemphill determined what school buildings would be used for what grades. As often
happened in other districts, the previously all-White Manning High became the
high school for all the district's grade 9–12 students. The previously all-Black
Manning Training School would be zoned for the district's middle school students. The various primary schools would be zoned to accommodate as many
students as possible, including the use of portable classrooms for all but the
new high school.[66]

Predictably the district objected, this time by calling for progressive integration of the schools starting with the first grade in 1970–71 and adding a
grade each year thereafter. Robinson privately suggested that the district "make
plans to sell the community on the plans. This might include a dignified press
release, appearances before parent-teacher groups, civic clubs, etc." At the
same time, he recommended that "the Board should explore the possibility of
submitting alternate plans for 1970–71 and thereafter. One such plan might be
the assignment of pupils on the basis of impartially administered educational
achievement tests." In August, Robinson wrote school board attorney Marion
Riggs again, noting that in Charleston, Judge Martin allowed the district to
have one high school for college prep and another for vocational work. Perhaps,
he suggested, Clarendon 2 could try the same thing. In September, Robinson,
still trying to develop alternatives to the court-ordered plan, continued to
worry that Hemphill's plan would drive White children from the schools or
lead to mass resignations of White teachers. When Riggs revealed the board's
grade-a-year plan to Robinson in October, Robinson responded that Hemphill
would reject it out of hand, since other courts had consistently rejected such

plans. When the proposal was revealed, Perry pointed out that all the parties had to agree before such an alternative could be proposed and called the plan a "mockery."[67]

In the fall of 1969, the schools of Clarendon 1 remained virtually segregated. The Black schools remained all-Black; the White schools had achieved no more than token integration. (Summerton Elementary had 12 Black students out of 157; Summerton High had 16 out of 127.) Perry demanded an end to further delay based on fears of "White flight" and requested that the defendants be given only three days to respond to his motion.[68]

Desperately, Robinson wrote to Clarendon District 1 superintendent H. A. Roberts in November. He proposed a plan to assign students based on zoning that would also "provide that any child assigned to a school where his race was in the majority could transfer to any other school." In doing this Robinson hoped that "the result would be a school system with which the people could live." He went on:

> If the Negroes prefer to go to their own schools those assigned in 1970 to Summerton High and Summerton Elementary could elect to transfer out since Negroes would be in the majority in those schools (as in all other schools). This might leave a majority white in these two schools. Admittedly this plan would leave a minority white in all other schools because the Court, under existing decisions, cannot give a child who is in the minority in a school the right to transfer out. These white children might elect to go to private school. However there is a chance of keeping some whites in the public schools under this plan.[69]

In January, Robinson remained hopeful of gaining Perry's consent to continuing the freedom of choice plan, even though Perry had told him that many Black parents were still opposed to it. In *Alexander v. Holmes County Board of Education*, a case from Mississippi decided in October 1969, the Supreme Court had ruled that operation of unitary school districts must begin immediately. Perry submitted his motion to force the immediate administration of a unitary district. Riggs's only hope was that the hearing on the motion could not be held in time to bring about integration for the spring of 1970. Robinson agreed that delaying the hearing to prevent transferring students in midterm was the best approach.[70]

In July 1969 Judge Simons issued a new order in the *Brunson* case, deciding that the freedom of choice plan should remain in effect for 1969–70. He ordered the district to confer with representatives from the Department of Health, Education, and Welfare, but they were unable to develop an acceptable desegregation plan by the summer. He did, however, address the issue of faculty desegregation, directing the board to apply to HEW for funds to improve the facilities and to supplement teacher salaries. He also directed the district to continue to meet with HEW to develop a workable desegregation plan for the fall of 1970.[71] On March 6, 1970, he issued a final order to desegregate the schools of Clarendon 1 in the *Brunson* case: the HEW plan for a unitary system in which students would be assigned schools based on attendance zones would go into effect in the fall of 1970, but not before an unsuccessful appeal to the Fourth Circuit.[72]

The *Adams* case from Orangeburg District 5 was also in Judge Simons's court. Orangeburg 5 schools still had not devised a terminal plan for desegregation by the end of the 1968–69 year. In June Simons invited the parties to an informal hearing in which he directed the school board "to reopen consultations with officials from the Office of Education" in order to determine a solid final plan. District superintendent W. J. Clark wrote to Jesse Jordan of the Division of Equal Educational Opportunities of the Office of Education to inform him that the school board had agreed to accept and implement the 1969–70 portion of the office's proposed plan. The district was also working with the Desegregation Consulting Center established with federal funds at the University of South Carolina to develop a final plan. Clark realized that a terminal plan for 1970 had to be developed but was daunted by the problems associated with implementation. The school board favored a unitary high school, but that would require an expensive new building, as well as a change in the debt limit. Pairing of schools would also be workable—as well as more "acceptable" to the people of the district—but would also require "extensive modifications" to the existing physical plant. Clark pleaded for a postponement to October.[73]

Instead, in August 1969 Simons issued his final order in *Adams v. Orangeburg*. Adopting the HEW plan for desegregation for the district, Simons essentially quoted the plan into the record. Implementation would take place over two years. In 1969–70 the plan was designed "to prepare the community for accepting school desegregation with a more positive attitude" as well as to prepare the administration and teachers to deal with a new system. The transitional year consisted of summer workshops for teachers and administrative staff. Phase two required the establishment of a biracial advisory committee for the district, human relations councils for each school, pairing of faculties as much as possible to achieve greater parity, and regular meetings of administrators to map out the next year's moves, followed by "intensive curriculum workshops" in the summer of 1970. Attorneys for the plaintiffs argued that a zoning plan should be implemented in 1969. Simons, still dragging his feet, was "convinced that the defendants have acted in good faith in the operation of the District's schools under its freedom of choice plan" and allowed the less-drastic

1969 plan to go forward. He realized that the freedom of choice plan had not achieved appreciable integration (less than 7 percent Black population in White schools, no White students in Black schools), but the administrative difficulties of immediate implementation were, he thought, insurmountable. Nevertheless he only gave the district until November 1 to develop a "desegregation plan conformable to the constitutional rights of all of the pupils in its school systems."[74]

The district's proposal for 1970 included plans for zoning of the elementary schools, which in most cases created relatively well-balanced student racial populations. The one exception, Nix Elementary, would have a twenty-four-to-one ratio of Black to White students. Students in middle and high schools, with the exception of rising ninth graders, would be allowed to continue at their present schools or transfer. The reasons given for this plan were that both high schools were full, curricula had differed over the years, and students were involved in extracurricular activities.[75]

With a few modifications recommended by HEW, the plan was accepted in December 1969. The *Adams* plaintiffs, joined by a group of White parents calling itself HOPE (Help Orangeburg Public Education), filed an appeal of Judge Simons's order, arguing that "in the light of *Green* . . . the Orangeburg schools should, and must be, completely integrated *'now'*. . . . The plan approved by the District Court . . . violates . . . Supreme Court mandates, in that the plan provides integration *in form* but creates and maintains segregation *in fact*."[76] The HOPE parents' motives must ultimately be questioned, however. The schools to which their children would go under the new plan were all schools that would have Black majorities, including Nix Elementary, which would only have 27 White students in a body of 731. The parents felt "strongly that they [were] not afforded equal protection of the laws . . . by having their children used as the tokens by which token integration [was] achieved."[77]

The Nixon administration, despite its reliance on a southern electoral strategy, did not initiate drastic changes in the federal government's school desegregation policy. Constrained by the Supreme Court, there was not much the administration could do, although Nixon's remaking of the Court during his foreshortened administration had some effect later. After Simons's March 1970 ruling in *Brunson*, Robinson also appealed to Robert Mardian, the executive director of the Cabinet Office on Education for the Vice President. To Mardian, Robinson reiterated much of his standard argument and asked for "the help of [his] committee in working out some solution to this problem," although he was unconvinced of Mardian's ability to help. Robinson's assessment turned out to be correct.[78] In other instances the new administration provided some hope. When Robert Finch took over at HEW, he was more willing to compromise with southern school districts than Harold Howe, his predecessor. When funds for two South Carolina districts (along with three other southern districts) were to be cut off, Finch allowed the districts to submit plans within sixty days and have the funds retroactively restored. Although there were possibilities for compromise, the Nixon administration was not a puppet of southern segregationists. Compromise in the form of diplomatic enforcement, technical assistance, and new attention to northern states, all without turning away from the issues in the South, was more likely, but desegregation was now the paradigm. In April 1970 Jerris Leonard, a Justice Department attorney, told South Carolina officials flatly that districts still in noncompliance had to submit plans in ten days or be in serious negotiations by that time or face a federal lawsuit. "The plan must be completely implemented before you open your school doors next fall."[79]

Meanwhile Robinson appealed the *Brunson* case once again to the Fourth Circuit and continued to argue for a freedom of choice plan as well as to invoke his old arguments of parental preference for freedom of choice, the vast disparity in the numbers of Black and White students, the educational achievement differences between the two groups, and the threat of White flight. The White children of the district would be faced with "a 'Hobson's choice'—he must stay in a class with a group two years behind him in education . . . or pay some five hundred dollars a year to go to a small parochial school." Admitting that educational achievement was irrelevant to the issue of desegregation was one thing. Robinson had no choice after *Brown v. Charleston* but to do so; but, he argued, educational achievement could be used to determine what desegregation plan would be used. Robinson further argued that "in efforts to solve desegregation problems some Courts and some HEW officials have become more interested in racial balance than in education." Citing the Civil Rights Act of 1964, Robinson, echoing Darlington's attorney Benny Greer, said that "'desegregation' shall not mean the assignment of students to public schools in order to overcome racial imbalance." Both men, following what Judge Parker had done in his *Briggs* dictum, attempted to cloak commitment to segregation in color blindness. By April, Judge Simons still had not passed on Perry's motion. Robinson promised Riggs that he would continue to push for some measure of testing to allow the district to place students into different sections within a grade "in order to salvage some education for your white children."[80] Perry countered that the case should finally be put to death: the arguments that Robinson depended on were not legally relevant, and to continue to rely on them was essentially a waste of time. Contending that the appeal was "frivolous," Perry argued that double costs and fees should be awarded: sixteen years was simply too long a time to wait for meaningful desegregation.[81]

Despite favorable rulings, Black people were not completely confident that desegregation would actually take place. The Clarendon County NAACP branch petitioned the Education Committee of the NAACP State Conference to ask Perry to seek modifications to the plan, including a requirement for 30 percent Black enrollment at Summerton Elementary and Summerton High School, transfer of teachers, an advisory committee, and periodic review of the plan by Simons.[82] The Fourth Circuit, in two separate opinions, upheld Judge Simons's March 1970 order in *Brunson*. The case was heard and decided on June 5, but Robinson appealed to the Supreme Court for a writ of certiorari and was given an extension to October 1 to file.[83] The Supreme Court ultimately denied the petition.

By September 1970 Clarendon 1's desegregation plan was in place and close to implementation. At this point the plans for Clarendon 1 and 2 intersected. About thirty White children who lived in Clarendon 1 wanted to go to school in Clarendon 2. Only about fifteen White children went to school in Clarendon 1, and the thirty students in question did not go to school at all and could not afford private school. Therefore they wished to transfer to Clarendon 2 schools. Robinson considered their desire to transfer as a positive for the Clarendon 2 case, because adding their numbers to the extremely small White population would enhance the appearance of desegregation. Riggs thought the transfers would be "questionable." It is not known what happened to these students, although Hemphill did schedule a hearing for later in September.[84]

Outside the diehard segregationist districts, as a result of an order from the Fourth Circuit, Greenville developed a plan that called for a White-Black ratio of four to one in its schools. The schools were closed temporarily but reopened to a successful "integration with grace and style." Darlington County, however, was under the same order and did not submit a plan by the February 1970 deadline set forth by the appeals court. As a result Darlington's schools were integrated under an HEW-designed plan. Gov. Robert McNair, who in 1968 had enrolled his daughter in a desegregated school in Columbia, expressed his realization to the people of the state in a televised address on Valentine's Day, 1970: "We've run out of courts, and we've run out of time, and we must adjust to new circumstances."[85]

Despite local White resistance, by the fall of 1970, twelve districts had unitary systems, forty-eight were readying HEW-approved plans, twenty-two districts operated under court-approved plans, and another eleven were waiting for court orders. Fifteen were still without plans, and there were brief delays in some districts as last-minute details were worked out.[86] In the fall of 1970, twenty years after Harry Briggs filed his lawsuit against Clarendon County on behalf of his son, who was now twenty-nine years old, the schools of South Carolina were finally desegregated—at least on paper.

The *Southern Education Report* published its final issue in June 1969. In it W. D. Workman wrote that "the threat of future discord stems not so much from the prospect of continued and accelerated compliance with the Supreme Court decisions of 1954 and 1955 as from pressures generated by zealots whose obsession for mixing the races goes far beyond the scope of the original court decrees." He went on to complain about the movement of emphasis from education to "integration *per se*," arguing that federal bureaucrats had moved away from the original emphasis to the detriment of the entire process. He went so far as to quote the ruling in *Plessy* that "if the races are to meet upon terms of social equality, it must be the result of natural affinities."[87] Clearly even if desegregation had come, attitudes of journalists such as Workman and the continuing White flight away from the public schools revealed that attitudes, unlike the law (at least at times), are painfully slow to change.

In April 1970, with desegregation less than five months away, Robinson wrote, in despair over his failure to maintain segregation, that

in this country we have created a white man's civilization. That is natural because we came from white Europe and 88 percent of the people in this country are white. . . . This civilization has developed a highly industrialized society. . . . It has developed giant corporations and influential labor unions . . . and a democratic form of government. Its failures have also been significant—pollution, wars, poverty, unrest.

Three hundred years ago we brought to this country as slaves black people. . . . These black people have different talents from the white population; talents not necessarily superior or inferior to the white majority but different. The black man excels in physical coordination as professional sports . . . demonstrate[d] on television each week-end. He wins the dashes and the jumps but seldom competes in the distance runs. The black man is a major factor in popular music but seldom appears with a symphony or orchestra. . . .

Because this is a white civilization the curriculum in our public schools is a white curriculum. The average black child has great difficulty in keeping up with the white child particularly in subjects such as mathematics, physics and chemistry. The figures published by HEW show that in educational achievement he lags two to three years behind the white child of the same age. . . .

It is now generally accepted that where blacks voluntarily move into a white school and do not constitute more than 30 percent the black benefits from the association with the better prepared white children. But where this percentage is higher than 30 the school rapidly becomes substantially all black and the advantage to the black child is lost and the education of the minority white is adversely affected. . . .

The white child does not flee the black school because it is black but because he cannot obtain an adequate education where the majority has a substantially lower educational achievement.

Among his last-ditch recommendations, Robinson suggested allowing rural districts with less than a 20 percent White population to retain freedom of choice. "This will result in some schools with a white majority," but "[Black students] have the power to convert the student body to a majority black school at any time." He also believed that faculty desegregation based on following district population lines was less desirable than basing it on the population of the student body at a given school. "Many of our black teachers received their education at all black colleges where educational standards are well below that of the average State University. . . . To throw these black teachers into classes predominantly white is to force them to teach more advanced pupils at a considerable disadvantage." (Of course, when Robinson was arguing for the creation of a law school at South Carolina State rather than let John Wrighten into the University of South Carolina Law School twenty-three years earlier, he emphasized the basic equality of the two schools.) Robinson claimed to be interested only in the improvement of education and criticized HEW for "emphasiz[ing] percentages of racial integration. . . . Increased racial integration percentages may not mean better education for either race." To Robert Mardian he wrote:

I am very much disturbed about the plight of the rural school district where there is not residential segregation. In my judgment the policy of the United States courts and that of HEW is effectively destroying public education for white children in these districts. I cannot believe that this is the purpose of the equal protection clause of the Fourteenth Amendment.[88]

As Robinson and many other White people had predicted, White flight from the various districts became the unfortunate reality. By the end of May 1970, only eighty-nine White students remained in Clarendon 1's public schools. There were no more courts; there was no more time. In September 1970 Robinson said he would not file a certiorari petition since the state would not fund it. In September 1970 there were eight White students in the district, and by 1974 the number was down to one. Even as late as 1980, there was only one White student in the public schools of Clarendon County.[89]

More than any other aspect of civil rights challenges, White South Carolinians resisted the desegregation of schools the longest. While their reasons, as this work shows, were complex, the core was White supremacy. Holding unchecked power over generations of Black South Carolinians had resulted in both material and psychological benefits to White people that were priceless. The mindset that justified slavery could not be wrong, and that same system perpetuated White supremacy in the aftermath of the Civil War and Reconstruction. In the aftermath of emancipation in the late nineteenth century, White South Carolinians deliberately created a separate and unequal society. White supremacy justified it because White people could not conceive of a world where Black people were their equals. As the tenacity in these beliefs of David Robinson and others demonstrate, White supremacy informed their way of life. Preserving it was worth the resistance.

8

DESEGREGATION, NOT INTEGRATION

South Carolina Since 1968

Although in 1968 the courts made clear that desegregation in schools had to occur, segregation did not magically disappear there or in other areas of South Carolina life. Although Maurice Bessinger lost the case over desegregation of his restaurants in 1964, that was not the end of public accommodations segregation. Roper Hospital in Charleston, privately owned and operated by the Medical Society of South Carolina, had never opened its doors to Black in-patients, although some African Americans had received physical therapy and X-rays there.[1] The prospect of federal funds becoming available inspired the hospital's chief of staff in 1964 to recommend desegregation, but the society refused, because it would mean federal intervention in hospital operations. In March 1965 the hospital announced that it would not participate in programs initiated by the Department of Health, Education and Welfare.[2]

In 1968 US Attorney General Nicholas Katzenbach sued the hospital to force it to accept Black patients and to desegregate its workforce. The hospital accepted patients from out of state, and their out-of-state visitors were served in the cafeteria. The professional staff, with the exception of one Black registered nurse, was all White. There were numerous egregious examples of employment discrimination as well. For example, African Americans were employed as orderlies and nurses' aides and in menial positions. Until 1968 the hospital maintained separate toilet facilities for its Black and White employees, as well as separate locker rooms for Black employees. Black workers in the hospital laundry were required to punch time cards, while White laundry workers were not.[3]

On March 10, 1969, a week before African American workers struck against Charleston County's two other hospitals, Judge Robert Martin ordered the hospital to end discrimination "against Negroes on account of their race in relation to their admission or treatment as patients at Roper Hospital and with respect to their employment at Roper Hospital." The hospital was not allowed to ask patients if they had a racial preference for a roommate, and White patients were not allowed to be moved from rooms with Black patients. Martin required the hospital to use a somewhat cumbersome but fair procedure to ensure nondiscrimination in employment as well. Black employees in the laundry and dietary departments were allowed into jobs that they previously could not hold based on seniority. The hospital had to provide evidence of compliance quarterly for the next two years.[4] With the end of this suit, in the words of Judge Ashton H. Williams, the fight for racial equality won in the courts. But even after winning in courts, Black South Carolinians still faced challenges in "press[ing] the victory."

The effect of litigation on both Black and White South Carolinians, as well as the state itself, has been profound. Black South Carolinians' efforts to bring about equality through the legal system reveal their determination to fight for equal justice. However, White resistance to equality reveals the fierce determination of White South Carolinians to maintain White supremacy. White South Carolinians used the legal machinery of the state and nation to delay its decline. In many ways obstruction by White people in the 1950s and 1960s—to say nothing of the era of Jim Crow that preceded World War II—was successful at minimizing Black progress.

Black voting increased following the *Elmore* and *Brown* cases from the 1940s, but it grew slowly. By 1970, because of increasing activism and the effects of the Voting Rights Act, there were 213,000 registered Black voters in the state, but that represented less than a quarter of those eligible.[5] Black voters, as they increased in numbers in the late 1960s, also increased in power. Despite efforts to dilute the strength of a minority bloc by revising systems of representation— like at-large elections—African Americans, for the first time since the 1890s, elected three Black representatives to the General Assembly in 1970.[6] Four years later there were thirteen Black legislators. Black members of the state House of Representatives formed a caucus in 1974 as well. By 1990 there were 322 elected Black officials across the state.[7] The reentry of Black voters into the political system fractured the state's Democratic consensus. Because of the state's racial history, the fragmentation of the Democratic Party did not lead to a genuine dual-party system but rather a realignment of White voters, who now vote for Republican candidates by wide margins. In essence, outlawing the White primary, coupled with the leftward swing of the Democratic Party nationally, set off a chain of events that resulted in White flight from the Democratic Party.

South Carolina has become a secure bastion for the Republican Party. The closest a Democratic presidential candidate came to receiving a majority of South Carolina's White vote since 1964 was in 1976, when Jimmy Carter carried 44 percent of the White vote (and nearly all the Black vote) and won the state. By 1995, however, only 42 percent of local Democratic Party managers could say with confidence that their party was getting stronger; 85 percent of Republicans believed their party was rising. However, while most Republicans were confident that their party could attract Black votes, Democrats were equally confident that Black voters would remain predominantly Democratic. During the early 1990s, the Democratic Party hemorrhaged White politicians: eighteen sitting Democratic politicians left the party, fourteen of them for the Republicans.[8] The governor's office has been comfortably Republican, with a one-term interlude, since the mid-1980s. The state House of Representatives has had a Republican majority since 1994 and the Senate since 2000. Even those seemingly late dates are misleading, though, as many of those Democrats in office before the Republican majorities took over were conservatives who only ran as Democrats to garner support from people who traditionally voted for that party. Voting rights have been a key instrument in Black southerners keeping issues of racial oppression on the national agenda. Voter ID requirements and other efforts at restricting minority voting show that voting rights are still under assault. In *Rucho v. Common Cause,* the Supreme Court ruled that partisan gerrymandering is a political question unreachable by the courts. In the South, where the Republican Party is predominantly White and the Democratic Party mostly Black, partisan gerrymandering is tantamount to racial gerrymandering.

In other areas tactics put in place to justify unequal treatment during resistance to civil rights have been legitimized as "color-blind" by conservative jurists. Teacher testing, implemented by White administrators, then targeted in the 1940s and early 1950s for its deleterious effect on Black teachers' salaries, continued to be an issue. In 1966 the Palmetto Education Association sued Clarendon County District 1 because the district passed a resolution that gave salary supplements to teachers based on their scores on the National Teacher Exam: the higher the score, the greater the supplement. Judge Robert W. Hemphill ruled that the mere fact that the supplements were based on NTE scores was not enough to justify an injunction to prevent enforcement of the school board's resolution.[9] In 1977 a three-judge panel upheld the system against a suit brought by the Justice Department, which the South Carolina Educational Association, the National Education Association, and several individual teachers joined. A new generation of judges—Clement Haynsworth, Donald Russell, and Charles E. Simons—were "unable to find any discriminatory intent" and concluded that "defendants' use of the NTE for salary purposes bears the necessary relationship to South Carolina's objectives with respect to its public school teaching force."[10] The use of the NTE as a factor in determining salaries may have been legal, but its disparate impact remained.

School desegregation is another difficult area. Although the state moved toward full desegregation in 1970, South Carolina continued to deal with the historic effects of discrimination. For example, when desegregation came to Darlington County in the fall of 1970, White students by the thousands boycotted schools. However, after a group of White rioters attacked and overturned a school bus the following March, an all-White jury found them guilty. Elsewhere in the state, guards were necessary to control violence as individual incidents had the potential to turn into racial unrest—and often did.[11]

One effect of the creation of unitary school districts was the frequent destruction of community-related identities for many schools, White and, especially, Black. Some high schools—most of them Black—held their last graduations in June 1970. Other formerly Black schools were combined with others to form new entities. Many former Black high schools became junior high schools, for example. Students would then go through the process of renaming school mascots, newspapers, and yearbooks. Finally, as David Robinson predicted, many White parents took their children out of the public school system entirely. The number of private schools grew from twenty-five White schools and ten Black schools (all but six of the thirty-five were religiously affiliated) to fifty White schools and twelve Black schools in 1964. All of the Black schools were religiously affiliated; nineteen of the White schools, more than three times the number ten years previously, were not religious. Although it is difficult to determine which private schools were formed as a direct response to integration, South Carolina in 1966–67 had only about forty-four private schools with approximately 4,500 students.[12] Nearly two hundred new private schools were built during the late 1960s. By 1971 the number of nonreligious private schools had grown to eighty-four, and by 1975 South Carolina had a higher than average percentage of students attending private schools. Though of course their histories no longer indicated that these schools were segregated, that likelihood is quite high. According to the Southern Education Foundation, most students attending private schools went to schools that were 90 percent or greater White.[13]

In Summerton, for example, following integration in the fall of 1965, a private school run by the Summerton Baptist Church opened its doors. By 1967 the school had one hundred students in twelve grades. Two of the five members of the public school board of trustees enrolled their children in the private school. However, even by then some White parents had returned their children to the public schools, and one confessed to Dwayne Walls of the *Charlotte Observer* that he would have taken his children out of the private school if he could do so without "losing face."[14]

Some private school graduates in South Carolina, including those of the flagship of the "integration private schools," Wade Hampton Academy in

Orangeburg, received a small pin with a representation of the Confederate battle flag with the word "SURVIVOR" engraved along the bottom of a circular frame around the flag. It symbolized the fact that they had survived a second incursion of the federal government into the affairs of the South.[15]

In Williamsburg County, which had never been subject to lawsuits to bring about desegregation, initial attempts at integration began in 1965. However, like most districts in the state, Williamsburg did not begin a full-scale effort at desegregating its schools until the fall of 1970. More than one thousand students left the system that fall, nearly eight hundred of them White. In the words of John Egerton, writing for the Southern Regional Council in 1976, "it appeared likely that the schools would soon be left to struggle along ineffectively with a woefully unprepared, overwhelmingly Black, totally poor student body."[16]

Despite that, Egerton was hopeful. By 1976 Williamsburg had managed to develop an efficient desegregated system in which Black and White students—the latter in small numbers, to be sure—were successfully educated in the same classrooms. Early White flight had by 1975 actually reversed into an increase in the number of White students in the system. Declines in Black enrollment due to emigration were also leveling out. Unlike many other school districts in South Carolina and elsewhere, Williamsburg did not close formerly all-Black schools, and it did not reduce the numbers of Black teachers and administrators. Discipline was no problem, and the percentage of students who went on to higher education doubled over the eight years since 1968 to 25 percent. While two of the most rural schools were still almost all Black, most of the schools had reasonable Black-White ratio of students and staff. District Superintendent R.C. Fennell was generally pleased, but he cautioned that mere desegregation without efforts to improve the quality of education would not have been enough to bring about the positive changes that Williamsburg experienced. Mary Harper, who had been hired in 1968 to initiate a kindergarten program, summed it up best when she said, "I personally believe that the best thing that ever happened to the public schools was the 1954 Supreme Court decision outlawing segregation. We're very slow to internalize it, slow to change our attitudes and our behavior, but the changes are taking place, and we'll be the better for them."[17]

In the laments of David Robinson, W. D. Workman, and many other White South Carolinians were the seeds of a new Lost Cause as White South Carolinians decried the passing of a system that had created political, economic, social, and educational advantages for their ancestors, themselves, and their heirs. Children are impressionable and learned the ways of White supremacy and the necessity of segregation along with their ABCs in White schools across the South. The denial of education for enslaved African Americans and the denial of equal education for their freed descendants were the cornerstones of South Carolina's White "civilization" as Black ignorance undergirded White supremacy's claims of innate Black inferiority.

Today South Carolina ranks near the bottom in many statistical categories that measure educational quality. As late as 1985, one of the many cases that went to federal court made its way back. The case of *Whittenberg v. Greenville,* which had been settled in 1963 without a trial, was heard in the courtroom of Judge George Ross Anderson in 1984. The fact that the districts remained under court-ordered desegregation suggests that communities were not trusted to do the right thing. A number of groups including the NAACP attempted to intervene in the case, arguing that the county continued to operate a dual school system. Despite rulings from Judge Martin in 1970 establishing an eighty-to-twenty ratio of White to Black students (and a subsequent ruling in 1976 by Judge Robert F. Chapman to lower the ratio of White to Black students to seventy-six to twenty-four), several groups petitioned Judge Anderson for the alleviation of a number of grievances. Essentially the various groups were concerned about continuing inadequacies at some schools, the alleged closing of some Black schools while new schools were built or old ones expanded in White neighborhoods, the allegedly disproportionate burden of busing on Black students, the relaxation of racial ratios, and general discrimination against Black students regarding educational opportunities. One of the groups represented White parents from predominantly White areas near the city of Greenville who intervened in the case to "protect their interests."[18]

Anderson held several hearings on the matter and ordered the district to prepare student assignment plans to minimize busing, student dislocation, and costs. Public hearings held concurrently led to the adoption of a plan designed to meet Anderson's directives while making some adjustments to the racial mix in the county's schools. Anderson ruled that Greenville County was maintaining racial balances "to a remarkable degree since Judge Martin's Order in 1970." The school closings and conversions, he ruled, were not the result of discriminatory intent. He ultimately found that the intervenors' concerns were important but that "they involve questions which do not rise to Constitutional status and which are properly heard in the administrative or political forum."[19] School desegregation, which the state had spent so much time and energy arguing should be taken out of the hands of the courts, had become so detailed and involved that the courts were now content to allow districts to make their own way.

Stanley v. Darlington County provides another example of the increasing complexities of the issues of desegregation. In 1974 Judge Simons reaffirmed the 1970 desegregation order, which was based on a modified HEW plan. The plaintiffs chose not to follow up, and in 1976 Simons moved the case to the inactive docket. In 1984, however, plaintiffs challenged the district's implementation of the 1970 plan, arguing that in at least seven instances, the district had failed to follow it.[20] After a hearing the plaintiffs withdrew their complaint, but a few years later the federal government intervened. Eventually in June 1994 a consent decree was filed with the approval of Judge Cameron Currie, establishing a new desegregation agreement and establishing Mayo High School, formerly a Black high school, as a magnet school for the district. A year later Currie reaffirmed that plan.

Desegregated schools struck at the very heart of every other type of discrimination that South Carolinians had emplaced. Even after the legal battle for segregation had ended, vestiges of the cultural attitudes that created it remained. Decades later Black South Carolinians returned to the courts to challenge the failure of educational reform, which had resulted in a "Corridor of Shame" in which students in impoverished majority-Black counties sued because of ongoing educational inequities. "The South Carolina Constitution requires there be a system of free public schools that affords each student the opportunity to receive a minimally adequate education." So stated the South Carolina Supreme Court in 1999 and again in 2014.[21] As of 2018 the state's schools, especially those in the Corridor of Shame, were still extremely segregated. According to the *Charleston News and Courier,* almost 80 percent of South Carolina's schools were more than 90 percent minority. White flight to private schools and charter schools funded with public money continues at a remarkable rate. The Corridor of Shame, where segregation is most intense, produces underprepared and struggling students, while students in wealthier parts of the state enjoy much greater success. But even wealthier districts are subject to some of the same ills that have befallen impoverished parts of the state. Statewide only a little more than one-third of eighth-grade students meet the state's own math requirements.[22]

Racial incidents have not disappeared despite cautious optimism among some that South Carolina has become a society with racial equality. In 1989 a restaurant in Aiken refused to serve Black customers, and an integrated youth group was denied access to a pool in Saluda County. Other incidents have arisen from time to time. Each time outrage from the public was immediate, and action by the government was swift and decisive: for example the Aiken restaurant soon found itself without a liquor license, and Republican governor Carroll Campbell, who in 1969 had led a motorcade to the capital to protest the end of freedom of choice plans, invited the Saluda youth group to a picnic at the governor's mansion.[23]

Differences over race and justice continue in other areas as well. In 1962 a resolution of the General Assembly called for the flying of the Confederate battle flag over the State House. It was intended, ostensibly, as a celebration of the Confederate centennial. It remained in place during and long after that centennial as Black and White South Carolinians engaged in civil war in the courts.[24] Yet until July 2000, the flag still flew above the capital city. Its removal likely cost the Republican governor, David Beasley, his reelection that fall. A different, "more traditional" version of the flag was moved to the front of the State House until 2015. It was finally removed from State House grounds altogether following the murders at the Emanuel African Methodist Episcopal Church in Charleston. "Mother Emanuel," as many called the church, was one of the epicenters in the state of the civil rights movement, including being the home church of Denmark Vesey, who was alleged to have plotted a slave uprising in 1822.[25] All the while, proponents of the flags ignored their historical context and argued that their position is based on "heritage not hate." Those who wanted the flag removed contended that the symbolic racism it represents insults the dignity and humanity of many South Carolinians, and not just those of African descent. The fact that the metaphorical battle over the flag ended with a very real and devastating massacre perpetrated by a White supremacist, in the state that touted its "integration with dignity," is perhaps emblematic of the civil rights era.

The Second Reconstruction was in many ways as futile as the first. By indulging White South Carolinians in their obstruction, judges were able to run out the clock on federal officials and Black South Carolinians who sought transformative racial change. Richard Nixon appointed bureaucrats who were more flexible than Lyndon Johnson's appointees. Nixon seeded the courts with conservative lifetime appointees who contributed to the protracted struggle that, for many, continues—and ultimately failed in many ways. That the original plaintiffs in whose names the cases continue are often old enough to be grandparents raises the question of "dignity for whom" in South Carolina's ongoing struggle for civil rights.

The South Carolina Conference of the NAACP, which was so important in the litigation campaign throughout the thirty years covered in this work, remains an important advocacy organization for Black South Carolinians. While the organization does not enjoy a vast membership (it never has), it remains an important force for civil rights and justice in the state. Its activism still makes it a target of some White hostility. Local issues such as the mistreatment of alleged criminals in Greenville County as well as statewide issues like the Confederate flag controversy and state boycott continue to mobilize members of the organization and sometimes a sympathetic public as well.

Black and White South Carolinians contended in the courts over issues of law and justice from the 1940s through 1970 and beyond by appealing to their respective but differing interpretations of the rule of law. The nature of civil rights after 1970 supports a contention that ultimately the rule of law triumphed. White supremacy could successfully be challenged in court. The rule of law did not consistently bend "the arc of moral universe" toward equal justice for all, but it did create a legal process that decreased many obvious racial disparities that consistently favored White people. Civil rights issues continue to be heard in the federal courts. White people seeking to challenge affirmative action couch their attacks in the language of civil rights and take to the courts, which increasingly support their claims. The legal complexities of school desegregation, as illustrated by the 1985 iteration of the *Whittenberg* case and the mid-1990s decisions in the *Stanley* case, have demonstrated the virtual impossibility of solving such problems administratively without community support, despite judicial admonitions to the contrary. The ongoing problems encountered by mostly Black students in the Corridor of Shame are sufficient evidence that decades of neglect are just as problematic as active discrimination ever was. The legal struggle over civil rights began as a strategy to win justice through the courts. It has left us with a long tradition of litigation but a much less clear-cut meaning of justice.

ABBREVIATIONS USED IN THE NOTES

CUSC   Clemson University Special Collections, Robert M. Cooper
            Library
DWR Papers David W. Robinson Papers, South Carolina State Library
NARA   National Archives and Records Administration, College Park,
            Maryland
NARA-MA   National Archives and Records Administration, Mid-Atlantic
            Region, Philadelphia, Pennsylvania
NARA-SE   National Archives and Records Administration, Southeast
            Region, Atlanta, Georgia

NOTES

Introduction

1. Since the turn of the century, several new works have explored South Carolina's role in the civil rights movement. Burke, *All for Civil Rights,* and Burke and Gergel, *Matthew J. Perry,* explore how Black lawyers were instrumental in the movement, building somewhat on the older but still important work by Tinsley Yarbrough, *A Passion for Justice.* On Judge J. Waties Waring, Hicks, *In Darkest South Carolina,* explores his involvement in voting rights cases in the 1940s and school desegregation in the 1950s, along with the personal toll his stands exacted. Lau, *Democracy Rising,* is a valuable source for background and context. Winfred B. Moore Jr. and Orville Vernon Burton's edited collection from the Citadel Conference on Civil Rights, *Toward the Meeting of the Waters,* contains many vital articles on that subject. Ophelia De Laine Gona's *Dawn of Desegregation* offers an account based on the life of her father, Rev. J. A. De Laine, who was central to the *Briggs v. Elliott* case. Baker, *Paradoxes of Desegregation,* covers several legal cases from Charleston while examining "educational equity" in the city through much of the twentieth century. The most well-known instance of violence in South Carolina took place in Orangeburg in 1968. While there have not been any recent reexaminations of those events, Bass and Nelson, *Orangeburg Massacre,* remains an excellent source despite its original publication date of 1970. In the March 2005 issue of the *Journal of American History,* Jacquelyn Dowd Hall expanded on an idea she had first introduced four years earlier in the *Chronicle of Higher Education*—that of the "long civil rights movement," starting with migrations of African Americans in the early twentieth century and continuing well past the 1970s. See Hall, "Long Civil Rights Movement." The *Chronicle* article is "Broadening Our View of the Civil Rights Movement."

2. Peltason, *Fifty-Eight Lonely Men,* offers a contemporary view of district and appellate judges grappling with desegregation. South Carolina judges are mentioned a few times, but the emphasis is primarily on other states. Hamilton, *Bench and the Ballot,* explores voting rights within the same context. Finally, Bass, *Unlikely Heroes,* looks at judges on the Fifth Circuit Court of Appeals. As such it does not look at South Carolina, which was in the Fourth Circuit.

3. Newby, *Black Carolinians,* 229–73; Hayes, *South Carolina and the New Deal.*

4. Hoffman, "Genesis of the Modern Movement."

5. Bartley, *Rise of Massive Resistance,* 174, 176.

6. Edgar, South Carolina, xx.

7. Bartley, *Rise of Massive Resistance*, 19, quoting Boyce Alexander Drummond Jr., "Arkansas Politics: A Study of a One-Party System" (PhD diss., University of Chicago, 1957), 8. Bartley emphasized how the characteristics of the Arkansas elite could be carried over generally to a description of neo-Bourbonism.

8. South Carolina State College was chartered as the Colored, Normal, Agricultural, Industrial, and Mechanical College of South Carolina. Founded in 1895 under the 1890 Morrill Act, it served the purposes of preparing teachers, like Winthrop, the public White women's college, as well as teaching agriculture and the mechanic arts, like Clemson, the land-grant college for White men.

9. Johnston, "Communism vs. Segregation."

10. *Henry v. Greenville Airport Commission* 175 F. Supp. 343 (1959) at 347.

11. McNeill, Paul Wesley. "School Desegregation in South Carolina, 1963–1970" (Ed.D. dissertation, University of Kentucky, 1979), 79.

Chapter 1

1. Complaint against the Board of Commissioners of Elections of Columbia, filed April 22, 1932, quoted in Aba-Mecha, "Black Woman Activist," 161. See also ibid., 216n20. See *Nixon v. Herndon* and *Nixon v. Condon,* both Texas cases regarding voting rights. While *Condon* was decided shortly after the attempts in Columbia to vote, both cases were probably inspirational for the Black Columbians.

2. Aba-Mecha, "Black Woman Activist," 162–63. In Texas the Democratic Party's status as a private entity was constitutionally approved in *Grovey v. Townsend.* On Frederick, see Burke, *All for Civil Rights,* 142, 145.

3. Hayes, *South Carolina and the New Deal,* 169. See also Weiss, *Farewell to the Party of Lincoln,* 213.

4. "Business Men of City Wage Fight on Housing Proposal," *Greenville (SC) News,* March 31, 1939, at the Greenville Housing Authority, https://www.tgha.net/1930 -1940 (accessed April 28, 2020).

5. Hoffman, "Genesis of the Modern Movement," 368. For more on the establishment and growth of the NAACP in South Carolina, see Lau, "Mr. NAACP"; see also Lau, *Democracy Rising.*

6. O. H. Doyle to the Attorney General, July 13, 1939. File 144-68-1, Box 17601, Department of Justice Central Files, Classified Subject Files, Correspondence, RG 60, National Archives. Hereafter NARA.

7. Ibid.

8. "Greenville Chief to Ask Klan for Fewer Parades," *Spartanburg (SC) Herald,* November 22, 1939. See Huff, *Greenville,* 357. See also Baker, *What Reconstruction Meant,* 103–9 for more on the Klan terrorism that followed the voter registration drive in Greenville. Klan leader Johnson was arrested some months later in connection with the "abduction and flogging" of a mechanic from Anderson named Lanier Pruitt. Forty or more people were involved in the lynching. "Alleged Chief of Klan Re-arrested," *Spartanburg (SC) Herald,* January 14, 1940.

9. Baker, *What Reconstruction Meant,* 103–4; Kennedy, *Southern Exposure,* 175; NAACP Subject File: KKK (Clippings), 54–55. NAACP Papers, Library of Congress.

10. *Newberry v. United States* concerned the validity of a Michigan law regulating the amount that candidates and their agents could spend on a political campaign for US senator or representative. Narrowly the Court overturned the Michigan statute, which regulated both primary and general elections; the Court was evenly divided on whether primary elections were reachable under federal law. Thurgood Marshall to Henry Schweinhaut, July 11, 1939; O. John Rogge to Marshall, July 31, 1939; Walter White to Schweinhaut, August 9, 1939; Marshall to Rogge, August 5, 1939. File 144-68-1, RG 60, NARA.

11. Marshall to Rogge, October 2, 1939; Rogge to Marshall, October 11, 1939. File 144-68-1, Box 17601, Department of Justice Central Files, Classified Subject Files, Correspondence, RG 60, NARA. Emphasis added.

12. "Federal Criminal Jurisdiction over Violations of Civil Liberties," memo accompanying Circular No. 3356 (Supplement 1), O. John Rogge, Assistant Attorney General, to All United States Attorneys, May 21, 1940, quoted in Kato, *Liberalizing Lynching*, 140-41.

13. For example, electors who were eligible in 1898 could continue to vote unless subsequently disqualified. Also counties were to have three-member boards of electors, and those boards had the authority to "judge . . . the legal qualifications of all applicants for registration." Compiled Code of South Carolina, 1930, 785. https://archive.org/details/compiledcodeofs002unse/page/788 (accessed July 17, 2019).

14. E. A. Dawkins to Walter White, September 11, 1939; Lottie P. Gaffney to NAACP, August 25, 1940. NAACP Papers, Library of Congress. To avoid confusion between Lottie Gaffney and the town of Gaffney, I use "Gaffney" to refer to the town and refer to Lottie Gaffney by her full name.

15. Roy Wilkins to Lottie P. Gaffney, August 28, 1940; Wilkins to Gaffney, September 7, 1940; Affidavit of Lottie P. Gaffney and Bernice Bonner, October 8, 1940. NAACP Papers, Library of Congress.

16. *United States v. Classic* affirmed the right of the federal government to regulate primary elections, because Louisiana officials did not count the votes of certain White voters in a congressional primary. The narrow ruling held that Congress could regulate primaries if a federal office were involved.

17. Lottie Gaffney to Thurgood Marshall, February 28, 1942; Marshall to Gaffney, March 10, 1942. NAACP Papers, Library of Congress. For Judge Cecil C. Wyche's opinion on the defendants' motion to quash the indictment, see *United States v. Ellis*.

18. Marshall to Gaffney, March 10, 1942. NAACP Papers, Library of Congress.

19. Lottie Gaffney to NAACP, June 4, 1942. NAACP Papers, Library of Congress.

20Assistant Attorney General Wendell Berge to Marshall, July 11, 1942. NAACP Papers, Library of Congress.

21. Jones-Branch, "'To Speak When and Where I Can,'" 204-9.

22. Report of Special Agent Gordon Lee Smith, May 18, 1943, File 72-67-7, Box 12404, RG 60, NARA. Quotation on p. 3.

23. E. A. Adams et al. to the Attorney General, August 25, 1942; Wendell Berge to Claude N. Sapp, October 2, 1942; Berge to Sapp, February 15, 1943; Report of Special Agent Gordon Smith, August 12, 1943, File 72-67-7, Box 12404, RG 60, NARA. See 18 U.S.C. 242 Deprivation of rights under color of law.

24. Thurgood Marshall to Sam S. Minter, May 10, 1944, quoted in Lawson, *Black Ballots*, 46. See also D. Hine, *Black Victory*.

25. Exhibit C to plaintiff's original complaint, Proclamation and Speech by Governor Olin D. Johnston to South Carolina General Assembly, April 12 and 14, 1944, respectively. *George Elmore v. Clay Rice, et al.*, Civil Action Number 1702, Eastern District of South Carolina, Columbia Division, Record Group 21, Records of the District Courts of the United States, NARA-SE. Emphasis added.

26. "Speech of Senator Benjamin R. Tillman, March 23, 1900," *Congressional Record*, 56th Congress, 1st Session, 3223–24. Reprinted in Richard Purday, ed., *Document Sets for the South in U.S. History* (Lexington, MA: D.C. Heath and Company, 1991), 147.

27. Olin Johnston quoted in Borsos, "Support for the National Democratic Party," 11; emphasis added. In 1948, when South Carolina's Strom Thurmond ran for the presidency under the aegis of the States' Rights Democratic Party (also known as the Dixiecrat Party), Johnston never specifically endorsed Thurmond's candidacy. His "loyalty" to the Democratic Party was rewarded, but he made it clear that he did not support President Truman's stance on civil rights. Johnston and his wife, who was vice-chair of the Jefferson-Jackson Day event, refused to attend the reception in February 1949 after hearing that it would be integrated and trying unsuccessfully to ensure that none of the senator's group would be seated next to Black guests.

28. The constitution was amended by popular vote on February 14, 1945.

29. Complaint, February 21, 1947. *Elmore v. Rice*, C/A 1702.

30. Fred G. Folsom to Thurgood Marshall, January 17, 1947. NAACP Papers, Library of Congress.

31. Exhibit B of Plaintiff's Complaint; Complaint. *Elmore v. Rice*, C/A 1702.

32. Complaint. *Elmore v. Rice*, C/A 1702.

33. See also *Williams v. Mississippi*, which upheld the legality of that state's poll tax and literacy test requirements for voting.

34. Defendants' Answer, April 11, 1947. *Elmore v. Rice*, C/A 1702. In 1944 Black South Carolinians created the Progressive Democratic Party, largely in response to encouragement from John McCray, publisher of the *Lighthouse and Informer*. In May 172 delegates representing 39 of the state's 46 counties convened in Columbia. The PDP proposed to send delegates to the national Democratic convention that summer but were persuaded not to. See Richards, "Progressive Democrats in Chicago," for background on the PDP.

35. Testimony of William P. Baskin, June 3, 1947. *Elmore v. Rice*, C/A 1702. Baskin, the chairman of the state's Democratic Party and a future defendant in the follow-up to the *Elmore* case, was also one of the attorneys for the defense in this case. Judge J. Waties Waring called him as an informational witness to testify regarding differences between the operations of the party before and after the legislature repealed state laws concerning the party.

36. Findings of Fact and Conclusions of Law, July 12, 1947. *Elmore v. Rice*, C/A 1702.

37. *Elmore v. Rice*, C/A 1702, at 527–28.

38. Waring's role and the price he paid personally for that role in the voting cases are ably covered in Yarbrough, *Passion for Justice*, 60–75. See also Hicks, *In Darkest South Carolina*, 146–77.

39. Argument for Appellants. *Elmore v. Rice*, no. 5664, Filed October 13, 1947. 11 United States Circuit Court of Appeals, Fourth Circuit. RG 276, NARA-MA.

40. For example, see William Workman's excoriation of the Fourteenth and Fifteenth Amendments in Workman, "State Regulation of the Right to Vote." He argues that the amendments were punitive, particularly the Fourteenth, "sponsored in Congress by a vengeful group of Republicans who sought to punish further the defeated South" (393)

41. Reply Brief for Appellants. *Elmore v. Rice*, no. 5664, Filed October 13, 1947. United States Circuit Court of Appeals, Fourth Circuit. RG 276, NARA-MA. Emphasis added.

42. *Prigg v. Pennsylvania*. When northern states invoked states' rights in fugitive slave cases, the South was quick to reject. Constitutional theory went one way: what was good for the goose was not necessarily good for the gander.

43. Brief for Appellee, November 4, 1947. *Elmore v. Rice*, no. 5664. United States Circuit Court of Appeals, Fourth Circuit. RG 276, NARA-MA.

44. William H. Hastie to Thurgood Marshall, 19 July 1947. NAACP Papers, Library of Congress.

45. Complaint, July 8, 1948. *David Brown v. W. P. Baskin, et al.*, C/A 1964, Eastern District of South Carolina, Charleston Division, RG 21, Records of the District Courts of the United States, NARA-SE.

46. Boulware memo. NAACP Papers, Library of Congress.

47. See Brown, "Wishin', Hopin', Prayin' and Votin'," 10; Complaint. *Brown v. Baskin*, C/A 1964.

48. Quoted in Cohodas, *Strom Thurmond*, 177.

49. Return to Rule to Show Cause, July 16, 1948. *Brown v. Baskin*, C/A 1964. Waring had allowed segregation to continue in South Carolina's higher education, specifically mandating the establishment of a separate law school at the state's Black South Carolina College (*Wrighten v. Board of Trustees*). Only one of the four counties that filed for exemption from the case—Jasper—was in the lowcountry, where historically most Black South Carolinians lived, and it was not dismissed from the case because the county's committee did not address the oath issue in its legal filings.

50. Transcript of hearing for preliminary injunction. *Brown v. Baskin*, C/A 1964.

51. Ibid.

52. Ibid.

53. Ibid. In his opinion Waring referred specifically to rules 6 and 7, among others. Rule 6 limited "club membership" to White Democrats; rule 7 specified that White Democrats, that is, members of the "club," could vote in their precincts. Black voters, since they still could not join the club, had to produce general election voting certificates. *Brown v. Baskin*, 78 F. Supp 933, 936 (1948).

54. Transcript of hearing for preliminary injunction. *Brown v. Baskin*, C/A 1964.

55. Ibid.

56. Order. *Brown v. Baskin,* C/A 1964.

57. Defendants' Answer. *Brown v. Baskin,* C/A 1964.

58. Affidavit of John E. Stansfield, October 20, 1948. *Brown v. Baskin,* C/A 1964.

59. Hearing on Motions, (filed) October 26, 1948; Findings of Fact, Conclusions of Law, and Order, 26 November 1948. *Brown v. Baskin,* C/A 1964.

60. Robert McC. Figg, Jr. to Claude M. Dean (Clerk, Fourth Circuit Court of Appeals), June 15, 1949. *Brown v. Baskin,* no. 5861. Box 502, RG 276, NARA-MA. On Dorn's reaction see Quint, *Profile in Black and White,* 6.

61. There were about 722,000 African Americans in the state in the 1950 census.

62. Newby, *Black Carolinians,* 286–87.

63. Report of Special Agent Francis W. Matthys, September 13, 1948; Report of Special Agent Roy M. Osborn, September 9, 1948; Report of Special Agent Edwin R. Groves, September 30, 1948, File 144-62-19, Box 1376, RG 60, NARA.

64. Report of Special Agent James T. Magher, October 28, 1948; Alexander Campbell to Oscar Doyle, March 25, 1949; Doyle to Campbell, April 14, 1949, File 144-67-19, Box 1376, RG 60, NARA.

65. Key, *Southern Politics in State and Nation,* 632–43.

66. Newby, *Black Carolinians,* 291.

Chapter 2

1. South Carolina, among other states, was investigated for public school discrimination in the mid-1930s, but the NAACP's emphasis remained focused on teacher salaries, higher education, and transportation. See McNeil, *Groundwork,* 153–54. For the 1950s see Dobrasko, "Upholding 'Separate but Equal,'" which explores the state's school equalization program in the early 1950s.

2. *Alston v. School Board of the City of Norfolk* Decision of the County Board of Education, p. 2, *Thompson v. Gibbes,* Civil Action Number 1273, Eastern District of South Carolina, Charleston Division, RG 21, Records of the District Courts of the United States, NARA-SE; Ihle, "Teacher Salary Equalization Movement in Virginia"; Kirk, "NAACP Campaign for Teachers' Salary Equalization." Aline Black, plaintiff in the Norfolk case, also sued for equal pay. See "Petitions Filed in Covington and Norfolk," *Washington Afro-American,* March 11, 1939. In 1936 Marshall represented William Gibbs in a Maryland case, *Gibbs v. Broome,* to equalize teacher salaries. The school district settled, and salaries were raised over the following two years. Klinger, "William B. Gibbs, Jr."

3. Tushnet, *Making Civil Rights Law,* 117–21; Tushnet, *NAACP's Legal Strategy,* 58–103.

4. Education General, July–September 1937 File, 35. NAACP Administrative File. NAACP Papers, Library of Congress.

5. NAACP Branch Files, Columbia, SC, 1938–1940, NAACP Papers, Library of Congress; Teachers' Salaries-South Carolina-Charleston, 1943–1944. NAACP Papers, Library of Congress; Tushnet, *NAACP's Legal Strategy,* 92–93; Katherine Mellen Charron, *Freedom's Teacher,* 157–63.

6. "South Carolina Defies the Supreme Court," *Phoenix (AZ) Index,* June 7, 1941; *Chronicling America: Historic American Newspapers.* Library of Congress. https://

chroniclingamerica.loc.gov/lccn/sn96060866/1941-06-07/ed-1/seq-8/. See also Charron, *Freedom's Teacher*, 154–55.

7. Hoffman, "Genesis of the Modern Movement," 367–68; *Columbia (SC) State*, February 7, 1945; Decision of School Board (Answer Exhibit C), *Thompson v. Gibbes*, C/A 1273; Tushnet, *NAACP's Legal Strategy*, 92; Yarbrough, *Passion for Justice*, 43–44.

8. Plaintiff's exhibit 3, Facts about Schools and Teachers; Defense exhibits A–D. *Thompson v. Gibbes*, C/A 1273.

9. Decision of School Board. *Thompson v. Gibbes*, C/A 1273.

10. *Columbia (SC) State*, February 7, 1945; Yarbrough, *Passion for Justice*, 44.

11. Complaint. *Thompson v. Gibbes*, C/A 1273.

12. Shadrack Morgan was a Howard University graduate who had returned to the state to practice law. Admitted to the bar in 1919, he took on a few civil rights cases and became a local counsel for the NAACP in the 1940s when Harold Boulware was serving in the war. See Burke, *All for Civil Rights*, 146; Complaint. *Thompson v. Gibbes*, C/A 1273.

13. Tushnet, *Making Civil Rights Law*, 121; Tushnet, *NAACP's Legal Strategy*, 92–93; Baker, *Paradoxes of Desegregation*, 56–58.

14. Request for Admission of Facts by Defendants, April 11, 1945. *Thompson v. Gibbes*, C/A 1273.

15. Findings of Fact and Conclusions of Law; Order. *Thompson v. Gibbes*, C/A 1273. The *Thompson* case file contains salary information for White and African American teachers for 1944–45. The highest-paid Black teacher earned $1,200; the lowest-paid White teachers also earned $1,200. Average salaries for White teachers were nearly $400 higher. The school district argued that the difference was based on experience.

16. Hearing before the State Board of Education, October 24, 1949. The figure of 801 comes from the defense answer. The answer also puts the number of keys discovered at various testing sites at 7. *Shirer v. Anderson*, C/A 2392, Eastern District of South Carolina, Charleston Division, Record Group 21, Records of the District Courts of the United States, National Archives-Southeast Region.

17. Complaint. *Shirer v. Anderson*, C/A 2392.

18. Complaint; Exhibit A, Transcript of Board of Education Hearing, October 24, 1949. *Shirer v. Anderson*, C/A 2392.

19. Testimony at Trial, January 23, 1950. *Shirer v. Anderson*, C/A 2392; *Pettiford v. State Board of Education*; "State High Court Hears Teacher Cheating Case," *Spartanburg (SC) Herald*, November 16, 1950. See also *State v. Hightower*, in which Willar [sic] Howard Hightower unsuccessfully appealed his fraud conviction to the state Supreme Court. http://law.justia.com/cases/south-carolina/supreme-court/1952/16589-1.html (accessed August 2, 2015).

20. Trial Transcript, Testimony of Pearl Green Shirer. *Shirer v. Anderson*, C/A 2392.

21. Trial Transcript, Testimony of John A. McHugh. *Shirer v. Anderson*, C/A 2392.

22. Trial Transcript. *Shirer v. Anderson*, C/A 2392.

23. Ibid.

24. *Shirer v. Anderson*, 88 F. Supp. 858, 861 (1950).

25. Tushnet, *NAACP's Legal Strategy*, 56–58; Entin, "*Sweatt v. Painter*," 18–19. See also G. R. McNeill, *Groundwork*, 137–39.

26. Tushnet, *NAACP's Legal Strategy*, 71–72. *Missouri ex. rel. Gaines v. Canada*.

27. NAACP Administrative File, American Fund for Public Service-University of South Carolina, 1938–40; Burke, *All for Civil Rights*, 168–70. Charles H. Houston died on April 22, 1950. G. R. McNeill, *Groundwork*, 211.

28. South Carolina Constitution, Article XI, Section 7.

29. There were ten students in the law school around 1873. See Hollis, *University of South Carolina*, 65–79, for a biased account of African Americans at the university during Reconstruction.

30. On South Carolina State's founding and history, see W. Hine, *South Carolina State University*.

31. DeCosta, "Education of Negroes in South Carolina," 411; DeCosta, "Negro Higher and Professional Education in South Carolina," 351.

32. Newby, *Black Carolinians*, 350. *Sipuel v. Board of Regents* held that Ada Lois Sipuel must be admitted to the University of Oklahoma's law school despite the segregated nature of that institution. The case was on appeal to the US Supreme Court while John Wrighten's case was still being heard.

33. James M. Hinton to Thurgood Marshall, November 29, 1946; Robert L. Carter to Hinton, December 2, 1946; Hinton to Carter, December 21, 1946. NAACP Papers, Library of Congress.

34. Complaint, n.d. (filed January 8, 1947). *John H. Wrighten v. Board of Trustees of the University of South Carolina, et al.*, C/A 1670, Eastern District of South Carolina, Columbia Division, Record Group 21, Records of the District Courts of the United States, NARA-SE.

35. Answer. *Wrighten v. Board of Trustees*, C/A 1670. Emphasis added. The "substantially equal" requirement was the standard set in the *Gaines* case.

36. Ibid.

37. Ibid. None of the six Black representatives at the 1895 constitutional convention signed the constitution. Instead they made impassioned speeches against racism. Thomas Miller made a deal with Ben Tillman to create South Carolina State College.

38. Transcript of Pretrial Conference, May 15, 1947. *Wrighten v. Board of Trustees*, C/A 1670; Robert L. Carter to J. W. Waring, May 22, 1947; Waring to Carter, May 26, 1947. NAACP Papers, Library of Congress.

39. Transcript of Pretrial Conference. *Wrighten v. Board of Trustees*, C/A 1670.

40. Deposition of Miller F. Whittaker, May 31, 1947. *Wrighten v. Board of Trustees*, C/A 1670.

41. Ibid.

42. Deposition of Norman M. Smith; Deposition of Samuel L. Prince, May 31, 1947. *Wrighten v. Board of Trustees*, C/A 1670.

43. *Pearson v. Murray*, 169 Md. 478; *Missouri ex rel. Gaines v. Canada*, 305 U.S. 337 (1938), quoted in Plaintiff's Memorandum of Law, *Wrighten v. Board of Trustees*, C/A 1670.

44. Transcript of Trial, June 5–6, 1947, Testimony of Miller F. Whittaker. *Wrighten v. Board of Trustees*, C/A 1670.

45. Ibid.

46. Ibid.

47. Ibid.

48. Transcript of Trial, June 5-6, 1947, Testimony of John H. Wrighten, *Wrighten v. Board of Trustees,* C/A 1670.

49. Transcript of Trial, June 5-6, 1947, Testimony of W. C. Bethea. *Wrighten v. Board of Trustees,* C/A 1670. "New Angle Reported in Law School Case," unknown date, from unknown newspaper. NAACP Legal File, Universities-University of South Carolina Newspaper Clippings 1946-48. NAACP Papers, Library of Congress.

50. Transcript of Trial, June 5-6, 1947, Testimony of S. L. Prince. *Wrighten v. Board of Trustees,* C/A 1670.

51. Ibid.

52. Transcript of Trial, June 5-6, 1947, Testimony of Jack Lott. *Wrighten v. Board of Trustees,* C/A 1670.

53. Order, July 12, 1947. *Wrighten v. Board of Trustees,* C/A 1670; *Wrighten v. Board of Trustees,* 72 F. Supp. 948, 950-53 (1947).

54. *Sipuel v. Board of Regents of the University of Oklahoma;* Irons, *People's History of the Supreme Court,* 371; Tushnet, *NAACP's Legal Strategy,* 121-23.

55. Wrighten to Carter, n.d. (received August 20, 1947); Carter to Wrighten, August 8, 1947; Wrighten to Marshall, September 27, 1947; Marshall to Wrighten, September 29, 1947; Memorandum, Marshall to Hinton, Boulware, and Beard, September 30, 1947. NAACP Legal File, Universities-University of South Carolina, Correspondence, 1946-49. NAACP Papers, Library of Congress. The Charleston NAACP executive board members pressuring Wrighten were probably Beard and John Green. Green had written John McCray in December 1944 that the Progressive Democrats should "forget or bury our court procedures." Beard wrote McCray in May 1945 of his belief that "we have many fair-minded white people in S.C." lacking "MORAL COURAGE to take a stand." Green to McCray, December 31, 1944; Beard to McCray, May 11, 1945. John Henry McCray Papers, 1929-1989, box 03, folder 29, 1944-1950. University of South Carolina Digital Collections. See also Moore, "Thorn in the Side of Segregation."

56. Wrighten to Marshall, October 1, 1947; Wrighten to Marshall, October 6, 1947; Wrighten to Hinton, October 8, 1947; Boulware to Edward Dudley, October 13, 1947; Wrighten to Hinton, October 8, 1947. NAACP Papers, Library of Congress.

57. Marshall to Boulware, March 3, 1948. NAACP Papers, Library of Congress.

58. Moore, "Thorn in the Side," 2, 45-48.

59. Wrighten to Mrs. J. Waites [sic] Waring, February 6, 1949; J. Waties Waring to Wrighten, February 8, 1949; Marshall to Wrighten, February 21, 1949. NAACP Papers, Library of Congress.

60. Synnott, "Federalism Vindicated," 297. Football player Deacon Jones, among others, lost his scholarship after participating in a demonstration in 1958. See Donnelly, *Deacon Jones,* 26-29. See also W. Hine, *South Carolina State University,* 192-95.

61. In 1948 State Teachers College became Alabama State College for Negroes. Since 1969 it has been Alabama State University.

62. G. E. Metz to Board of Trustees, February 17, 1948, Clemson University Archives, S10, Admissions, Folder 148, CUSC.

63. "Negro Asks Admission to Clemson College," unidentified newspaper clipping, n.d. (probably April 28, 1948), Clemson University Archives, S10, Folder 148, CUSC.

64. James M. Hinton to R. F. Poole, April 28, 1948, Clemson University Archives, S10, Folder 99, CUSC.

65. Daniel R. Moorer to R. F. Poole, April 29, 1948, Clemson University Archives, S10, Folder 99, CUSC.

66. T. B. Young to R. F. Poole, June 10, 1948, Clemson University Archives, CUSC.

67. There are multiple references in Poole's correspondence to the lack at Clemson of the programs both Braceys desired. Undoubtedly SC State's program in civil engineering was started because of Edward Bracey's expressed desire to pursue that program. See particularly correspondence between Poole and South Carolina State president Miller F. Whitaker between May 11 and May 22, 1948, Clemson University Archives, S10, Folder 148, CUSC.

68. Minutes of the Clemson College Board of Trustees, June 18, 1948, Clemson University Archives, CUSC.

Chapter 3

1. See, for example, various stories on *Smith v. Allwright, McLaurin v. State Board of Regents,* and *Sweatt v. Painter* in the *Lighthouse and Informer,* April 25, 1948, October 24, 1948, October 31, 1948, and July 7, 1951.

2. Smithsonian Institution, "Separate Is Not Equal." https://americanhistory .si.edu/brown/history/4-five/clarendon-county-2.html (accessed July 15, 2019).

3. For the *Pearson* case, see Kluger, *Simple Justice,* 3–17. The suit was dismissed on technical grounds because the plaintiff, Levi Pearson, although he lived in the district targeted in the suit, paid taxes to a different district. See also Gona, *Dawn of Desegregation.*

4. Kluger, *Simple Justice,* 18–24. For a brief discussion of the *Briggs* case and some of the other cases from South Carolina, see Wolters, *Burden of Brown,* 129–74. Wolters's factual background is based on many of the same sources I have used, but his perspective is that of one who believes that *Brown v. Board of Education* was flawed and that the results have largely been negative. Jack Greenberg, a lawyer in the NAACP's Legal Defense Fund beginning in 1949 and director of the LDF from 1962 to 1984, approaches the problem from the perspective of an insider in his *Crusaders in the Courts,* 85–194. For contemporary personal accounts of Clarendon County and the aftermath of *Brown,* see Rowan, *Go South to Sorrow,* 3–23, 110–15, and Martin, *Deep South Says "Never,"* 43–77.

5. "James F. Byrnes Stands Firmly against Change: Separating in Schools Must Be Maintained," *Orangeburg (SC) Times and Democrat,* June 7, 1950; "South Carolina," *Southern School News,* September 1954; Synnott, "Federalism Vindicated," 298; Newby, *Black Carolinians,* 306–7. See Byrnes's inaugural address, January 16, 1951, http://dc.statelibrary.sc.gov/bitstream/handle/10827 /704/Inaugural_Address_1951-1-16.pdf?sequence=1&isAllowed=y (accessed August 3, 2015). See also his address to the General Assembly, January 24, 1951, http://dc.statelibrary.sc.gov/bitstream/handle/10827/730/State_of_the_State_Address _1951-1-24.pdf?sequence=1&isAllowed=y (accessed August 3, 2015).

6. Kluger, *Simple Justice,* 303–4.

7. Quoted in "South Carolina," *Southern School News,* September 1954.

8. Kluger, *Simple Justice,* 347–48.

9. Ibid., 331–32, 351–53.

10. Ibid., 352–53.

11. Ibid., 317, 330–31, 353, 355–56; Wolters, *Burden of Brown,* 135.

12. Kluger, *Simple Justice,* 363–65.

13. *Briggs v. Elliot,* 98 F. Supp. 529. Waring's dissent is at pp. 538–48.

14. Bartley, *Rise of Massive Resistance,* 44–46.

15. "Inaugural Address of the Honorable George Bell Timmerman, Jr. as Governor of South Carolina," January 18, 1955, http://dc.statelibrary.sc.gov/bitstream/handle /10827/705/Inaugural_Address_1955-1-18.pdf?sequence=1&isAllowed=y (accessed August 3, 2015).

16. "Orangeburg Equalization Program Is 95% Complete," *Columbia State,* February 10, 1956.

17. Ashmore, *Negro and the Schools,* 150–53, 159 (tables 6–8, 14).

18. "Substandard Schools in SC Now Few," *Columbia State,* October 13, 1956.

19. Synnott, "Federalism Vindicated," 298.

20. Kluger, *Simple Justice,* 365–66.

21. Robert McC. Figg to Judge Eugene S. Blease, December 10, 1953. *Briggs v. Elliott* digital collection, University of South Carolina Library, https://digital.tcl.sc.edu /digital/collection/p17173coll24/id/10 (accessed August 5, 2019).

22. J. P. "Jack" Hightower to Edgar A. Brown, May 20, 1954, Edgar A. Brown Papers, MSS 91, Box 36, Folder 475, CUSC (Brown papers hereafter).

23. Brown to Hightower, May 24, 1954, Brown papers, Box 36, Folder 475.

24. Irvine F. Belser to Brown, May 24, 1954, Brown papers, Box 36, Folder 475.

25. Brown to Belser, May 27, 1954, Brown papers, Box 36, Folder 475.

26. Dissent, *Briggs v. Elliott,* 540.

27. Evermae B. Robertson to Brown, May 24, 1954, Brown papers, Box 36, Folder 475.

28. Clara Annie Childs to Brown, May 25, 1954, Brown papers, Box 36, Folder 475.

29. Quint, *Profile in Black and White,* 74–75.

30. Ibid., 83–84.

31. Ibid., 82.

32. "South Carolina," *Southern School News,* July 1954; "South Carolina," *Southern School News,* November 1954.

33. Quoted in "South Carolina," *Southern School News,* December 1954; Modjeska Simkins, "Column on Schools in South Carolina, January 25, 1947"; Modjeska Simkins Papers, Topical Papers, Journal and Guide, Norfolk, VA, Columns, January–May 1947. https://digital.tcl.sc.edu/digital/collection/mmsimkins/id/4123 (accessed August 5, 2019).

34. Quoted in Rowan, *Go South to Sorrow,* 87.

35. "South Carolina," *Southern School News,* September 3, 1954; Synnott, "Federalism Vindicated," 299; Quint, *Profile in Black and White,* 93; Synnott, "Desegregation in South Carolina," 57.

36. David W. Robinson to James F. Byrnes, July 13, 1954. Correspondence. DWR Papers.

37. Robinson to T. C. Callison and Robert McC. Figg, June 5, 1954. Correspondence. DWR Papers.

38. Ibid.; Callison to Robinson, June 11, 1954. Correspondence. DWR Papers.

39. Undated memorandum. Legal Memoranda, ca. 1954 . . . 1962–70. DWR Papers.

40. Memorandum—Re: Segregation, n.d. Legal Memoranda. DWR Papers.

41. "South Carolina," *Southern School News,* October 1954.

42. "South Carolina," *Southern School News,* February 1955; "South Carolina," *Southern School News,* April 1955. Waring quotation from Rowan, *Go South to Sorrow,* 105. For a brief look at a variety of state laws passed to maintain segregation in the aftermath of *Brown,* see Bardolph, *Civil Rights Record,* 373–93. Bardolph also covers in brief several civil rights cases from federal and state courts during the 1950s and 1960s.

43. "South Carolina," *Southern School News,* May 1955; "South Carolina," *Southern School News,* June 1955; Wolters, *Burden of Brown,* 143.

44. *Brown v. Board of Education,* 349 U.S. 294 (1955).

45. "Lower Court Decrees Mark Busy Month," *Southern School News,* August 1955.

46. "South Carolina," *Southern School News,* February 1955, quoted in Quint, *Profile in Black and White,* 95. Timmerman speech before a Joint Meeting of the Association of School Boards and Association of School Administrators, November 3, 1955, Brown papers, Box 36, Folder 476. Emphasis added.

47. "Resistance to Desegregation Is Increasing in South Carolina," *Southern School News,* September 1955.

48. Quoted in Wolters, *Burden of Brown,* 145.

49. Smyth, "Segregation in Charleston in the 1950s," 110–11.

50. "Marshall Cites Strategy," *Southern School News,* September 1955. The observer was William D. Workman, a correspondent for the *News and Courier* who went on to become the editor of *Columbia State* newspaper and South Carolina correspondent for the *Southern School News.*

51. Bartley, *Rise of Massive Resistance,* 92–94; McMillen, *Citizens' Council,* 74–80.

52. "Resistance to Desegregation Is Increasing in South Carolina"; Petition, 31 July 1955; Affidavit of Wilhelmenia Jones, August 30, 1955; Matthew D. McCollom (Orangeburg NAACP president) to Larry Wells (chair, Orangeburg District 5 Board of Trustees), September 6, 1955. DWR Papers, File Calhoun County/Orangeburg County *U.S.A. v Calhoun School District #2, U.S.A. v. Elloree School District #7* 1966, 1968–69; Quint, *Profile in Black and White,* 83–85.

53. "Citizens' Council Movement Is Spurred in South Carolina," *Southern School News,* October 1955; "'Clarendon Case' Figure Quits S.C. over Shooting Incident," *Southern School News,* November 1955; "Lines Sharply Drawn on School Question in South Carolina," *Southern School News,* December 1955. For more on the state's attacks on the NAACP, see Quint, *Profile in Black and White,* 60, 87–91; on Travelstead see also Rowan, *Go South to Sorrow,* 177–80.

54. "South Carolina Officials Stand Firm against Court Decree," *Southern School News,* July 1955.

55. J. M. Moorer to Edgar A. Brown, February 16, 1956, Brown papers, Box 36, Folder 476.

56. Southern Manifesto on Integration, from *Congressional Record, 84th Congress Second Session*, vol. 102, pt. 4, 4459–60. Washington, DC: Governmental Printing Office, 1956. http://www.pbs.org/wnet/supremecourt/rights/sources_document2.html (accessed August 4, 2015).

57. Joint Resolution, S. 514, South Carolina state legislature, Copy in Brown papers, Box 36, Folder 476, Special Collections. The full title of the resolution is "A Joint Resolution Condemning and Protesting the Usurpation and Encroachment on the Reserved Powers of the States by the Supreme Court of the United States, Calling upon the States and Congress to Prevent This and Other Encroachment by the Central Government and Declaring the Intention of South Carolina. To Exercise All Powers Reserved to It, to Protect Its Sovereignty and the Rights of Its People." *Acts and Joint Resolutions of the General Assembly of the State of South Carolina, Regular Session of 1956*. https://babel.hathitrust.org/cgi/pt?id=uc1.b3692994&view=1up&seq=7 (accessed May 8, 2020).

Chapter 4

1. *Flemming v. South Carolina Electric & Gas Company*, 128 F. Supp. 469, 470 (1955). Emphasis added. The case was appealed, and a three-judge panel of the Fourth Circuit (John J. Parker, Morris Ames Soper, and Armistead Mason Dobie) ruled that *Brown* and *Bolling v. Sharpe* (347 US 497) had abrogated *Plessy*. The appellate ruling is at 224 F.2d 752 (1955).

2. State of South Carolina, *Report of the State Commission of Forestry for the Year July 1, 1951 to June 30, 1952*. Columbia, SC, 1952, pp. 81–83. https://dc.statelibrary.sc.gov/bitstream/handle/10827/13881/SCFC_Annual_Report_1952.pdf?sequence=1&is Allowed=y (accessed May 12, 2019).

3. E. M. DeAli, "Seek Beach Resort on Coast for Race," *Lighthouse and Informer*, January 19, 1952.

4. M. E. Brown, "Civil Rights Activism in Charleston," 163, 174. Brown herself was instrumental as the named plaintiff in *Brown v. School District No. 20*, 226 F. Supp. 819 (1963), which desegregated public schools in Charleston and was the public-school desegregation suit that led to actual desegregation.

5. "South Carolina," *Southern School News*, April 7, 1955; Testimony for Plaintiffs at Trial, February 6, 1956; Donald B. Cooler to Mrs. Etta Clark, May 21, 1955. Exhibit P-1; Amended Complaint, July 22, 1955, p. 2. *Etta Clark, et al. v. C. H. Flory, et al.*, C/A 5082, Eastern District of South Carolina, Charleston Division, Record Group 21, NARA-SE. Hunting Island State Park is more than eighty miles from Charleston.

6. Defendants' Answer, August 17, 1955. *Clark v. Flory*, C/A 5082. While not the subject of this work, *Plessy*'s separation of civic versus social equality citing *Strauder v. West Virginia* does not acknowledge that the latter decision made no such distinction. The Court in *Strauder* asserted that the Fourteenth Amendment "was designed to assure to the colored race the enjoyment of all the civil rights that, under the law, are enjoyed by white persons, and to give to that race the protection of the general government in that enjoyment whenever it should be denied by the States" and that when discriminatory laws were enacted, it placed a "brand" upon Black citizens. "It not only gave

citizenship and the privileges of citizenship to persons of color, but it denied to any State the power to withhold from them the equal protection of the laws." *Strauder v. West Virginia,* 100 U.S. 303, 306 (1880).

7. Defendants' Answer, August 17, 1955. *Clark v. Flory,* C/A 5082

8. Transcript of Hearing, August 23, 1955. *Clark v. Flory,* C/A 5082.

9. Ibid. The article to which Williams referred is F. P. Graham, "Need for Wisdom." On Graham see Link, "Frank Porter Graham."

10. Transcript of Hearing, August 23, 1955. *Clark v. Flory,* C/A 5082.

11. *Dawson v. Mayor and City Council of Baltimore City,* 220 F. 2d 386 (Court of Appeals, Fourth Circuit, 1955).

12. Testimony for Plaintiffs at Trial, February 6, 1956. *Clark v. Flory,* C/A 5082.

13. Ibid.

14. Ibid.

15. Ibid.

16. Ibid.

17. Transcript of Trial, February 6, 1956. *Clark v. Flory,* C/A 5082.

18. Edgar A. Brown to Fulton B. Creech, February 16, 1956, MSS 91, Brown papers, Box 36, Folder 476.

19. *Acts and Joint Resolutions of the General Assembly of South Carolina,* 1956, Section 14, pp. 1955–56.

20. Ashton H. Williams to John H. Wrighten, W. Newton Pough, T. C. Callison, and James S. Verner, March 2, 1956. *Clark v. Flory,* C/A 5082.

21. Wrighten to Williams, March 5, 1956. *Clark v. Flory,* C/A 5082.

22. Transcript of Hearing, March 21, 1956. *Clark v. Flory,* C/A 5082.

23. "Edisto Park Case Action Is Deferred Indefinitely," *Columbia State,* March 22, 1956.

24. Katie Vloet, "Before Rosa Parks."

25. Philip Wittenberg to Arthur B. Caldwell, June 13, 1956; Arthur Caldwell to Warren Olney III, June 15, 1956; James M. Hinton to Herbert Brownell, August 10, 1956. File 144-67-183, Record Group 60, NARA.

26. "In the matter of the bus suit involving separate transportation facilities." Docket No. 9994, Order No. 10120, Public Service Commission of South Carolina. File 144-67-183, RG 60, NARA.

27. *Browder v. Gayle,* 142 F. Supp. 707 (1956); *Gayle v. Browder,* 352 U.S. 903 (1956). See Currie, "Before Rosa Parks."

28. *Columbia State,* February 9, 1956.

29. An Act to Make Unlawful the Employment by the State, School District or any County or Municipality Thereof of Any Member of the National Association for the Advancement of Colored People, and to Provide Penalties for Violations. R. 819, H. 1998. Approved March 17, 1956. *Acts and Joint Resolutions of S.C.* 1956. pp. 1747–49.

30. *Columbia State,* March 22, 1956.

31. H. 2100. A Concurrent Resolution Requesting the Attorney General of the United States to Place the National Association for the Advancement of Colored People on the Subversive List for Reasons Set Forth Herein. *Journal of the Senate of the Second Session of the 91st General Assembly of the State of South Carolina,* 1956, 387–88.

32. *Columbia State,* February 23, 1956.

33. Synnott, "Federalism Vindicated," 301–2.

34. South Carolina Code of Laws, 1957 Supplement, § 21-230(9).

35. J. Edgar Hoover to Assistant Chief of Staff for Intelligence, Department of the Army, File 144-67-182, RG 60, NARA.

36. Quint, 51.

37. Quint, Profile *in Black and White,* 51–54; Bartley, *Rise of Massive Resistance,* 230. Bartley also covers the state's attempts to undermine academic freedom at Allen University and Benedict College (ibid., 231–32). Gordon, "Boycotts Can Cut Two Ways." On the counter-boycott by Black citizens in Clarendon and Elloree, see Carmen V. Harris, "'You're Just Like Mules,'" 257–60.

38. "Little Major Activity Reported in South Carolina during Month," *Southern School News,* July 1956.

39. Lewis McMillan, for example, was fired for publishing a book, *Negro Higher Education in the State of South Carolina,* in 1952. South Carolina State president Benner C. Turner said, according to McMillan's account, "Now, Doctor, the policy of the administration—that is, of the president is to forbid any member of the staff to vilify the College or any sister institution in the State. If your book is of such a character, your case will be brought before the Trustee Board for action. Remember, now, Doctor McMillan, that you have a good job here at the College." "Negro Historian Fired for Attack on South Carolina College System," *Harvard Crimson,* June 17, 1954. http://www.thecrimson.com/article/1954/6/17/negro-historian-fired-for-attack-on/ (accessed August 24, 2015).

40. Report of Special Agent E. Fleming Mason, October 25, 1955, File 144-67-46, Box 1378, RG 60, NARA. Quotation from letter, R. A. De Laine to J. Edgar Hoover, October 13, 1955, quoted on p. 18. Gona, *Dawn of Desegregation,* 167–89. Timmerman quotation from "US Won't Arrest Carolina Pastor," *New York Times,* November 4, 1955.

41. Quint, *Profile in Black and White,* 36, 40–41. Memorandum, J. Edgar Hoover to Assistant Attorney General William F. Tompkins, July 26, 1957. File 144-67-223, Box 1386, RG 60, NARA.

42. Complaint, *Bryan v. Austin,* Civil Action Number 5792, RG 21, NARA-SE.

43. Ibid.

44. Answer, *Bryan v. Austin,* C/A 5792.

45. Ibid.

46. Ibid.

47. Memorandum of Points and Authorities, *Bryan v. Austin,* C/A 5792. *Wieman* v. *Updegraff,* 344 U.S. 183 (1952); *Slochower* v. *Board of Higher Education,* 350 U.S. 551 (1956). In the quotation from *Slochower,* the emphasis was added by Marshall.

48. Memorandum of Points and Authorities. *Bryan v. Austin,* C/A 5792. Excerpt from Frankfurter's opinion in *Wieman* from pp. 195–96 of that case.

49. *American Sugar Refining Co. v. Louisiana,* 179 US 89, 92 (1900); *Kotch v. River Port Pilot Commissioners,* 330 US 552, 556 (1947). Cited by Marshall in Memorandum of Points and Authorities, *Bryan v. Austin,* C/A 5792.

50. *Cummings v. Missouri,* 4 Wall 277 (1867); *Ex Parte Garland,* 4 Wall 333 (1866).

51. *United States v. Lovett*, 328 U.S. 303, 315–16. Cited by Marshall in Memorandum of Points and Authorities. *Bryan v. Austin*, C/A 5792.

52. Quoted in "Two S.C. Lawsuits Hold Spotlight during Month," *Southern School News*, November 1956. Brackets in article.

53. "New Legislation on Schools, Court Tests Occupy South Carolina," *Southern School News*, February 1957.

54. "S.C. Legislature Weights More School Bills, Repeals Earlier One," *Southern School News*, May 1957; Bartley, *Rise of Massive Resistance*, 217–18; Tushnet, *Making Civil Rights Law*, 293.

55. J. Edgar Hoover to Assistant Chief of Staff for Intelligence, US Army, September 27, 1957, File 144-67-223, Box 1386, RG 60, NARA.

56. "Two S.C. Lawsuits Hold Spotlight During Month."

57. "New Legislation on Schools, Court Tests Occupy South Carolina"; "S.C. Legislature Passes New Act Aimed at NAACP," *Southern School News*, March 1957; "S.C. Legislature Acts to Strengthen Resistance to Desegregation," *Southern School News*, April 1957; "NAACP Certified; Attorney General Sees Check-Rein," *Southern School News*, March 1959. See also Murphy, "South Counterattacks," 374–76, for South Carolina's and other states' laws on barratry and other matters pertaining to bringing lawsuits.

58. For an extensive contemporary analysis of anti-NAACP laws throughout the South, see Murphy, "South Counterattacks." For Alabama see Tushnet, *Making Civil Rights Law*, 283–89.

59. *Congressional Record*, April 15, 1959, pp. 1427–28. Copy in Brown papers, MSS 91, Box 15, Folder 200. Gressette, in addition to being chair of the state segregation committee, was chair of the state Senate Judiciary Committee. McNair was chair of the state House equivalent, while Pope was chair of the state Democratic Party.

60. The federal judges in question were George Bell Timmerman Sr., Ashton H. Williams, and Charles Cecil Wyche. Julius Waties Waring had entered senior status in 1952. Born in 1885, Wyche was nominated to the bench in 1937 by Franklin Roosevelt. He was serving as the US attorney for South Carolina's Western District at the time. He served until 1967. Williams was born in 1891, was nominated to the bench by Harry S. Truman in 1952, and served until his death in 1962. https://www.fjc.gov/history/courts/u.s.-district-courts-districts-south-carolina-judges-all-districts (accessed July 15, 2019).

Chapter 5

1. Motion hearing, September 14, 1960. *Richard B. Henry v. Greenville Airport Commission, et al.*, C/A 2491, Western District of South Carolina, Greenville Division, RG 21, Records of the District Courts of the United States, NARA-SE.

2. Proceedings of Hearing, July 20, 1959. *Henry v. Greenville Airport Commission*, C/A 2491.

3. Ibid.

4. *Plessy v. Ferguson*, 163 US 537 551 (1896).

5. Proceedings of Hearing, July 20, 1959. *Henry v. Greenville Airport Commission*, C/A 2491.

6. For example, *Williams v. Howard Johnson* (268 F.2d 845 [1959]), in which a three-judge panel of the Fourth Circuit admitted that the customs of the people of a state do not constitute state action.

7. Proceedings of Hearing, July 20, 1959. *Henry v. Greenville Airport Commission*, C/A 2491.

8. "Negroes Ask Reassignment in Clarendon's Schools," *Southern School News*, September 1959. While Henry's appeal was pending, another incident brought national attention to the Greenville Airport. Jackie Robinson, the great baseball player, was in Greenville to address the state convention of the NAACP in October 1959, and while there he traveled through the airport. At the airport Robinson was escorted out of the White waiting room and made to wait in the colored waiting area. By December the Department of Justice had become interested in the Robinson case and was "making a preliminary investigation." "Clarendon Reassignment Petitions Rejected; Officials Say Too Late," *Southern School News*, November 1959; "Clarendon County Action May Be Renewed in Courts," *Southern School News*, December 1959. See Robinson's op-ed in the "Afro Magazine" section of the *Baltimore Afro-American*, November 10, 1959.

9. George Bell Timmerman Sr. to Lincoln Jenkins, July 12, 1960. *Henry v. Greenville Airport Commission*, C/A 8009. U.S. District Court, Greenville Division. RG 276, Records of the US Courts of Appeal; Fourth Circuit; Richmond, VA. Box 672. NARA-MA.

10. Motion Hearing, September 14, 1960, Testimony of Richard Henry. *Henry v. Greenville Airport Commission*, C/A 2491.

11. Motion Hearing, September 14, 1960. *Henry v. Greenville Airport Commission*, C/A 2491.

12. Motion Hearing, September 14, 1960, Testimony of Rev. J. S. Hall. *Henry v. Greenville Airport Commission*, C/A 2491.

13. *Henry v. Greenville Airport Commission*, 175 F. Supp. 343 (1959). Emphasis added.

14. *Henry v. Greenville Airport Commission*, 175 F. Supp. 347 (1959).

15. *Henry v. Greenville Airport Commission*, 175 F. Supp. 349–51 (1959).

16. *Henry v. Greenville Airport Commission*, 191 F. Supp. 146 (1961). Quotation from circuit court's opinion from *Henry v. Greenville Airport Commission*, 279 F. 2nd 751,752, emphasis added by Timmerman. See also the same case at 284 F. 2nd 631 (1960).

17. For a discussion of the waning role of NAACP attorneys in initiating litigation, see Tushnet, *Making Civil Rights Law*, 301–6.

18. "Demonstrations by Negro Groups Bring Legislative, Other Action," *Southern School News* 6:10 (April 1960): 4. "Cross burned at Benedict," *Baltimore Afro-American*, March 12, 1960, p. 8. "Negroes Batter Cars At White Drive-In At South Carolina City," *Ocala Star-Banner*, March 6, 1960, p. 14. The *Southern School News* reported the cross-burning as a hoax. Other papers could not confirm the burning, and some ignored that aspect altogether, choosing to focus on the attacks by Black students. For example, see "Negroes Batter Cars at Drive-in: Pre-dawn Violence Flares at Columbia, S.C." *New York Times*, March 6, 1960.

19. Brief for Plaintiff, August 27, 1962; Complaint, 30 June 1962. *Harvey B. Gantt v. The Clemson Agricultural College of South Carolina*, Civil Action Number 4101,

Western District of South Carolina, Anderson Division, Record Group 21, NARA-SE; Synnott, "Federalism Vindicated," 302–3. Other sources put the number at 189.

20. "Demonstrations by Negro Groups Bring Legislative, Other Action," *Southern School News,* April 1960, 5.

21. "Historical Markers Help Civil Rights Activists Make Better Memories," *Columbia Regional Business Report,* October 23, 2017.

22. *Anderson v. City of Greenville* (WD S.C., #2787), September 1, 1960. The case was dismissed as moot on September 19. *Civil Liberties Docket* 6, no. 1, November 1960. http://sunsite.berkeley.edu/meiklejohn/meik-6_1/meik-6_1-4.html#551.SC2b (accessed June 21, 2019).

23. George M. Eberhart, "The Greenville Eight: The Sit-in That Integrated the Greenville (SC) Library," *American Libraries Magazine,* June 1, 2017. https://american librariesmagazine.org/2017/06/01/greenville-eight-library-sit-in/.

24. Burke Marshall to Solicitor General [Lee Rankin], July 13, 1962. File 144-62, Box 1299, RG 60, NARA.

25. "First Negroes Admitted to Five Public Colleges," *Southern School News,* July 1962; United States Commission on Civil Rights, *Equal Protection of the Laws in Higher Education,* 50–96. South Carolina's status in 1960 is treated on pp. 82–84.

26. Brief for Plaintiff, August 27, 1962; Complaint, June 30, 1962. *Gantt v. Clemson,* C/A 4101; Synnott, "Federalism Vindicated," 302–3.

27. "Desegregation of Clemson College," Report of FBI, December 27, 1962, File 144-100-68-1, Box 1809, RG 60, NARA.

28. Affidavit of Harvey B. Gantt, June 30, 1962; Brief for Plaintiff, August 27, 1962. *Gantt v. Clemson,* C/A 4101.

29. Testimony, Hearing for Preliminary Injunction, August 22, 1962; Appellant's Appendix; Complaint, June 30, 1962. *Gantt v. Clemson,* C/A 4101.

30. Robert C. Edwards to Gov. E. F. Hollings, June 21, 1961; Harry C. Walker to Edwards, July 17, 1961; R. C. Edwards, memorandum to Clemson Board of Trustees, July 11, 1961. Clemson University Archives, Office of President R. C. Edwards, Correspondence 1959–1965, Folder 189. CUSC.

31. Answer, July 28, 1962, Exhibit P; quotation from Clemson attorney in Brief for Plaintiff. *Gantt v. Clemson,* C/A 4101.

32. Testimony, Hearing for Preliminary Injunction, August 22, 1962; Appellant's Appendix; Complaint, June 30, 1962. *Gantt v. Clemson,* C/A 4101.

33. Ibid.

34. Minutes of the Meeting of the Board of Trustees of the Clemson Agricultural College, June 18, 1948. https://tigerprints.clemson.edu/cgi/viewcontent.cgi?article=1431 &context=trustees_minutes (accessed August 6, 2019).

35. Testimony, Hearing for Preliminary Injunction, August 22, 1962, Appellant's Appendix; Opinion and Order, September 6, 1962, Appellant's Appendix. *Gantt v. Clemson,* C/A 4101; Edgar Brown to Charles F. Young, October 2, 1962. Brown papers, Folder L399.

36. Edwards to Charles L. Horn, James O. Wynn, and Ralph Clark, 15 October 1962. Clemson University Archives, Office of President R. C. Edwards, Correspondence 1959–1965, Folder 190. CUSC.

37. "Judge Orders Speed in Clemson Suit," *Southern School News,* December 1962; Charles S. Wickenberg, "Judge Says Gantt Case Won't Cover All Others," *Columbia State,* November 20, 1962. Vickery had been director of admissions when the first Black applicants tried to get into Clemson in 1948.

38. "Judge Wyche Promises Ruling in Clemson Case by January," *Southern School News,* December 1962; Edgar A. Brown to Charles Fielding Young, November 28, 1962. Brown papers, Folder L398.

39. J. Herbert Nelson to Matthew Perry, September 15, 1960, and Mary Elizabeth Norris et al. to Perry, June 16, 1961. *J. Arthur Brown, et al. v. South Carolina State Forestry Commission, et al.,* C/A AC-774, Eastern District of South Carolina, Columbia Division, RG 21, NARA-SE.

40. Deposition of Harold White; Deposition of Mary Nesbitt. *Brown v. State Forestry Commission,* C/A AC-774.

41. Deposition of Jerrivoch C. Jefferson. *Brown v. State Forestry Commission,* C/A AC-774.

42. Deposition of Sam Leverette. *Brown v. State Forestry Commission,* C/A AC-774.

43. Penn Community Service, Inc., "Public Parks and Recreational Facilities: A Study in Transition," p. 2. Records of the South Carolina Council on Human Relations, South Caroliniana Library, Columbia.

44. Deposition of J. Arthur Brown. *Brown v. State Forestry Commission,* C/A AC-774.

45. Eugene B. Sloan, "State Parks Ordered Integrated," *Columbia State,* July 11, 1963; *Brown v. South Carolina State Forestry Commission,* 226 F. Supp. 646, 650 (1963).

46. Report of the State Commission of Forestry for July 1, 1963, to June 30, 1964, John R. Tiller, State Forester, in *Reports and Resolutions of South Carolina for Fiscal Year Ending June 30, 1964 to the General Assembly of the State of South Carolina for the Regular Session Commencing January 12, 1965,* 23; Marion A. Wright, *Public Parks and Recreational Facilities: A Study in Transition* (Frogmore, SC: Penn Community Service, 1963) 3, 7.

47. Transcript of Motion Hearing, Testimony of J. Roy Gibson; Depositions, Testimony of Classie Rae Walker; Depositions, Testimony of James Allen Carter. *Classie Rae Walker, et al. v. Gerald W. Shaw, et al.,* C/A 2983, RG 21, NARA-SE.

48. Complaint and Answer. *Walker v. Shaw,* C/A 2983. Quotations from pp. 5 and 2, respectively.

49. Depositions, Testimony of Mary Elizabeth Norris. *Walker v. Shaw,* C/A 2983.

50. Opinion and Order, October 17, 1962. p. 3. *Walker v. Shaw,* C/A 2983.

51. *Rackley v. Board of Trustees of Orangeburg Hospital,* No. 8731. November 9, 1962. Box 726, RG 276, NARA-MA.

52. E. H. Beardsley, "Good-Bye to Jim Crow," 368–71.

53. Letters from Chapman J. Milling Jr., Librarian to F. C. James, E. M. Miller, and B. T. Williams, September 4, 1962, Plaintiffs' Exhibit A. *James v. Carnegie Public Library,* C/A AC-1163, RG 21, NARA-SE.

54. Answer, n.d. (filed June 25, 1963); Notice to Plaintiffs, n.d. (filed July 5, 1963); and Order, November 25, 1964. *James v. Carnegie Public Library,* C/A AC-1163.

55. Lofton, "Calm and Exemplary," 76–81.

56. Ibid., 379–81. Toomey quoted on p. 381. Of course, Beardsley's interview with Toomey took place in 1979, so there are issues of selective memory and genuine forgetfulness to consider. On Daniel see "Over There and Back at Home, Charlie Daniel Marched for Change," *Greenville (SC) Journal*, December 15, 2016. https://greenville journal.com/2016/12/15/back-home-charlie-daniel-marched-change/. On Greenville's business community, see O'Neill, "Memory, History, and the Desegregation of Greenville."

57. Joseph O. Rogers (attorney for the district) to David W. Robinson, August 28, 1959; Lincoln Jenkins to M. L. Marvin (member of board of trustees), October 8, 1959; Robinson to Marion Gressette, Joseph O. Rogers, and Charles Plowden, September 1, 1959, and enclosed form letter. DWR Papers, *Miller v. Clarendon 2*.

58. Jenkins to Marvin, October 8, 1959; Rogers to Robinson, October 12; anon. to Jenkins (template or copy), October 16, 1959; Gressette to Rogers, October 17, 1959. DWR Papers, *Miller v. Clarendon 2*.

59. Complaint, filed April 13, 1960. DWR Papers, File *Brunson v. Clarendon School District #1*, 1958, 1960, 1962–70.

60. Motion to Strike, May 2, 1960; Order, May 31, 1962, *Brunson v. Clarendon School District #1*. DWR Papers, File *Brunson v. Clarendon School District #1*, 1958, 1960, 1962–70; "Lull in Legal Action Ends; 2 Suits Filed," *Southern School News*, June 1962; "Negroes to Appeal Wyche Ruling in Clarendon Suit," *Southern School News*, July 1962.

61. "Massive Boycott Underscores Demands for Improved Schools," *Southern School News*, November 1960.

62. "Thurmond Renamed to U.S. Senate Seat," *Southern School News*, July 1960.

63. "Massive Boycott Underscores Demands for Improved Schools," *Southern School News*, November 1960. See Baker, *Paradoxes of Desegregation*, 142–46.

64. Requests for Transfer, n.d.; Thomas A. Carrere (Superintendent of Charleston City Schools) to J. Arthur Brown, October 21, 1960; Request for transfer, May 1, 1961. DWR Papers, File Charleston County *Brown v. Charleston School District #20/Johnson v. Charleston School District #20, 1960–66, 1968–69*. Answer, Appellant's Appendix, p. 13; Opinion and Order, August 22, 1963, p. 3. *Brown v. Charleston*, C/A 7210.

65. No title: the document is a report of the Special Committee of the Board of Trustees of School District No. 20 regarding the requests for transfer of six students in the district, July 29, 1961. DWR Papers, File Charleston County *Brown v. Charleston School District #20/ Johnson v. Charleston School District #20, 1960–66, 1968–69*.

66. Ibid.; "Negro Transfer Requests Opposed in Charleston," *Southern School News*, December 1961. There is a bit of confusion in the chronology. The sources in the Robinson papers indicate that the hearings with the parents and children took place in July, but the *Southern School News* reports that they took place on November 21 after the requests were rejected in July. At any rate a final decision by the county board had yet to be made, though it was highly unlikely that the board would grant the transfers.

67. "Lull in Legal Action Ends; 2 Suits Filed"; "Public Schools Mark First Peaceful Year," *Southern School News*, June 1962.

68. "South Carolina Figures Hint Favor for 'Flexibility,'" *Southern School News*, January 1962.

69. "Officials React Adversely to Aid Withdrawal Threat," *Southern School News,* April 1962.

70. "Lull in Legal Action Ends; 2 Suits Filed"; Complaint, *Stanley v. Darlington County School District* (referred to hereafter as *Stanley v. Darlington*). DWR Papers, File Darlington County.

71. Brief and Appendix for Appellees Motion to Dismiss Appeal, September 1962. DWR Papers, File *Brunson v. Clarendon School District #1,* 1958, 1960, 1962–70.

72. Ibid.

73. Plaintiffs' Brief, *Brunson v. Board of Trustees,* 22 January 1963. DWR Papers, File *Brunson v. Clarendon School District #1,* 1958, 1960, 1962–70.

74. "Baptist Convention Asks College to Delay Planned Desegregation," *Southern School News,* December 1963.

75. "School Desegregation Suit Draws Officials' Answer," *Columbia State,* April 17, 1964. *Adams, et al. v. School District Number 5, Orangeburg County, South Carolina.* Civil Action No. 8301. DWR Papers, Desegregation Files, 1954–74. File Orangeburg County, *Adams v. Orangeburg.* Orangeburg's District 5 consisted of the city of Orangeburg itself. Hereafter I will refer to the case as *Adams v. Orangeburg* and the file as DWR Papers, Orangeburg County.

Chapter 6

1. Edwards to Clemson Board of Trustees, January 17, 18, and 19, 1963. R. C. Edwards, Correspondence 1959–65, Folder 191. CUSC.

2. Statement of Senator L. Marion Gressette, Chairman, South Carolina School Committee, January 23, 1963. R. C. Edwards, Folder 191; Agenda of Board of Trustees Meeting, January 24, 1963. R. C. Edwards, Correspondence 1959–65, Folder 191. CUSC.

3. Charles H. Wickenberg, "Clemson's Attorneys Will Try Last Legal Resort on Monday," *Columbia State,* January 20, 1963.

4. William Watkins to Robert C. Edwards, January 25, 1963. Brown papers, Folder L397.

5. "Alabama Leader: Another Oxford," *Christian Science Monitor,* October 2, 1962, p. 7.

6. "Alabama Leader: Another Oxford," *Christian Science Monitor,* October 2, 1962.

7. McMillan, "Integratation with Dignity," 20–21.

8. For example, "High Marks for South Carolina," Los Angeles Times, January 30, 1963, said that Gantt's matriculation at Clemson was "marked by decency and dignity." The *Louisville Courier-Journal,* in a piece titled "Clemson and Tulane Show the Way" on the same date on its editorial page, remarked on the "dignity and order" with which Clemson desegregated.

9. Miller, "Raised for Activism." Late in the evening of August 26, 1963, a bomb exploded in the front yard of Dr. H. D. Monteith, Henrie's uncle who lived about two hundred yards from her house, leaving a crater a foot deep and five feet long and shattering windows.

10. Lesesne, *History of the University of South Carolina,* 149.

11. "State Senators Attack Plan To Build On-Base Schools," *Southern School News* (March 1963): 16.

12. Ron Wenzell, "Winthrop College Admits 1st Negro," *Columbia State*, July 21, 1964; "Winthrop Registers 2 Negroes," *Columbia State*, September 17, 1964.

13. "USC Acknowledges Admission Denied Because of Race," *Southern School News*, July 1963; "State Baptists to Consider Desegregation of Furman," *Southern School News*, November 1963; "Baptist Convention Asks College to Delay Planned Desegregation," *Southern School News*, December 1963; Tollison, "Moral Imperative and Financial Practicality," 88–124.

14. "Negro Girl Applies at Lander College," *Columbia State*, May 14, 1964.

15. "North Charleston Plans Fully Voluntary Action," *Southern School News*, July 1964; "Methodist College Registers Negro," *Southern School News*, September 1964; "15 Districts Desegregate, All But Four Voluntarily," *Southern School News*, September 1964; "Segregation-Desegregation Status [table]," *Southern School News*, December 1964; "State Baptists Vote Against College Desegregation," *Southern School News*, December 1964; "Furman to Defy Baptist Vote Against Desegregation," *Southern School News*, January 1965. On Milliken's offer to cover the shortfall in donations, see Wechsler, *Qualified Student*, 320.

16. "Baptist Convention Asks College to Delay Planned Desegregation."

17. "Paper Attacks 'Marginal Mixing,'" *Southern School News*, January 1965.

18. Synnott, "Federalism Vindicated," 292–93.

19. Newby, *Black Carolinians*, 330; Cox, "1963—The Year of Decision."

20. "General Assembly Completes Session without Enacting New School Laws," *Southern School News*, June 1959.

21. George McMillan, "Integration with Dignity," *Saturday Evening Post*, March 16, 1963.

22. *Report of the State Commission on Forestry for 1964*, 23–26; 111 Race Relations Law Reporter 1578, 1579; South Carolina Code of Laws, 1966, Section 51-2.5.

23. See, for example, "The Birmingham Campaign," Black Culture Connection, PBS. http://www.pbs.org/black-culture/explore/civil-rights-movement-birmingham -campaign/ (accessed July 14, 2019).

24. Richard Reid, "The Gloria Rackley-Blackwell Story," *Orangeburg (SC) Times and Democrat*, February 22, 2011. https://thetandd.com/the-gloria-rackley-blackwell -story/article_356cbc9e-3e10-11e0-883e-001cc4c03286.html.

25. Transcript of Trial, Testimony of Gloria Rackley Fraser, September 2, 1965. *Rackley v. School* District 5, C/A 8458. Record Group 21, NARA-SE.

26. Transcript of Trial, Testimony of Gloria Rackley Fraser, September 2, 1965, 23 ff. *Rackley v. School District 5*, C/A 8458.

27. Ibid. For the "jail-no-bail" approach, see "Rock Hill Sit-ins and Jail-No-Bail," SNCC Digital Gateway, SNCC Legacy Project and Duke University, https://snccdigital .org/events/rock-hill-sit-ins-and-jail-no-bail/ (accessed July 14, 2019). For a contemporary account of events in Rock Hill, see "The Student Protest Movement: A Recapitulation," Special Report of the Southern Regional Council, September 1961, 10.

28. Defendants' Brief, *Rackley v. Orangeburg*, C/A 8458.

29. Testimony of Harris Marshall. *Rackley v. School District 5*, C/A 8458.

30. Defendants' Brief. *Rackley v. School District 5*, C/A 8458. Emphasis added.

31. *Washington Afro-American*, October 29, 1963.

32. Eugene B. Sloan, "Orangeburg Has First Civil Rights Challenge," *Columbia State*, July 30, 1964; Resolution of the Board of Directors of Orangeburg Theatres, Inc., August 31, 1964, *C. H. Thomas, et al. v. Orangeburg Theatres, Inc.*, C/A 8421, RG 21, NARA-SE.

33. Transcript of Trial, Testimony of Gloria Rackley Fraser, September 2, 1965. *Rackley v. School District 5*, C/A 8458.

34. Ibid. For Marshall's attitude on school closing, see the *Spartanburg (SC) Herald*, May 21, 1964.

35. Testimony in Reply for Plaintiff, Testimony of Rackley. *Rackley v. School District 5*, C/A 8458.

36. *Rackley v. School District Number 5, Orangeburg County, S.C.*, 258 F. Supp. 676 (1966).

37. See Felder, *Civil Rights in South Carolina*, chap. 18.

38. Complaint. *Irene Williams v. Sumter School District Number 2, et al.*, C/A AC-1534, RG 21, NARA-SE.

39. Brief in Behalf of Defendants; Deposition of Benjamin Robinson. *Williams v. Sumter School District Number 2*, C/A AC-1534.

40. Complaint. *Irene Williams v. Sumter School District Number 2, et al.*, C/A AC-1534, RG 21, NARA-SE.

41. Plaintiff's exhibits. *Williams v. Sumter School District Number 2*, C/A AC-1534.

42. Brief in Behalf of Defendants; Deposition of Pitts Delorme. *Williams v. Sumter School District Number 2*, C/A AC-1534.

43. Brief in Behalf of Defendants. *Williams v. Sumter School District Number 2*, C/A AC-1534; *Sarratt v. Cash*, 88 S.E. 256 (1916).

44. Opinion of Judge Robert W. Hemphill; Plaintiff's Exhibit 9, Transcript of June 16, 1964 Sumter County School Board Meeting. *Williams v. Sumter School District Number 2*, C/A AC-1534.

45. Opinion of Judge Robert W. Hemphill. *Williams v. Sumter School District Number 2*, C/A AC-1534. Quotation from *Willa Johnson v. Joseph Branch*, 364 F. 2d 177 (1966).

46. Opinion. *Williams v. Sumter School District Number 2*, C/A AC-1534.

47. Synnott, "Federalism Vindicated," 292–93; "Proposed Tuition-Grants Plan Arouses Heavy Debate," *Southern School News*, May 1963.

48. *Brunson et al. v. Board of Trustees of School District No. 1 of Clarendon County, et al.*, 311 F.2d 107 (4th Cir. 1962).

49. *Brown v. School Dist. 20* and *Stanley v. Darlington Co. School Dist. No. 1*.

50. "USC Acknowledges Admission Denied Because of Race," *Southern School News*, July 1963; "Greenville Rejects Transfers," *Southern School News*, September 1963; "Sumter County Faces Lawsuit by Negro Airman," *Southern School News*, October 1963, 16. On Shaw Airfield see Owens, "G.I. Joe v. Jim Crow," 112–36.

51. "Address by Governor Ernest F. Hollings to the General Assembly of South

Carolina, January 9, 1963," 38, South Carolina State Library Digital Collections https://dc.statelibrary.sc.gov/bitstream/handle/10827/672/State_of_the_State_Address_1963-1-9.pdf?sequence=1&isAllowed=y (accessed May 21, 2019).

52. "Segregation-by-Sex Proposal Voted Down by State Senate," *Southern School News*, May 1963.

53. *Columbia State*, August 21, 1955. Quoted in Wolters, *Burden of Brown*, 145.

54. For a detailed analysis of the impact of scientific racism on *Brown v. Board*, see Jackson, *Science for Segregation*.

55. Newby, *Challenge to the Court*, 65. For material on Kilpatrick and the citizens' councils, see ibid., 183. See also McMillen, *Citizens' Council*, 159–88, for more on the pro-segregation argument, especially the scientific justifications for segregation.

56. Newby, *Challenge to the Court*, 191–97. For a complete analysis of the *Stell* case, see ibid., 191–212. See Newby, *Development of Segregationist Thought*, 146–53, for excerpts from the Pleas and Answers to Intervenors and the Brief and Argument of Intervenors in the *Stell* case.

57. *Stell v. Savannah-Chatham County Board of Education*, 220 F. Supp. 667 (1963). *Ralph Stell et al., Appellants, v. Savannah-Chatham County Board of Education et al., Appellees*, 318 F.2d 425 (1963). Motion to Intervene and Proposed Answer of Intervenors, Appellant's Appendix. *Brown v. Charleston*, C/A No. 7210.

58. Answer. *Brown v. Charleston*. Appendix of Appellants. *Charleston v. Brown*, United States Court of Appeals, Fourth Circuit, No. 9216; see also Wolters, *Burden of Brown*, 145–46. Emphasis in the quotation is added.

59. Answer. *Brown v. Charleston*. Appendix of Appellants, pp. 16–17. *Charleston v. Brown*, United States Court of Appeals, Fourth Circuit, No. 9216.

60. Answer. *Brown v. Charleston*. Appendix of Appellants, pp. 18–19. *Charleston v. Brown*, United States Court of Appeals, Fourth Circuit, No. 9216.

61. "Schools Quietly Desegregated in Charleston; First in State," *Southern School News*, September 1963.

62. See Garrett, "SPSSI and Racial Differences," in which Garrett argues that "the evidence for Negro-White equality in intelligence under comparable conditions —far from being overwhelming—is not even moderately convincing." Abstract, https://psycnet.apa.org/record/2005-11891-003 (accessed July 14, 2019). For additional background, see Zuberi and Bonilla-Silva, *White Logic, White Methods*, especially the essay by William H. Tucker, "To Win the War: Racial Research and the Pioneer Fund," 283–94.

63. "Schools Quietly Desegregated in Charleston; First in State"; Wolters, *Burden of Brown*, 146–47. Garrett quoted on p. 146.

64. Garrett, "Equalitarian Dogma," 480. Journalist John Lear observed in an opinion piece in *New Scientist* that the issue of *Perspectives* would "become a weapon in the hands of White extremists." *New Scientist*, 11 (1961): 340.

65. Augustus T. Graydon, "A Plan in Regard to the Integration Push in the Public Schools of South Carolina," August 22, 1963. DWR Papers. File Achievement Testing 1963.

66. Ibid.

67. Ibid.

68. Augustus T. Graydon, "Memorandum on Testing as a Method of Achieving Some Measure of Racial Segregation in Public Schools," n.d. DWR Papers. File Achievement Testing 1963. On Wilson, see Owens, "G.I. Joe v. Jim Crow," 125–8.

69. Opinion and Order, *Brown v. Charleston,* August 22, 1963. DWR papers, File Charleston County *Brown v. Charleston School District #20/ Johnson v. Charleston School District #20,* 1960–66, 1968–69. For a contemporary academic take on freedom of choice, see R. W. Brown, "Freedom of Choice in the South."

70. Opinion and Order, *Brown v. Charleston,* August 22, 1963. DWR papers, File Charleston County *Brown v. Charleston School District #20/ Johnson v. Charleston School District #20,* 1960–66, 1968–69.

71. Final Draft of Intervenors'—Appellants' Portion of Brief in the United States Court of Appeals for the Fourth Circuit, n.d. DWR papers, File Charleston County *Brown v. Charleston School District #20/ Johnson v. Charleston School District #20,* 1960–66, 1968–69.

72. Ibid.

73. Ibid. "Charleston Holds Segregation Aids Negroes; Appeal Rejected," *Southern School News,* February 1964.

74. "Hearings Begin on Darlington County Desegregation," *Southern School News,* January 1964.

75. United States Commission on Civil Rights, "Public Education," 188–89.

76. Answer, *Adams v. Orangeburg,* April 11, 1964. DWR papers, File Orangeburg County.

77. Ibid.

78. Pleas and Answer of Intervenors, filed April 22, 1964. *Adams v. Orangeburg,* DWR papers, File Orangeburg County.

79. Transcript of Pretrial Conference, July 14, 1964, *Adams v. Orangeburg.* DWR papers, File Orangeburg County.

80. Ibid.

81. *Randall v. Sumter School District 2,* C/A 1240. RG 21, NARA-SE.

82. Thomas N. McLean, "U.S. Sues Sumter School District," *Columbia State,* July 8, 1964; "Darlington County Gets Orders to Admit Negroes with Whites," *Southern School News,* August 1964.

83. "School Quietly Desegregated in Charleston; First in State," *Southern School News,* September 1963; Wolters, *Burden of Brown,* 149.

84. "Darlington County Gets Orders to Admit Negroes with Whites"; "Orangeburg's Private School Plan Continues," *Columbia State,* July 2, 1964; "Private or Public School?" *Columbia State,* July 15, 1964.

85. *Evers v. Jackson Municipal Separate School District,* 232 F. Supp. 241 (1964).

86. "Summary Judgments Asked in Two Lawsuits," *Southern School News,* June 1964.

87. "Desegregation Suit Filed against Orangeburg County," *Southern School News,* April 1964; "Greenville Desegregation Set for Next September," *Southern School News,* May 1964; Opinion and Order, April 27, 1964, *Whittenberg v. School District of Greenville County,* Civil Action No. 4396. DWR Papers, Folder Greenville County: School System Review, *Whittenberg v. Greenville,* 1961, 1964.

88. "Darlington County Gets Orders to Admit Negroes with Whites"; United States Commission on Civil Rights, "Public Education," 189–90.

89. "Thurmond Calls Off-Limits Order 'Raw Blackmail,'" *Detroit Free Press,* July 28, 1963.

90. "North Charleston Board Sets Up State's First All-Voluntary Plan," *Southern School News,* July 1964.

91. "Strongest Civil-Rights Bill Becomes Law," *Southern School News,* July 1964. See also P. W. McNeill, "School Desegregation in South Carolina," 19.

92. Opinion and Order, *Stanley v. Darlington.* DWR Papers, Darlington County.

93. Plaintiffs' Motion to Vacate or Amend and Plaintiffs' Objections to Plan, *Stanley v. Darlington.* DWR Papers, Darlington County.

94. "Desegregation Plan Attacked by Negroes," *Columbia State,* July 29, 1964.

95. Mont Morton, "City Schools to Consider Applications," *Columbia State,* August 19, 1964; "4 Negroes Admitted in Oconee," *Columbia State,* August 20, 1964.

96. "15 Districts Desegregate, All But Four Voluntarily"; "Segregation-Desegregation Status [table]"; "State Baptists Vote Against College Desegregation."

97. "Transfer Plan Attacked by Negro Attorneys," *Southern School News,* September 1964; Plaintiffs' Motion to Vacate or Amend and Plaintiffs' Objections to Plan, August 20, 1964, *Adams v. Orangeburg.* DWR Papers, Orangeburg County.

98. "Supreme Court Rejects Ethnic Difference Plea," *Southern School News,* November 1964.

99. Robinson to Gressette, October 13, 1964. DWR Papers, Correspondence.

100. *Newman v. Piggie Park Enterprises, Inc.,* 256 F. Supp. 941, 944, 947 (1966); William B. Williams, "FBI Gets Complaint from Local Negro," *Columbia State,* July 10, 1964.

101. Cortner, *Civil Rights and Public Accommodations.*

102. *Newman v. Piggie Park Enterprises, Inc.,* 256 F. Supp. 941, 945 (1966), 377 F. 2d 433, 435–36 (1967).

103. "Civil Rights Bill: Little S.C. Opposition," *Columbia State,* July 10, 1964.

Chapter 7

1. *Watson v. City of Memphis,* 373 US 526 (1963). Note, however, that the Court did not overrule its own opinion in *Brown II.*

2. United States Commission on Civil Rights, "Nondiscrimination in Federally-Assisted Programs"; United States Commission on Civil Rights, *Survey of School Desegregation,* describes the requirements of the desegregation plans on pp. 20–22. https://archive.org/details/surveyofschooldeoounit/page/n13 (accessed July 22, 2019).

3. *Rogers v. Paul,* 382 US 198 (1965).

4. *Singleton v. Jackson Municipal Separate School District,* 355 F. 2d 865 (1966).

5. "Officials Stirred by Guidelines," *Southern School News,* May 1965; "Gov. Russell Criticizes Return of District Desegregation Plans," *Southern School News,* April 1965; *Stanley v. Darlington County School District,* 9 Race Rel L Rep 1293 (1964).

6. "Gov. Russell Criticizes Return of District Desegregation Plans"; *Survey of School Desegregation, 1965–66,* 30; Southern Regional Council, "School Desegregation

1966—The Slow Undoing," December 1966, 3–13. https://files.eric.ed.gov/fulltext/EDo 19345.pdf (accessed August 8, 2019).

7. "Almost All Districts May Be Desegregated in September," *Southern School News,* May 1965.

8. "Schoolmen Struggle to Comply with Civil Rights Act," *Southern School News,* June 1965.

9. "Official Says Form Calls for Full Desegregation," *Southern School News,* February 1965. On the football game, see P. W. McNeill, "School Desegregation in South Carolina," 62. There were at least two St. John's High Schools in South Carolina at the time, one in Charleston County, the other in Darlington County. The latter school is the more likely St. John's involved in the football game's cancellation.

10. *Regents of the University of California v. Bakke,* 438 U.S. 265, 407 (1978), additional opinion of Justice Harry Blackmun.

11. "Desegregation," *Southern Education Report,* July–August 1965; Jim Leeson, "Desegregation," *Southern Education Report,* September–October 1965, 32.

12. Plaintiffs' Motion to Vacate or Amend and Plaintiffs' Objections to Plan, August 28, 1965. DWR Papers, Desegregation Files, 1954–74. File *Brunson v. Clarendon School District #1* 1958, 1960, 1962–70.

13. Answer, *Miller v. Clarendon* 22, September 8, 1965. DWR Papers, Clarendon County.

14. Order Fixing Times and Dates of Hearings. *In re Barbour County Board of Education, et al.,* September 10, 1965; Supplemental Order Fixing Times and Places of Hearings, In *re Barbour County Board of Education, et al.,* September 17, 1965; Francis Keppel to J. P. Dufford, (received) September 20, 1965; Gressette to Robinson, September 22, 1965. DWR Papers, Desegregation Files, 1954–74. File Calhoun County/Orangeburg County *U.S.A. v Calhoun School District #2, U.S.A. v. Elloree School District #7,* 1966, 1968–69.

15. Leeson, "Desegregation," 32. Status of Compliance, November 8, 1965 (table); Leeson, "Desegregation: Faster Pace, Scarcer Records," *Southern Education Report,* January–February 1966, 30–31 (tables 2 and 3).

16. Department of Health, Education, and Welfare, "Revised Statement of Policies for School Desegregation Plans: Under Title VI of the Civil Rights Act of 1964, December 1966, as Amended for the School Year 1967–68," various pages. Department of Health, Education, and Welfare, "Guidelines for School Desegregation: Hearings before the Special Subcommittee on Civil Rights of the Committee on the Judiciary, House of Representatives, Eighty-Ninth Congress, Second Session," A55–58.

17. Robinson to Gressette, September 23, 1965; Return, *In re Cameron School District No. 2.,* October 1, 1965. DWR Papers, Calhoun County/Orangeburg County.

18. *Survey of School Desegregation, 1965–66,* 45–46.

19. "Guidelines for School Desegregation," December 14–16, 1966; "Slow Undoing," 3–19.

20. *Survey of School Desegregation, 1965–66,* 1.

21. "Slow Undoing," 2–5.

22. Ibid., 3.

23. William E. Rone Jr., "Integration Plan Dismissed by Judge," *Columbia State*, April 25, 1966.

24. Plaintiff-Intervenor's Trial Brief, March 10, 1966, referring to transcript of trial conference, testimony of Weldon. DWR Papers, Clarendon County. The case in question was *Miller v. School District Number 2, Clarendon Co., SC* 256 F. Supp. 370 (1966).

25. W. E. Durant to W. H. Weldon, March 2, 1966 (two letters of that date). The amounts were $1,023,279.71 for the Black schools and $671,950.33 for the White schools; Plaintiff-Intervenor's Trial Brief, March 10, 1966. DWR Papers, Clarendon County.

26. Plan for Pupil Assignment, Transfer and Re-assignment in Compliance with Civil Rights Act of 1964 for School District Number 2, Clarendon County, South Carolina, n.d., adopted March 3, 1966; Memorandum for the Defendants, filed March 25, 1966. DWR Papers, Desegregation Files, 1954–74. DWR Papers, Clarendon County.

27. Motion for a Rehearing, for the Amending of the Court's Findings and Conclusions, and for the Amending of the Judgment, *Miller v. Clarendon 2*, April 28, 1966. DWR Papers, Clarendon County.

28. Order, *Miller v. Clarendon 2*, filed June 14, 1966, DWR Papers, Clarendon County. Emphasis added. *Miller v. School District Number 2, Clarendon County, SC*, 253 F. Supp. 552.

29. John Doar to F. O. Hutto, May 2, 1966; Robinson to Gressette, May 10, 1966. DWR Papers, Calhoun County/Orangeburg County.

30. The Supreme Court, in *Brown II*, was more specific: "Problems related to administration, arising from the physical condition of the school plant, the school transportation system, personnel, revision of school districts and attendance areas into compact units to achieve a system of determining admission to the public schools on a nonracial basis, and revision of local laws and regulations which may be necessary in solving the foregoing problems" were all considerations that lower courts could take into account. *Brown v. Board of Education*, 349 US 294, 300–301 (1955).

31. Order, *Miller v. Clarendon*, filed June 14, 1966. DWR Papers, Clarendon County.

32. Report of School District Number 2, Clarendon County, to United States District Court Pursuant to Order of the Court Dated June 14, 1966, n.d. (enclosed with Petition, August 3, 1966). DWR Papers, Clarendon County. According to the Defendants' Reply to Comments of Plaintiff-Intervenors, n.d., the one Black student whose request was denied was actually granted his first choice. The transfer to a White school was his second choice.

33. David S. Seeley, Assistant Commissioner, Equal Ed Opportunities Program, to Joseph Rogers, December 12, 1966; Rogers to Seeley, December 14, 1966. DWR Papers, Clarendon County.

34. Answers to Interrogatories, *Brown v. Charleston*, June 17, 1966; Clark to Robinson. DWR Papers, Desegregation Files, 1954–74. File Charleston County *Brown v. Charleston School District #20/ Johnson v. Charleston School District #20*, 1960–66, 1968–69.

35. P. W. McNeill, "School Desegregation in South Carolina," 48.

36. Jim Leeson, "Desegregation: Guidelines and a New Count," *Southern Education Report* January–February 1967, 31 (table 2), 32; Jim Leeson, "Desegregation: The

Pace Quickens in the South," and accompanying table: Rate of Desegregation Versus Rise in Negro Enrollment, *Southern Education Report,* April 1967, 35. Southern Education Reporting Service, *Statistical Summary,* 28.

37. P. W. McNeill, "School Desegregation in South Carolina," 41–43; *Whittenberg v. Greenville, Brown v. Charleston,* and *Stanley v. Darlington,* 12 Race Rel L Rep 268 (1966).

38. Brief of Defendants on Motion to Dismiss Amicus Curiae and in Reply to Amicus Curiae Brief, *Stanley v. Darlington;* Answers to Defendants' Interrogatories, *Stanley v. Darlington.* DWR Papers, Desegregation Files, 1954–74. File Darlington County: *Stanley v. Darlington, USA v. Darlington County Board of Education,* 1958, 1961–69.

39. P. W. McNeill, "School Desegregation in South Carolina," 41–43. *Whittenberg v. Greenville, Brown v. Charleston,* and *Stanley v. Darlington,* 12 Race Rel L Rep 268, 276–80 (1966).

40. P. W. McNeill, "School Desegregation in South Carolina," 56.

41. Answers to Interrogatories, July 25, 1967, DWR Papers, Clarendon County.

42. Order, *Brunson v. Board of Trustees,* February 20 or 28, 1967; Modified School Desegregation Plan, *Brunson v. Board of Trustees.* DWR Papers, *Brunson v. Clarendon School District #1.*

43. Order, *Miller v. Clarendon,* n. d. [March 24, 1967]. DWR Papers, Clarendon County.

44. W. J. Clark to David W. Robinson, September 5, 1968. DWR Papers, Orangeburg County. The numbers were 3,837 parents in favor of freedom of choice, 501 parents in favor of zoning. At the all-Black schools, the percentages were 82.1 to 17.9 in favor of freedom of choice, while at the (minimally) integrated schools, the percentages were 95.7 to 4.3 in favor of freedom of choice.

45. *Green v. County Sch. Bd. of New Kent County,* 391 US 438, 437, 441; Wolters, *Burden of Brown,* 156–58.

46. Complaint [as plaintiff-intervenors in *Stanley v. Darlington*], *U.S. v. Darlington County School District,* filed April 15, 1968; Benny Greer to Peter Libassi (Director of the Office for Civil Rights in HEW), February 14, 1968. DWR Papers, Darlington County.

47. Answer, *Stanley v. Darlington,* May 3, 1968, pp. 2–3. DWR Papers, Darlington County. See section 407 of the Civil Rights Act of 1964, Suits by the Attorney General, for more information on the restrictions on governmental authority to "achieve a racial balance in any school by requiring the transportation of pupils or students from one school . . . or school district to another."

48. Answers to Interrogatories Propounded by the Plaintiff, August 1, 1968. DWR Papers, *Brunson v. Clarendon School District #1;* Wolters, *Burden of Brown,* 159–60.

49. Order, *Whittenberg v. Greenville,* September 13, 1968. DWR Papers, *Brunson v. Clarendon School District #1.*

50. Those districts were Anderson 3, Barnwell 29, Calhoun 1 and 2, Dillon 2 and 3, Georgetown County, Hampton 1, Lancaster County, Laurens 56, and Saluda County. *Whittenberg v. Greenville County School District,* 298 F. Supp. 784, 794 (1969).

51. Augustus Graydon to David W. Robinson, December 4, 1968; Graydon to J. P. Dufford (Superintendent, Cameron Public Schools), December 4, 1968; Graydon

to Dufford, January 21, 1969; Graydon to M. G. Austin (Superintendent, Elloree Public Schools), December 4, 1968; Graydon to Klyde Robinson, November 7, 1968. DWR Papers, Calhoun County/Orangeburg County. The new administration, of course, was the Nixon administration, which came to power using the Southern Strategy, which appealed to the racial prejudices and fears of the White South. Strom Thurmond, a Republican for four years at that time, endorsed Nixon and may have expected a quid pro quo.

52. School Enrollment Plan for Elloree District for 1969–70, *U.S. v. Elloree School District Number 7 Orangeburg County, South Carolina;* Plaintiffs' Objections to Defendants' School Enrollment Plan for 1969–70. *U.S. v. Elloree School District Number 7 Orangeburg County, South Carolina,* January 29, 1969. DWR Papers, Calhoun County/ Orangeburg County.

53. Interim Order, *U.S. v. School District Number Two, Calhoun County, South Carolina,* September 1968. DWR Papers, Calhoun County/Orangeburg County.

54. *U.S. v. School District Number Two, Calhoun County, South Carolina.* Desegregation Plan for 1969–70, n.d; Plaintiff's Objections to Defendants' Desegregation Plan for 1969–70. *U.S. v. Calhoun 2;* Graydon to Dufford, September 17, 1968; Graydon to Judge Donald Russell, September 19, 1968. DWR Papers, Calhoun County/Orangeburg County.

55. Return of the School District to the Order of September 13, 1968. *Brunson v. Board.* DWR Papers, *Brunson v. Clarendon School District #1.*

56. Ibid.

57. Plaintiffs' Memorandum in Opposition to Defendants' Plan, February 20, 1969, *Brunson v. Board.* DWR Papers, *Brunson v. Clarendon School District #1.*

58. Status Report of School Desegregation in South Carolina, March 27, 1969, Report of Program Officers OE, EEO, Title IV: Pretrial Conference of School Districts under Order of Court; Status Report on School Desegregation in South Carolina, 1964–65, 1969. DWR Papers, Desegregation Files, 1954–74; File Compliance, *Civil Rights Act of 1964—Title VI Court Orders.* The twelve districts were Charleston 20 (since integrated into the county); Clarendon 1, 2, and 3; Darlington; Dorchester 2 and 3; Greenville; Lexington 1; Orangeburg 5 and 7; and Sumter 2.

59. Graydon to Robinson, May 19, 1969; Graydon to Leon Panetta, May 19, 1969. DWR Papers, Calhoun County/Orangeburg County. Panetta at the time was director of the Civil Rights Office in HEW.

60. Plaintiff Intervenor's Motion for Supplemental Relief, n.d.; Return, n.d.; Rogers to Robinson, January 11, 1969. DWR Papers, Clarendon County.

61. Response to Plan of Desegregation Submitted by the United States Office of Education, n.d., Exhibit A, Proposed Decree. DWR Papers, Clarendon County.

62. Motion for a Rehearing, for Relief from Order or, in the Alternative, for an Amendment of the Order of the Court, *Stanley v. Darlington,* April 3, 1969; Greer to Judge Martin, May 30, 1969. DWR Papers, Darlington County; Robinson to Sidney B. Jones (attorney for Dorchester County), May 14, 1969. DWR Papers, Desegregation Files, 1954–74. File Dorchester County, *USA v. Dorchester District 1, DeLee v. Dorchester District 3, Dorchester District 2,* 1969.

63. Petition and Supporting Memorandum, June 3, 1969, *Brunson v. Board;* Robinson to Simons, October 28, 1969; Response to Plan of Desegregation Submitted by

the United States Office of Education, n.d. *Brunson v. Board*. DWR Papers, *Brunson v. Clarendon School District #1*.

64. Order, *Miller v. Clarendon Two*, July 23, 1969. DWR Papers, Clarendon County. Emphasis added.

65. Marion S. Riggs to Robert W. Hemphill, August 21, 1969; Order, July 23, 1969. DWR Papers, Clarendon County.

66. Order, July 23, 1969. DWR Papers, Clarendon County.

67. Substitute Plan, filed November 7, 1969; Robinson to Marion S. Riggs, July 24, 1969; Robinson to Riggs, August 12, 1969; Robinson to Riggs, September 12, 1969; Robinson to Riggs, October 7, 1969; Plaintiff's Opposition to Plan of Desegregation Submitted by Defendant, n.d. DWR Papers, Clarendon County.

68. H. A. Roberts to Robinson, September 8, 1969; Motion for Immediate Relief, n.d., *Brunson v. Board*. DWR Papers, *Brunson v. Clarendon School District #1*.

69. Robinson to Roberts, November 25, 1969. DWR Papers, *Brunson v. Clarendon School District #1*.

70. Robinson to Roberts, January 22, 1970. DWR Papers, *Brunson v. Clarendon School District #1*; Motion for Immediate Relief; Riggs to Robinson, February 3, 1970; Robinson to Riggs, February 5, 1970. DWR Papers, Clarendon County.

71. Order, July 18, 1969. *Brunson v. Board*, 3. DWR Papers, *Brunson v. Clarendon School District #1*.

72. *Brunson v. Clarendon School District #1*. DWR Papers, *Brunson v. Clarendon School District #1*.

73. W. J. Clark to Jesse Jordan, July 7, 1969. DWR Papers, File Orangeburg County. The Nixon administration also funded almost $5 million in grants to school districts, the Office of Technical Assistance, or to the Desegregation Consulting Center for making the transition to unitary districts.

74. Order, August 8, 1969, *Adams v. Orangeburg*. DWR Papers, Orangeburg County.

75. Desegregation Plan, October 15, 1969, *Adams v. Orangeburg*. DWR Papers, Orangeburg County.

76. Brief of Amicus Curiae, August[?] 1970, *Adams v. Orangeburg*. DWR Papers, Orangeburg County. Emphasis in original.

77. Ibid.

78. Robinson to Robert Mardian, March 31, 1970; Robinson to Roberts, March 31, 1970; Robinson to Roberts, April 9, 1970; Mardian to Robinson, April 15, 1970. DWR Papers, *Brunson v. Clarendon School District #1*.

79. P. W. McNeill, "School Desegregation in South Carolina," 74–78. Quotation on p. 77.

80. Order, March 6, 1970. *Brunson v. Board*, Brief of Appellants, May 1970, *Brunson v. Board*, quoting sections 401 and 407 of the Civil Rights Act of 1964. DWR Papers, *Brunson v. Clarendon School District #1*; Robinson to Riggs, April 6, 1970. DWR Papers, Clarendon County.

81. Brief for Appellees, n.d. (filed May 25, 1970), *Brunson v. Board*. DWR Papers, *Brunson v. Clarendon School District #1*.

82. L. B. Rivers, Mazie Solomon, and Annie Gibson to Omega F. Newman, May 13, 1970. DWR Papers, Clarendon County.

83. Application for an Extension of Time within Which to File a Petition for Writ of Certiorari; Order Extending Time to File a Petition for Writ of Certiorari. DWR Papers, *Brunson v. Clarendon School District #1*.

84. Petition, September 17, 1970; Riggs to Robinson, September 16, 1970; Robinson to Riggs, September 17, 1970. DWR Papers, Clarendon County.

85. P. W. McNeill, "School Desegregation in South Carolina," 71, 84. Quotation on p. 79.

86. Ibid.

87. W. D. Workman Jr., "The Decision and the Demands," *Southern Education Report*, June 1969, 18, 21. Workman was one of the leaders of the renascent Republican Party in South Carolina, running for US Senate in the early 1960s and governor in the early 1980s. The quotation from *Plessy* is at 163 US 537, 551.

88. Memorandum, Robinson to Gressette Committee, April 1970. DWR Papers, Desegregation Files, 1954–74. File Legal Memoranda. Robinson to Mardian, April 20, 1970. DWR Papers, Desegregation Files, 1954–74. File Correspondence.

89. Robinson to Charles N. Plowden, September 11, 1970; Roberts to Robinson, May 30, 1970; Roberts to Robinson, September 18, 1970; Robinson to Hon. J. Braxton Craven, August 16, 1974. DWR Papers, Correspondence; Wolters, *Burden of Brown*, 165.

Chapter 8

1. *United States v. Medical Society of South Carolina*, 298 F. Supp. 145. 147–48 (1969). This refers to the so-called New Roper Hospital. Old Roper, closed in 1957 (eleven years after New Roper opened its doors), had been the primary institution for Charleston's Black population needing hospital care. Since New Roper opened, however, Black patients had come to be cared for at three other hospitals in the area, one of them Black-owned.

2. Beardsley, "Good-Bye Jim Crow," 383–84; *United States v. Medical Society of South Carolina*, 298 F. Supp. 145, 148 (1969).

3. *United States v. Medical Society of South Carolina*, 298 F. Supp. 145, 149–51 (1969).

4. Beardsley, "Good-Bye Jim Crow," 383–84.

5. Even as late as 1979, state law listed nearly two dozen crimes for which conviction would exclude someone from voting. Those crimes ranged from adultery to murder and rape. See Underwood, *Constitution of South Carolina*, 115–19. South Carolina and other states in the former Confederacy remained under the preclearance requirement of the Voting Rights Act until the 2013 case of *Shelby County v. Holder*, 570 US 529 (2013). For the 1969 debate regarding extending the Voting Rights Act, which Strom Thurmond vigorously opposed, see Berman, *Give Us the Ballot*, 83–85.

6. On at-large elections and other means of undermining Black votes in South Carolina particularly, see Davidson, *Quiet Revolution in the South*, 201–2.

7. Edgar, *South Carolina*, 541–42, 563.

8. Ibid., 560–62.

9. *Palmetto Education Association, Inc., et al. v. School District Number 1, Clarendon County, South Carolina, et al.*, 12 Race Rel L Rep 2025 (1968).

10. *United States v. State of South Carolina*, 445 F. Supp. 1094, 1102, 1109 (1977).

11. Edgar, *South Carolina*, 544. See also Bass, "White Violence in Lamar."

12. Jim Leeson, "Private Schools for Whites Face Some Hurdles," *Southern Education Report*, November 1967, 15 (table).

13. State Department of Education, "School Directory for South Carolina," 1954–55, 197–99; 1964–65, 154–58; 1971–72, 143–50; Southern Education Foundation, "History of Private Schools."

14. Quoted in Leeson, "Private Schools for Whites Face Some Hurdles," 16.

15. Ibid., 13.

16. J. Egerton, *School Desegregation*, 21; United States Commission on Civil Rights, "School Desegregation in Williamsburg County," 10.

17. J. Egerton, *School Desegregation*, 22–23. Quotation on p. 24.

18. *Whittenberg v. School District of Greenville County, South Carolina*, 607 F. Supp. 289 (D.C.S.C. 1985), quotation on p. 293.

19. Ibid., quotations on pp. 295–96, 304.

20. *Stanley v. Darlington County*, 879 F. Supp. 1341 (1995). Those seven areas were "1) Construction and closing of school facilities, including specifically the construction of St. John's High School, the construction of the career center in Darlington, the construction of several elementary schools in the Hartsville area, and the closing of Butler High School; 2) Inconsistencies in attendance zone lines between HEW Plan B and the attendance zones used by the District including the attendance zone boundaries between the Carolina and Washington Street Elementary Schools; 3) The assignment of residents in the Country Club Estates area to the school zone containing St. John's High School, Brunson-Dargan Junior High School and Spring Elementary School; 4) The boundary lines between St. John's Elementary School, St. John's High School and Brunson-Dargan Junior High School, and Brockington Elementary School, Pine Middle School and Mayo High School; 5) The system-wide assignment of principals; 6) The system-wide assignment of teachers; and 7) The locations of the program for the gifted and talented in the elementary grades."

21. *Abbeville County School District v. State of South Carolina*, Opinion No. 27466, November 12, 2014.

22. Bowers et al., "Minimally Adequate."

23. Edgar, *South Carolina*, 567.

24. Ibid., 538; Bursey, "Day the Flag Went Up."

25. See D. R. Egerton, *He Shall Go Out Free*, 105–12, and D. R. Egerton, "Long, Troubled History." Dylann Roof stated, after he was captured, that he chose Emanuel because of its historic nature. Glenn Smith, Jennifer Berry Hawes and Abigail Darlington, "Dylann Roof Says He Chose Charleston, Emanuel AME for Massacre Because They Were Historic, Meaningful," *Charleston Post and Courier*, December 9, 2016. https://www.postandcourier.com/church_shooting/dylann-roof-says-he-chose-charleston-emanuel-ame-for-massacre-because-they-were-historic-meaningful/article_6fab532c-be05-11e6-ab05-575a173993ee.html.

BIBLIOGRAPHY

Archival Collections, Government Documents, and Online Manuscript Resources

Acts and Joint Resolutions of the General Assembly of the State of South Carolina, Regular Session of 1956

American Folklife Center, Library of Congress

Briggs v. Elliott digital collection, University of South Carolina Digital Collections

Civil Rights Digital Library

Clemson University Archives, Clemson University Special Collections

Congressional Record

David W. Robinson Papers: Desegregation Files, South Carolina State Library

Edgar A. Brown Papers, Clemson University Special Collections

Federal Court Records (Record Group 21), National Archives-Southeast Region

Federal Court Records-Fourth Circuit (Record Group 276), National Archives-Mid-Atlantic Region

General Records of the Department of Justice (Record Group 60), National Archives, College Park, Maryland

J. Waties Waring Papers. Moorland-Spingarn Library, Howard University

James A. Byrnes Papers, Clemson University Special Collections

John Henry McCray papers, 1929–1989, University of South Carolina Digital Collections

Journal of the Senate of the Second Session of the 91st General Assembly of the State of South Carolina

Minutes of the Meeting of the Board of Trustees of the Clemson Agricultural College

Modjeska Simkins Papers, digital collection, University of South Carolina Digital Collections

NAACP Papers, Library of Congress (and on microfilm)

Records of the South Carolina Committee on Human Relations, South Caroliniana Library

Reports and Resolutions of South Carolina

SNCC Digital Gateway, SNCC Legacy Project and Duke University

South Carolina Code of Laws

South Carolina Constitution

South Carolina Digital Library

South Carolina State Library Digital Collections

Southern Education Foundation

Southern Regional Council

Statutes at Large of South Carolina
Strom Thurmond Collection, Clemson University Special Collections
Tiger Prints, Clemson University Libraries
University of South Carolina Digital Collections
United States Code

Newspapers and Contemporary Periodicals

Baltimore Afro-American
Christian Science Monitor
Columbia (SC) Regional Business Report
Columbia (SC) State
Detroit Free Press
Greenville (SC) Journal
Greenville (SC) News
Harvard Crimson
Lighthouse and Informer
Los Angeles Times
Louisville (KY) Courier-Journal
The New York Times
Ocala (FL) Star-Banner
Orangeburg (SC) Times and Democrat (Orangeburg, South Carolina; online)
Phoenix (AZ) Index
Southern Education Report
Southern School News
Spartanburg (SC) Herald
Washington Afro-American

Websites

Archive.org
American Psychological Association
Blackpast.org
Civil Liberties Docket (Berkeley.edu)
Eric.ed.gov
Fjc.gov (Federal Judicial Center)
Greenville Housing Authority
PBS.org
Smithsonian Institution, americanhistory.si.edu
South Carolina Encyclopedia Online
Thirteen.org (WNET)

Principal Cases (in chronological order)

U.S. v. Ellis 43 F. Supp. 321 (1942)
Thompson v. Gibbes 60 F. Supp. 872 (1945)
Elmore v. Rice 72 F. Supp. 516 (1947)
Wrighten v. Board of Trustees of the University of South Carolina 72 F. Supp. 948 (1947)

Pearson v. County Board of Education (1947)

Brown v. Baskin 78 F. Supp. 933 (1948); 80 F. Supp. 1017 (1948)

Shirer v. Anderson 88 F. Supp. 858 (1950)

Briggs v. Elliott 98 F. Supp. 529 (1951); 103 F. Supp. 920 (1952); 132 F. Supp. 776 (1955)

Flemming v. South Carolina Electric & Gas Company 128 F. Supp. 469 (1955); 224 F. 2d 752 (1955)

Clark v. Flory 141 F. Supp. 248 (1956)

Bryan v. Austin 148 F. Supp. 563 (1957)

Henry v. Greenville Airport Commission 175 F. Supp. 343 (1959); 191 F. Supp. 146 (1960)

Gantt v. Clemson Agricultural College of South Carolina 208 F. Supp 416 (1962); 213 F. Supp. 103 (1962)

Walker v. Shaw 209 F. Supp. 569 (1962)

Brown v. South Carolina State Forestry Commission 226 F. Supp. 646 (1963)

Brown v. School District 20, Charleston 226 F. Supp. 819 (1963)

Adams v. School District 5, Orangeburg Co. 232 F. Supp. 692 (1964)

James v. Carnegie Public Library 235 F. Supp. 911 (1964)

Stanley v. Darlington County School District No. 1 9 Race Rel L Rep 1293 (1964)

Randall v. Sumter School District 2 232 F. Supp. 786 (1964); 241 F. Supp 787 (1965)

Rackley v. Trustees of Orangeburg Regional Hospital 238 F. Supp. 512 (1965)

Thomas v. Orangeburg Theaters 241 F. Supp. 317 (1965)

Bradford v. School District 20 Charleston 244 F. Supp. 768 (1965)

Brunson v. Board of Trustees of School District 1 of Clarendon County 244 F. Supp. 859 (1965)

Thomas v. Orangeburg Theatres, Inc. 241 F. Supp. 317 (1965)

Miller v. School District 2 Clarendon County 253 F. Supp. 552 (1966); 256 F. Supp. 370 (1966)

Williams v. Sumter School District 2 255 F. Supp. 397 (1966)

Newman v. Piggie Park Enterprises, Inc. 256 F. Supp. 941 (1966)

Rackley v. School District 5 of Orangeburg County 258 F. Supp. 676 (1966)

United States v. Medical Society of South Carolina 298 F. Supp. 145 (1969)

Whittenberg v. School District of Greenville County 607 F. Supp. 289 (1985)

Other cases (in Alphabetical Order)

Abbeville County School District v. State of South Carolina Opinion No. 27466 (South Carolina Supreme Court)

Alexander v. Holmes County Board of Education 396 US 1218 (1969)

Alston v. School Board of the City of Norfolk 112 F. 2nd 992 (1940)

American Sugar Refining Co. v. Louisiana 179 US 89 (1900)

Anderson v. City of Greenville (WD S.C., #2787)

Bolling v. Sharpe 347 US 497 (1954)

Browder v. Gayle 142 F. Supp. 707 (1956); *Gayle v. Browder* 352 US 903 (1956)

Brown v. Board of Education 347 US 483 (1954); 349 US 294 (1955)

Civil Rights Cases 109 US 3 (1883)

Cummings v. Missouri 4 Wall 277 (1867)

Dawson v. Mayor and City Council of Baltimore City 220 F. 2d 386 (1955)

Dred Scott v. Sandford 60 US 393 (1857)

Evers v. Jackson Municipal Separate School District 232 F. Supp. 241 (1964)

Ex Parte Garland 4 Wall 333 (1866)

Green v. County School Board of New Kent County 391 US 430 (1968)

Grovey v. Townsend 295 US 45 (1935)

Heart of Atlanta Motel, Inc. v. United States 379 US 241 (1964)

Kotch v. River Port Pilot Commissioners 330 US 552 (1947)

McLaurin v. State Board of Regents 339 US 637 (1950)

Missouri ex. rel. Gaines v. Canada 305 US 337 (1938)

Newberry v. United States 256 US 232 (1921)

Nixon v. Condon 286 US 73 (1932)

Nixon v. Herndon 273 US 536 (1927)

Palmetto Education Association, Inc., et al. v. School District Number 1, Clarendon County, South Carolina, et al. 12 Race Rel L Rep 2025 (1968)

Pearson v. Murray 169 Md. 478 (1936)

Pettiford v. State Board of Education 62 S.E. 2d 780 (Supreme Court of South Carolina 1950)

Plessy v. Ferguson 163 US 537 (1896)

Prigg v. Pennsylvania 41 US 539 (1842)

Regents of the University of California v. Bakke 438 US 265 (1978)

Rogers v. Paul 382 US 198 (1965)

Sarratt v. Cash 103 S.C. 531 (Supreme Court of South Carolina 1916)

Shelby County v. Holder 570 US 529 (2013)

Singleton v. Jackson Municipal Separate School District 355 F. 2d 865 (1966)

Sipuel v. Board of Regents of the University of Oklahoma 332 US 631 (1948)

Slochower v. Board of Higher Education 350 US 551 (1956)

Smith v. Allwright 321 US 649 (1944)

State v. Hightower 221 SC 91 (Supreme Court of South Carolina 1952)

Stell v. Savannah Chatham County Board of Education 220 F. Supp. 667 (1963)

Strauder v. West Virginia 100 US 303 (1880)

Sweatt v. Painter 339 US 629 (1950)

United States v. Lovett 328 US 303

United States v. State of South Carolina 445 F. Supp. 1094 (1977)

U.S. v. Classic 313 US 299 (1941)

U.S. v. Elloree School District Number 7 283 F. Supp. 557 (D.S.C. 1968)

Watson v. City of Memphis 373 US 526 (1963)

Wieman v. Updegraff 344 US 183 (1952)

Willa Johnson v. Joseph Branch 364 F. 2d 177 (1966)

Williams v. Howard Johnson 268 F.2d 845 (1959)

Williams v. Mississippi 170 US 213 (1898)

Secondary Works and Contemporary Published Works

Aba-Mecha, Barbara Woods. "Black Woman Activist in Twentieth Century South Carolina: Modjeska Monteith Simkins." PhD diss., Emory University, 1978.

————. "South Carolina Conference of NAACP: Origin and Major Accomplishments, 1939–1954." *Proceedings of the South Carolina Historical Association* (1981): 1–21.

Ashmore, Harry S. *The Negro and the Schools,* with a foreword by Owen J. Roberts. Chapel Hill: University of North Carolina Press, 1954.

Baker, E. Bruce. *What Reconstruction Meant: Historical Memory in the American South.* Charlottesville: University of Virginia Press, 2007.

Baker, R. Scott. *Paradoxes of Desegregation: African American Struggles for Educational Equity in Charleston, South Carolina, 1926–1972.* Columbia: University of South Carolina Press, 2006.

Bardolph, Richard, ed. *The Civil Rights Record: Black Americans and the Law, 1849–1970.* New York: Crowell, 1970.

Bartley, Numan V. *The New South, 1945–1980.* A History of the South, vol. 11. Baton Rouge: Louisiana State University Press, 1995.

————. *The Rise of Massive Resistance: Race and Politics in the South during the 1950s.* Baton Rouge: Louisiana State University Press, 1969.

————, and Hugh D. Graham, *Southern Politics and the Second Reconstruction.* Baltimore: Johns Hopkins University Press, 1975.

Bass, Jack. *Unlikely Heroes.* New York: Simon & Schuster, 1981.

————. "White Violence in Lamar." *New Republic,* March 28, 1970, 10–12.

————, and Jack Nelson. *The Orangeburg Massacre.* 2nd edition. Macon, GA: Mercer University Press, 1984.

Bast, Kirk K. "'As Different as Heaven and Hell': The Desegregation of Clemson College." *Proceedings of the South Carolina Historical Association* (1994): 38–44.

Beardsley, E. H. "Good-Bye Jim Crow: The Desegregation of Southern Hospitals, 1945–1970." *Bulletin of the History of Medicine* 60 (1986): 367–86.

Bell, Derrick A. *Race, Racism, and American Law.* 2nd ed. Boston: Little, Brown, 1980.

Berman, Ari. *Give Us the Ballot: The Modern Struggle for Voting Rights in America.* New York: Farrar, Straus & Giroux, 2015.

Berry, Mary Frances. *Black Resistance, White Law: A History of Constitutional Racism in America.* New York: Appleton-Century-Crofts, 1971.

Blaustein, Albert P., and Clarence Clyde Ferguson, Jr. *Desegregation and the Law: The Meaning and Effect of the School Segregation Cases.* New Brunswick, NJ: Rutgers University Press, 1957.

Bloom, Jack M. *Class, Race, and the Civil Rights Movement.* Blacks in the Diaspora. Bloomington: Indiana University Press, 1987.

Blumberg, Rhoda Lois. *Civil Rights: The 1960s Freedom Struggle.* Boston: Twayne, 1984.

Borsos, John E. "Support for the National Democratic Party in South Carolina during the Dixiecrat Revolt of 1948." *Southern Historian* 9 (1988): 7–21.

Bowers, Paul, et al. "Minimally Adequate." *Charleston News and Courier,* November 14, 2018. https://data.postandcourier.com/saga/minimally-adequate/page/1.

Branch, Taylor. *Parting the Waters: America in the King Years, 1954–1963.* New York: Simon & Schuster, 1988.

————. *Pillar of Fire: America in the King Years, 1963–1965.* New York: Simon & Schuster, 1998.

Breathett, George. "Black Educators and the United States Supreme Court Decision of May 17, 1954." *Journal of Negro History* 68, no. 2 (1983): 201–8.

Brown, Millicent Ellison. "Civil Rights Activism in Charleston, South Carolina, 1940–1970." PhD diss., Florida State University, 1997.

———. "Wishin', Hopin', Prayin' and Votin': Black Charleston's Efforts to Merge Politics and Race, 1940–1970." Unpublished paper presented at the Citadel Conference on the Civil Rights Movement in South Carolina, March 2003.

Brown-Nagin, Tomiko. *Courage to Dissent: Atlanta and the Long History of the Civil Rights Movement.* New York: Oxford University Press, 2011.

Brown, Richard W. "Freedom of Choice in the South: A Constitutional Perspective." *Louisiana Law Review* 28 (1968): 455–68.

Bullock, Henry Allen. *A History of Negro Education in the South: From 1619 to the Present.* New York: Praeger, 1967.

Burke, W. Lewis. *All for Civil Rights: African American Lawyers in South Carolina, 1868–1968.* Athens: University of Georgia Press, 2017.

Burke, W. Lewis, and Belinda Gergel, eds. *Matthew J. Perry: The Man, His Times, and His Legacy.* Introduction by Randall L. Kennedy. Columbia: University of South Carolina Press, 2004.

Bursey, Brett. "The Day the Flag Went Up." *Point*, no. 97 (1999), http://www.scpronet.com/point/9909/p04.html.

Burton, Orville Vernon. "'The Black Squint of the Law': Racism in South Carolina." In *The Meaning of South Carolina History: Essays in Honor of George C. Rogers, Jr.,* edited by David R. Chesnutt and Clyde N. Wilson, 161–85. Columbia: University of South Carolina Press, 1991.

———, and Lewie Reece. "The Palmetto Revolution: School Desegregation in South Carolina." In *With All Deliberate Speed: Implementing* Brown v. Board of Education, edited by Brian J Daugherity and Charles C. Bolton, 59–92. Fayetteville: University of Arkansas Press, 2008.

Chafe, William H. *Civilities and Civil Rights: Greensboro, North Carolina, and the Black Struggle for Freedom.* New York: Oxford University Press, 1980.

Chappell, David L. *Inside Agitators: White Southerners in the Civil Rights Movement.* Baltimore: Johns Hopkins University Press, 1994.

Charron, Katherine Mellen. *Freedom's Teacher: The Life of Septima Clark.* Chapel Hill: University of North Carolina Press, 2009.

Chesler, Mark, Joseph Sanders, and Debra Kalmuss. *Social Science in Court: Mobilizing Experts in School Desegregation Cases.* Madison: University of Wisconsin Press, 1988.

"Civil Rights and the South: A Symposium." *North Carolina Law Review* 42 (1963): 1–178.

Clark, Septima Poinsette, with LeGette Blythe. *Echo in My Soul.* New York: Dutton, 1962.

Clement, Rufus E. "The Impact of the War upon Negro Graduate and Professional Schools," *Journal of Negro Education* 11, no. 3 (1942): 365–74.

Cohodas, Nadine. *Strom Thurmond and the Politics of Southern Change.* New York: Simon & Schuster, 1993.

Cortner, Richard C. *Civil Rights and Public Accommodations: The* Heart of Atlanta Motel *and* McClung *Cases*. Lawrence: University Press of Kansas, 2001.

Cotter, Patrick R. "Southern Reaction to the Second Reconstruction: The Case of South Carolina." *Western Political Quarterly* 34, no. 4 (1981): 543–51.

Cox, Maxie Myron. "1963—The Year of Decision: Desegregation in South Carolina." PhD diss., University of South Carolina, 1996.

Currie, Cameron McGowan. "Before Rosa Parks: The Case of Sarah Mae Flemming." In *Matthew J. Perry,* edited by W. Lewis Burke and Belina F. Gergel, 81–103. Columbia: University of South Carolina Press, 2004.

Davidson, Chandler. *Quiet Revolution in the South: The Impact of the Voting Rights Act, 1965–1990*. Princeton, NJ: Princeton University Press, 1994.

DeCosta, Frank A. "The Education of Negroes in South Carolina." *Journal of Negro Education* 16, no. 3 (1947): 405–16.

———. "Negro Higher and Professional Education in South Carolina." *Journal of Negro Education* 17, no. 3 (1948): 350–60.

Dittmer, John. *Local People: The Struggle for Civil Rights in Mississippi*. Blacks in the New World. Urbana: University of Illinois Press, 1994.

Dobrasko, Rebekah. "Upholding 'Separate but Equal': South Carolina's School Equalization Program, 1951–1955." MA thesis, University of South Carolina, 2005.

Donnelly, Karen. *Deacon Jones*. New York: Rosen, 2002.

Eagles, Charles W, ed. *The Civil Rights Movement in America*. Jackson: University Press of Mississippi, 1986.

———. *Outside Agitator: Jon Daniels and the Civil Rights Movement in Alabama*. Chapel Hill: University of North Carolina Press, 1993.

Eberhart, George M. "The Greenville Eight: The Sit-in That Integrated the Greenville (SC) Library." *American Libraries Magazine,* June 1, 2017. https://americanlibraries magazine.org/2017/06/01/greenville-eight-library-sit-in/.

Edgar, Walter. *South Carolina: A History*. Columbia: University of South Carolina Press, 1998.

Egerton, Douglas R. *He Shall Go Out Free: The Lives of Denmark Vesey,* rev. and updated ed. Lanham, MD: Rowman & Littlefield, 2004.

———. "The Long, Troubled History of Charleston's Emanuel AME Church." *New Republic,* June 18, 2015. https://newrepublic.com/article/122070/long-troubled-history -charlestons-emanuel-ame-church.

Egerton, John. *School Desegregation: A Report Card from the South*. Atlanta: Southern Regional Council, 1976.

———. *Speak Now against the Day: The Generation before the Civil Rights Movement in the South*. New York: Knopf, 1994.

Entin, Jonathan L. "*Sweatt v. Painter,* the End of Segregation, and the Transformation of Education Law." *Review of Litigation* 5 (1986): 3–71.

Eskew, Glenn Thomas. *But for Birmingham: The Local and National Movements in the Civil Rights Struggle*. Chapel Hill: University of North Carolina Press, 1997.

Fairclough, Adam. *Race and Democracy: The Civil Rights Struggle in Louisiana, 1915–1972*. Athens: University of Georgia Press, 1995.

Felder, James L. *Civil Rights in South Carolina: From Peaceful Protests to Groundbreaking Rulings.* Charleston, SC: History Press, 2012.

Finnegan, Terence Robert. "'At the Hands of Parties Unknown': Lynching in Mississippi and South Carolina, 1881–1940." PhD diss., University of Illinois at Urbana-Champaign, 1996.

Freyer, Tony. *The Little Rock Crisis: A Constitutional Interpretation.* Westport, CT: Greenwood, 1984.

Garrett, Henry E. "The Equalitarian Dogma." *Perspectives in Biology and Medicine* 4 (1961): 480–84.

———. "The SPSSI and Racial Differences." American Psychologist 17 (1962): 260–63.

Gates, Robbins. *The Making of Massive Resistance: Virginia's Politics of Public School Desegregation, 1945–1956.* Chapel Hill: University of North Carolina Press, 1984.

Glennon, Robert Jerome. "The Role of Law in the Civil Rights Movement: The Montgomery Bus Boycott, 1955–1957." *Law and History Review* 9 (1991): 59–112.

Goldfield, David R. *Black, White, and Southern: Race Relations and Southern Culture, 1940 to the Present.* Baton Rouge: Louisiana State University Press, 1990.

Gona, Ophelia De Laine. *Dawn of Desegregation: J. A. De Laine and Briggs v. Elliott.* Columbia: University of South Carolina Press, 2011.

Gordon, Asa H. *Sketches of Negro Life and History in South Carolina.* 2nd ed. Columbia: University of South Carolina Press, 1971. Originally published in 1929.

Gordon, William. "Boycotts Can Cut Two Ways." *New South* 11 (1956): 5–10.

Graham, Frank Porter. "The Need for Wisdom: Two Suggestions for Carrying Out the Supreme Court's Decision against Segregation." *Virginia Quarterly Review* 3 (1955): 192–212.

Graham, Hugh Davis. *Civil Rights and the Presidency: Race and Gender in American Politics, 1960–1972.* New York: Oxford University Press, 1992.

———. *The Civil Rights Era: Origins and Development of National Policy.* New York: Oxford University Press, 1990.

Greenberg, Jack. *Crusaders in the Courts: How a Dedicated Band of Lawyers Fought for the Civil Rights Revolution.* New York: Basic Books, 1994.

Greene, Robert. "South Carolina and the Legacy of the Civil Rights Movement." *Patterns of Prejudice* 49 (2015): 486–501.

Hall, Jacquelyn Dowd. "Broadening Our View of the Civil Rights Movement." *Chronicle of Higher Education,* July 27, 2001, B7–11.

———. "The Long Civil Rights Movement and the Political Uses of the Past." *Journal of American History* 91 (2005): 1233–63.

Hamilton, Charles V. *The Bench and the Ballot: Southern Federal Judges and Black Voters.* New York: Oxford University Press, 1973.

Harris, Carmen V. "'You're Just Like Mules, You Don't Know Your Own Strength': Rural South Carolina Blacks and the Emergence of the Civil Rights Struggle." In *Beyond Forty Acres and a Mule,* edited by Debra A. Reid and Evan P. Bennett, 254–70. Gainesville: University Press of Florida, 2012.

Hayes, Jack Irby, Jr. *South Carolina and the New Deal.* Columbia: University of South Carolina Press, 2001.

Hicks, Brian. *In Darkest South Carolina: J. Waties Waring and the Secret Plan That Sparked a Civil Rights Movement.* Charleston, SC: Evening Post Books, 2018.

Hine, Darlene Clark. *Black Victory: The Rise and Fall of the White Primary in Texas.* Millwood, NY: KTO, 1978.

Hine, William. *South Carolina State University: A Black Land-Grant College in Jim Crow America.* Columbia: University of South Carolina Press, 2018.

Hoffman, Edwin D. "The Genesis of the Modern Movement for Equal Rights in South Carolina, 1930–1939." *Journal of Negro History* 44, no. 3 (1959): 346–69.

Hollis, Daniel Walker. *University of South Carolina,* vol. 2, *College to University.* Columbia: University of South Carolina Press, 1956.

Horwitz, Morton J. *The Transformation of American Law, 1870–1960: The Crisis of Legal Orthodoxy.* New York: Oxford University Press, 1992.

Huff, Archie Vernon. *Greenville: The History of the City and County in the South Carolina Piedmont.* Columbia: University of South Carolina Press, 1995.

Ihle, Elizabeth. "The Teacher Salary Equalization Movement in Virginia: The NAACP and the Virginia State Teachers Association, 1935–1941." Unpublished paper delivered at the American Educational Research Association, New Orleans, 1994. https://archive.org/stream/ERIC_ED370193#page/n1/mode/2up.

Irons, Peter. *A People's History of the Supreme Court.* New York: Penguin, 1999.

Jackson, John P., Jr. *Science for Segregation: Race, Law, and the Case against Brown v. Board of Education.* New York: New York University Press, 2005.

Jacoway, Elizabeth, and Colburn, David R., eds. *Southern Businessmen and Desegregation.* Baton Rouge: Louisiana State University Press, 1982.

Johnston, Joyce. "Communism vs. Segregation: Evolution of the Committee to Investigate Communist Activities in South Carolina." *Proceedings of the South Carolina Historical Association* (1993): 19–29.

Jonas, Gilbert. *Freedom's Sword: The NAACP and the Struggle against Racism in America, 1909–1969.* New York: Routledge, 2005.

Jones-Branch, Cherisse. "'To Speak When and Where I Can': African American Women's Political Activism in South Carolina in the 1940s and 1950s." *South Carolina Historical Magazine* 107 (2006): 204–24.

Kato, Daniel. *Liberalizing Lynching: Building a New Racialized State.* New York: Oxford University Press, 2016.

Kelly, Alfred H., et al. *The American Constitution: Its Origins and Development,* vol. 2, 7th ed. New York: Norton, 1991.

Kelman, Mark. *A Guide to Critical Legal Studies.* Cambridge, MA: Harvard University Press, 1987.

Kennedy, Stetson. *Southern Exposure.* Garden City, NY: Doubleday, 1946.

Key, V. O., Jr. *Southern Politics in State and Nation.* New York: Vintage Books, 1949.

Kilpatrick, James Jackson. *The Southern Case for School Segregation.* New York: Crowell-Collier, 1962.

King, Martin Luther, Jr. *The Words of Martin Luther King, Jr.,* selected by Coretta Scott King. New York: Newmarket, 1983.

King, David B., and Quick, Charles W., eds. *Legal Aspects of the Civil Rights Movement.* Detroit: Wayne State University Press, 1965.

Kirk, John A. "The NAACP Campaign for Teachers' Salary Equalization: African American Women Educators And The Early Civil Rights Struggle." In "Documenting the NAACP's First Century," special issue, *Journal of African American History* 94, no. 4 (2009): 529–52.

Klarman, Michael J. *Brown v. Board of Education and the Civil Rights Movement.* New York: Oxford University Press, 2007.

———. *From Jim Crow to Civil Rights: The Supreme Court and the Struggle for Racial Equality.* New York: Oxford University Press, 2004.

Klinger, Jerry. "William B. Gibbs, Jr. (1905–1984)." *Black Past,* April 6, 2009. https://www.blackpast.org/african-american-history/william-b-gibbs-jr-1905–1984/.

Kluger, Richard. *Simple Justice: The History of* Brown v. Board of Education *and Black America's Struggle for Equality.* 1975; repr., New York: Vintage Books, 1977.

Kousser, J. Morgan. *The Shaping of Southern Politics: Suffrage Restriction and the Establishment of the One-Party South, 1880–1910.* New Haven, CT: Yale University Press, 1974.

Lau, Peter F. *Democracy Rising: South Carolina and the Fight for Black Equality since 1865.* Lexington: University Press of Kentucky, 2006.

———. "Mr. NAACP: Levi G. Byrd and the Remaking of the NAACP in State and Nation, 1917–1960." in Moore and Burton, *Toward the Meeting of the Waters,* 146–55.

Lawson, Steven F. *Black Ballots: Voting Rights in the South, 1944–1969.* New York: Columbia University Press, 1976.

———. *Running for Freedom: Civil Rights and Black Politics in America since 1941.* Philadelphia: Temple University Press, 1991.

Lesesne, Henry H. *A History of the University of South Carolina, 1940–2000.* Columbia: University of South Carolina Press, 2001.

Link, William A. "Frank Porter Graham, Racial Gradualism, and the Dilemmas of Southern Liberalism." *Journal of Southern History* 86 (2020): 7–36.

Lofton, Paul S., Jr. "Calm and Exemplary: Desegregation in Columbia, South Carolina." In *Southern Businessmen and Desegregation,* edited by Elizabeth Jacoway and David R. Colburn, 70–81. Baton Rouge: Louisiana State University Press, 1982.

Logan, Rayford W., ed. *The Attitude of the Southern White Press Toward Negro Suffrage, 1932–1940.* Washington, DC: Foundation, 1940.

Martin, John Bartlow. *The Deep South Says "Never."* New York: Ballantine Books, 1957.

McMillan, George. "Integration with Dignity." *Saturday Evening Post,* March 16, 1963, 15–21.

McMillen, Neil R. *The Citizens' Council: Organized Resistance to the Second Reconstruction, 1954–64.* Urbana: University of Illinois Press, 1971.

McNeil, Genna Rae. *Groundwork: Charles Hamilton Houston and the Struggle for Civil Rights.* Philadelphia: University of Pennsylvania Press, 1983.

McNeill, Paul Wesley. "School Desegregation in South Carolina, 1963–1970." EdD diss., University of Kentucky, 1979.

Miller, Rebecca L. "Raised for Activism: Henrie Monteith and the Desegregation of the University of South Carolina." *South Carolina Historical Magazine* 109 (2008): 121–47.

Moore, Alfred D., III. "Thorn in the Side of Segregation: The Short Life, Long Odds, and Legacy of the Law School at South Carolina State College." PhD diss., University of South Carolina, 2016.

Moore, Winfred B., Jr., and Orville Vernon Burton, eds. *Toward the Meeting of the Waters: Currents in the Civil Rights Movement of South Carolina during the Twentieth Century.* Columbia: University of South Carolina Press, 2008.

Morris, Aldon D. *The Origins of the Civil Rights Movement: Black Communities Organizing for Change.* New York: Free Press, 1984.

Murphy, Walter F. "The South Counterattacks: The Anti-NAACP Laws." *Western Political Quarterly* 12 (1959): 371–90.

Newby, I. A. *Black Carolinians: A History of Blacks in South Carolina from 1895 to 1968.* Columbia: University of South Carolina Press, 1973.

———. *Challenge to the Court: Social Scientists and the Defense of Segregation, 1954–1966,* rev. ed. Baton Rouge: Louisiana State University Press, 1969.

———, ed. *The Development of Segregationist Thought.* Homewood, IL: Dorsey, 1968.

———. *Jim Crow's Defense: Anti-Negro Thought in America, 1900–1930.* Baton Rouge: Louisiana State University Press, 1965.

O'Neill, Stephen. "Memory, History, and the Desegregation of Greenville, South Carolina." In Moore and Burton, *Toward the Meeting of the Waters,* 286–99.

Owens, Randall George. "G.I. Joe v. Jim Crow: Legal Battles over Off-Base School Segregation of Military Children in the American South, 1962–1964." PhD diss., University of South Carolina, 2016.

Payne, Charles M. *I've Got the Light of Freedom: The Organizing Tradition and the Mississippi Freedom Struggle.* Berkeley: University of California Press, 1995.

Peltason, J. W. *Fifty-Eight Lonely Men: Southern Federal Judges and School Desegregation.* Urbana: University of Illinois Press, 1961.

Pratt, Robert A. *The Color of Their Skin: Education and Race in Richmond, Virginia, 1954–89.* Charlottesville: University Press of Virginia, 1992.

Quint, Howard H. *Profile in Black and White: A Frank Portrait of South Carolina.* Washington, DC: Public Affairs Press, 1958.

Richards, Miles S. "The Eminent Lieutenant McKaine." *Proceedings of the South Carolina Historical Association* (1992): 46–54.

———. "The Progressive Democrats in Chicago, July 1944." *South Carolina Historical Magazine* 102 (2001): 219–37.

Rowan, Carl T. *Go South to Sorrow.* New York: Random House, 1957.

Sarat, Austin, ed. *Race, Law, and Culture: Reflections on Brown v. Board of Education.* New York: Oxford University Press, 1997.

Sarratt, Reed. *The Ordeal of Desegregation: The First Decade.* New York: Harper & Row, 1966.

Simkins, Francis Butler. *Pitchfork Ben Tillman: South Carolinian.* Gloucester, MA: Peter Smith, 1964.

Sitkoff, Harvard. *The Struggle for Black Equality, 1954–1992.* New York: Hill & Wang, 1993.

Smyth, William D. "Segregation in Charleston in the 1950s: A Decade of Transition." *South Carolina Historical Magazine* 92 (1991): 99–123.

Southern, David W. "Beyond Jim Crow Liberalism: Judge Waring's Fight against Segregation in South Carolina, 1942–52." *Journal of Negro History* 66 (1981): 209–27.

Southern Education Foundation. "A History of Private Schools & Race in the American South." Southern Education Foundation. https://www.southerneducation.org
/publications/historyofprivateschools/ (accessed July 31, 2019).

Southern Education Reporting Service. *A Statistical Summary, State by State, of School
Segregation-Desegregation in the Southern and Border Area from 1954 to the Present,*
16th revision, February 1967.

Southern Manifesto on Integration. Congressional Record, 84th Congress, Second Session, vol. 102, part 4. Washington, DC: Governmental Printing Office, 1956.

Sullivan, Patricia. *Days of Hope: Race and Democracy in the New Deal Era.* Chapel
Hill: University of North Carolina Press, 1996.

Synnott, Marcia G. "Desegregation in South Carolina, 1950–1963: Sometime 'Between
'Now' and 'Never.'" In *Looking South: Chapters in the Story of an American Region,*
edited by Winfred B. Moore Jr. and Joseph F. Tripp, 51–64. New York: Greenwood,
1989.

———. "Federalism Vindicated: University Desegregation in South Carolina and Alabama, 1962–1963." *Journal of Policy History* 1, no. 3 (1989): 292–318.

Tindall, George Brown. *South Carolina Negroes, 1877–1900.* Baton Rouge: Louisiana
State University Press, 1966.

Tollison, Courtney Louise. "Moral Imperative and Financial Practicality: Desegregation
of South Carolina's Denominationally-Affiliated Colleges and Universities." PhD
diss., University of South Carolina, 2003.

Tushnet, Mark V. *Making Civil Rights Law: Thurgood Marshall and the Supreme
Court, 1936–1961.* New York: Oxford University Press, 1994.

———. *The NAACP's Legal Strategy Against Segregated Education, 1925–1950.* Chapel
Hill: University of North Carolina Press, 1988.

Underwood, James L. *The Constitution of South Carolina: The Struggle for Political
Equality.* Columbia: University of South Carolina Press, 1986.

United States Commission on Civil Rights, *Equal Protection of the Laws in Higher
Education.* Washington, DC: United States Commission on Civil Rights, 1960.

———. "Nondiscrimination in Federally-Assisted Programs of The Department of
Health, Education, and Welfare—Effectuation of Title VI of the Civil Rights Act of
1964." *Federal Register.* 29 Fed. Reg. 236 (December 4, 1964): 16–300.

———. "Public Education: 1964 Staff Report." October 1964.

———. "School Desegregation in Williamsburg County, South Carolina: A Staff Report
of the U.S. Commission on Civil Rights." 1977.

———. *Survey of School Desegregation in the Southern and Border States, 1965–66: A
Report.* February 1966.

Vloet, Katie. "Before Rosa Parks: Wittenberg, '50, Looks Back on Early Bus-Segregation
Case," *Law Quadrangle.* http://quadrangle.law.umich.edu/spring2015/class-notes
/before-rosa-parks/ (accessed August 4, 2015).

Ware, Gilbert. *William Hastie: Grace under Pressure.* New York: Oxford University
Press, 1984.

Wasby, Stephen L. *Race Relations Litigation in an Age of Complexity.* Charlottesville: University Press of Virginia, 1995.

Wechsler, Harold S. *The Qualified Student: A History of Selective College Admission in America.* Piscataway, NJ: Transaction, 2014.

Weisbrot, Robert. *Freedom Bound: A History of America's Civil Rights Movement.* New York: Norton, 1990.

Weiss, Nancy Joan. *Farewell to the Party of Lincoln: Black Politics in the Age of FDR.* Princeton, NJ: Princeton University Press, 1983.

Wolters, Raymond. *The Burden of Brown: Thirty Years of School Desegregation.* Knoxville: University of Tennessee Press, 1984.

Workman, W. D., Jr. "State Regulation of the Right to Vote: The Role of the Supreme Court in Civil Rights." *American Bar Association Journal* 35 (1949): 393–96, 439.

Wright, Marion A. *Public Parks and Recreational Facilities: A Study in Transition.* Frogmore, SC: Penn Community Service, 1963.

Yarbrough, Tinsley. *A Passion for Justice: J. Waites Waring and Civil Rights.* New York: Oxford University Press, 1987.

Zuberi, Tukufu, and Bonilla-Silva, Eduardo, eds. *White Logic, White Methods: Racism and Methodology.* Lanham, MD: Rowman & Littlefield, 2008.

INDEX

Abbeville County School District v. South Carolina, 8
Adams v. Orangeburg, 115, 143, 162, 171–72
Adams, Brenda, 115, see also *Adams v. Orangeburg*
Adams, E. A., 10
Adams, Rudolph, 115, see also *Adams v. Orangeburg*
Adams, Theodore, 115, see also *Adams v. Orangeburg*
Aiken County, hospital desegregation in, 109; and public accommodations, 184; public school desegregation in, 147
Alexander v. Holmes County Board of Education, 170
Allen University, 51, 100; and racial violence, 97; and sit-ins, 99
Alston v. School Board of the City of Norfolk, 33, 194n2
Anderson, George Ross, 183
Anderson, Jesse T., 35, 151–52
Anderson, Robert, 120
Anderson, SC, 106
Andrews, O. L., 92, 94–96; see also *Henry v. Greenville Airport Commission*
Arnold, W. H., 108
Austin, M. G., 85–86

Bailey, George, 39
Barratry, 82, 204n57; and anti-barratry bill, 83
Baskin, W. P., 24–26; see also *Brown v. Baskin*
Bates, Lester, 110
Beard, Jesse, 49, 197n55
Beasley, David, 185
Beaufort County, public school desegregation in, 68, 145; and White primary, 23–24

Belser, Irvine, 62
Benedict College, 15, 51; and racial violence, 97; and sit-ins, 99
Berge, Wendell, 15
Bessinger, Maurice, 8, 148–49, 178
Bethea, W. C., 46
Black National Lawyers Guild, 27
Bouie, Simon, 99
Boulware, Harold, 31, 49; and John Wrighten, 44, 49–50; and South Carolina State College Law School, 46; and *U.S. v. Ellis*, 15; and voting, 17–18, 22–23
Bracey, Edward, 52
Bracey, Spencer, 51–52, 103, 198n67
Brailsford, James M., 85
Brennan, William, 163
Briggs v. Elliott, 5, 6, 54–56, 62, 67, 69–70, 84, 87, 93, 111, 133, 136, 138, 147, 153–54, 173
Briggs, Harry, 55, 175; see also *Briggs v. Elliott*
Brown v. Baskin, 6, 23, 35
Brown v. Board of Education (Brown II), 7, 67, 68, 97, 150, 154, 156, 163
Brown v. Board of Education, 1, 6–7, 62, 73, 76, 79, 114, 141, 144, 198n4, 216n30
Brown v. Charleston, 135, 139, 143–44, 147, 157, 173
Brown, Alice, 122
Brown, Charles Henry, 15
Brown, David, 23–24, 38; see also *Brown v. Baskin*
Brown, Edgar A., 62, 79, 91, 102–03, 105, 119
Brown, J. Arthur, 5, 69; and public school desegregation, 113; and state park cases, 73–74, 78–79, 105–06
Brown, Millicent, 113, see also *Brown v. Charleston*

Brunson v. Board of Trustees, 114–15, 134, 153–54, 160, 164, 170–74
Brunson, Bobby, 112, 114
Bryan v. Austin, 82–90
Bryan, Ola, 89
Burke High School, 32, 68, 112
Byrnes, James F., 119; as Governor, 51, 55–56, 59–61, 64

Caldwell, Arthur, 81
Calhoun County, 56; public school desegregation in, 154, 158–60, 164–65
Callison, T. C., 65, 79–80
Cameron High School, 165
Cameron, SC, public schools in, 154, 158, 164–65
Campbell, Alexander, 28
Campbell, Carol, 184
Canty, Murray, 106
Carnegie Library, 110
Carolina Theater, 129
Carrere, Thomas A., 137–38
Carter, James, 107–08
Carter, Jimmy, 179
Carter, Robert, 18, 40, 42, 58
Cash, Paul, 120
Chapman, Robert F., 183
Charleston News and Courier, 184
Charleston, SC, 4, 8, 31; and Black voting, 10; city schools, 112; and establishment of state NAACP, 11; and law school desegregation, 48; NAACP membership in, 77; racial violence in, 98; resistance to desegregation in, 69; public school desegregation in, 134–47, 149, 153–54, 159–61, 169, 173; and sit-ins, 101; and state park desegregation, 73–76, 78–79
Charleston County, SC, 7, 146; and hospital strikes, 178
Charlotte Observer, 181
Cheraw, SC, 11, 147
Childs, Clara, 63
Chisolm, John, 74
Citizens Councils, 7, 69, 71, 83, 88, 136
Civil Rights Act of 1957, 29, 124
Civil Rights Act of 1960, 103
Civil Rights Act of 1964, 8, 99, 110, 128–29, 145, 148–49, 150–51, 154, 158–59, 163, 167, 173
Civil Rights Cases, 5, 22, 67
Claflin College, 39, 126–27

Clardy, George, 90
Clarendon County, 7, 23; public school desegregation in, 54–56, 58, 60, 62, 67–70, 111, 114–15, 135, 144, 147, 152, 153–54, 156, 159, 161–71, 174–77, 180
Clark v. Flory, 87, 109
Clark, Etta Mae, 74–77, 105; see also *Clark v. Flory*
Clark, Kenneth, 58, 136, 138
Clark, Ramsey, 155
Clark, William, 128, 162, 171
Clemson University, 7, 51–52, 82, 101–05, 117–20, 123–24, 127, 134
Cleveland Park (Greenville, SC), 107–08
Columbia College, 121
Columbia State, 122, 143, 149
Commission on Civil Rights, 29, 155–56
Committee for Interracial Cooperation, 64–65
Congress of Racial Equality, 97, 128
Cooler, Donald, 75
Cooper, R. M., 89, 102
Corridor of Shame, 184
Cruell, Claude, 84–85, 90
Currie, Cameron, 184

Daniel, Charles, 111
Darlington plan, 146, 152, 155, 157–59
Darlington, SC, public school desegregation in, 114, 134, 141, 145, 152, 160–61, 163, 166–67, 174, 181
Davis, Charles E., 85–86
Davis, Charles S., 121
Davis, Edith, 106
Dawson, Ralph, 113
DeLaine, J. A., 55, 84
Democratic Party, 12, 15, 17–29, 53, 179–80
Denmark Trade School, 122
Denmark, SC, 98
Department of Justice, 8, 84, 173, 180; Civil Rights Section/Division, 18, 81, 100; and Ku Klux Klan activity, 12; and school desegregation, 143, 153, 155–57, 163, 165–66; and voting rights, 13–16, 29
Desegregation, 6, 8, 33, 54, 63, 65–66, 68, 90, 100, 110, 114, 117, 119, 122, 127, 145, 150, 178; and gradualism, 63; of higher education, 7, 48, 51–53, 120, 122; opposition to, 7, 56, 62, 69, 70–73, 75, 80, 83, 91, 94, 97, 101, 104, 111, 123, 136, 138–39, 141, 175–77; and parochial

schools, 134; of public accommodations, 105, 108–09; of public schools, 7, 61, 67–68, 83, 114–16, 124, 133, 144, 146–47, 151–62, 164–68, 170–75, 181–86; and University of SC School of Education, 70
Desegregation Consulting Center, University of South Carolina, 171, 219n73
Dillon County, 126
Doar, John, 158
Dorn, Bryan, 27
Doyle, Oscar H., 11, 13–15, 28
Dred Scott v. Sandford, 5, 18, 22
Due process, 5, 35, 87, 133, 148, 167
Dufford, J. P., 154
Duvall, Viola, 32

Edisto Beach State Park, 73–82, 87, 105
Edisto Theater, 129
Egerton, John, 182
Elliott, R. W., see Briggs v. Elliott
Ellis, F. E., 14
Elloree, SC, 7; and citizens councils, 69, 83, 160, 164–65, 167; see also Elloree Training School
Elloree Training School, 85
Elmore v. Rice, 6, 19, 21–27, 35, 179
Elmore, George, 17, 21, 63
Emanuel African Methodist Episcopal Church, 185
Equal Protection Clause, 35, 41, 75, 88, 114, 133, 136, 148, 172, 176, 201n6
Evers, Medgar, 105–06

Fennell, R. C., 182
Finch, Robert, 172
Figg, Robert McC. 27, 56–58, 62, 87, 89, 102, 111, 120
Finney, Ernest J., 6
Fifth Circuit Court of Appeals, 136
Flemming, Sarah Mae, 7, 73, 80–81
Florence, SC, 106; desegregation in, 68, 83; and establishment of state NAACP, 11; reprisals over desegregation in, 63; and sit-ins, 98
Flory, C. H., 75, 79
Fludd, Cornelius, 101
Folsom, Fred, 18
Fourth Circuit Court of Appeals, 27, 101; and higher education cases, 50, 56, 104, 117–18, 134; and public accommodations, 81, 94, 97, 148; and public schools,

115, 140, 144, 146–47, 166, 171, 173–74; and White primary, 27
Frampton, G. Creighton, 35, 37
Frankfurter, Felix, 88
Frederick, Nathaniel J., 10
Furman University, 47, 122

Gaffney, Lottie P., 13–15
Gaffney, SC, 13
Gaines, Lloyd, 39
Gaither, Tom, 127–28
Gantt, Harvey, 7, 69, 101–05, 117–24, 134
Garrett, Charles, G., 81
Garrett, Henry, 138, 212n62
Gause, Harry, 84
Gibbs v. Broome, 31, 194n2
Gibson, 108
Gibson, J. Roy, 107
Gladden, Arnetta, 121
Glenn, Terrell, 153, 161
Glover, Lydia, 113
Graham, Baxter, 69–70
Graham, Donald, 84
Graham, Frank Porter, 76
Graydon, Augustus, 138–39, 164–65, 167
Green v. New Kent County, 8, 162–63, 168, 172
Greenberg, Jack, 89, 92–95, 103, 163, 198n4
Greenlee, Daisy, 37
Greenville Technical Education Center, 122
Greenville, SC, 7, 185; Democratic Party in, 24, 26; and desegregation of higher education, 122, 134; Ku Klux Klan activity in, 11–12; NAACP in, 11; and public accommodations, 74, 92–100, 107–11; public school desegregation in, 7, 68, 90, 134, 144–45, 147, 160–61, 174, 183; and racial violence, 84; voting by African Americans in, 11, 14; see also Whittenberg v. Greenville
Greenwood Index-Journal, 122
Greer, Benny, 160–61, 163, 166–67, 173
Gressette, James H., 129
Gressette, L. Marion, 5, 6, 56, 57, 91, 111, 114, 117–19, 135, 154–55, 204n59

Hall, J. S., 94–95
Harlan, John Marshall, 5
Harper, Mary, 182
Hart, John C., 82
Hart, Philip, 92

Haynsworth, Clement, 180
Health, Education, and Welfare, Department of, 145, 151–58, 163–76, 178, 184, 221n20
Heart of Atlanta Motel, Inc. v. United States, 148
Help Orangeburg Public Education (HOPE), 172
Hemphill, Robert, 2, 124, 180; and public school desegregation, 145, 147, 157–59, 162, 168–69, 174 and teachers' cases, 132–33
Henry v. Greenville Airport Commission, 7, 92–97
Henry, Richard, see *Henry v. Greenville Airport Commission*
Hicks, J. W., 47
Hightower, Jack, 62
Hill-Burton Act, 109
Hines, Clarice, 113
Hinton, James M., 15, 31, 40, 49, 51, 63, 82
Hollings, Ernest F., 29; as Governor, 99, 101, 114, 119, 134; as Lieutenant Governor, 70, 84
Horry County, 147
House Committee on Un-American Activities (HUAC), 82
Houston, Charles Hamilton, 1, 10, 30
Howe, Harold, 173
Hughes, Jerry M., 70
Hunt, Eugene, 31
Hust, Carl, 108
Hutto, F. O., 158

Iowa State University, 101, 105

Jackson, Jesse, 99
Jacocks, C. West, 75
James, C. F., 110
Jefferson, Jerivoch, 106
Jenkins, Lincoln, 15, 85, 94–95, 98, 106, 110–12
Johnson v. Branch, 130, 132
Johnson, Delores, 121
Johnson, Fred V., 11–12, 17, 190n8
Johnson, Lyndon, 124, 145, 185
Johnston, Olin D., 16–17, 20, 67, 192n27
Jones, Wilhelmenia, 70

Katzenbach, Nicholas, 178
Keppel, Francis, 154

Kilpatrick, James J., 136
King, Martin Luther, Jr., 97, 124
Knox, Ellis O., 57
Ku Klux Klan (KKK), 11–12, 69, 71, 76, 98

Lamar Riot, 8
Lander College, 122
Legal Defense and Education Fund (LDF), 2, 11, 16, 18, 30, 56, 58, 92, 97, 103, 106, 198n4
Leonard, George S., 135
Leonard, Jerris, 173
Leverette, Sam, 106
Lighthouse and Informer, 31, 192n34
Lincoln University, 44
Long, John, 119, 135
Lott, Jack, 47
Lucas, Luther, 86

Mance, R. W., 10
Manning High School, 152, 169
Manning Training School, 169
Mardian, Robert, 172, 176
Marion County, 22, 112
Marshall, Burke, 100
Marshall, Harris, 128, 130
Marshall, Thurgood, 11, 12, 30, 97; and desegregation of higher education, 38–41, 42–45, 47–51; and desegregation of public schools, 55–56, 58, 68; and public accommodations, 77; and teachers' cases, 31, 33, 85, 87–88; and voting rights, 14–18, 24–25
Martin, J. Robert, 2; and desegregation of public accommodations, 107, 178–79; and desegregation of public schools, 138–42, 144–46, 152, 160–63, 166, 169, 183
Maryland, 31, 38–39, 44–45, 77–80, 100
Maryland, University of, *see* Murray, Donald
Mason, Charles, 74
Maxwell, Cassandra, 15
Maybank, Burnett, R., 71
McCord, L. B., 152
McDonald, Samuel J., 11
McEachin, P.H., 87
McFadden, J. Means, 37
McGurck, Frank C. J., 135
McHugh, John A., 37
McKaine, Osceola, 24, 31

McLeod, Daniel, 102, 106, 140
McNair, Robert E., 8; as Governor, 174; as state representative, 91, 114, 204n59
McNally, Harold, 57
Medical Society of South Carolina, 178, 220n1
Meetze, T. E. 14
Metz, G. E., 51
Miller, E. M., 110
Milliken, Roger, 122
Missouri ex rel. Gaines v. Canada, 40, 45, 47–48
Mitchell, Clarence, 95
Mize, Sidney, 144
Monteith, Henrie, 120–21, 209n9
Moore, Leroy, 84
Moorer, Daniel, 51–52
Morgan, Shadrack, 33, 195n12
Morris College for Negroes, 64
Motley, Constance Baker, 103–04, 137
Mungin, J. W., 148
Murray, Donald, 38–39
Murray, John V., 70
Myrtle Beach State Park, 105–06

NAACP, 2, 4, 7, 12, 52, 77; criticism of, 70–71, 76, 81–85, 87, 116, 125; in Columbia, 10; and desegregation of higher education, 30, 38–40, 49–52, 103–05; and desegregation of public accommodations, 74, 92, 94–97, 105–08, 111, 149; local branches of, 3, 4, 31, 48, 69, 73, 78, 126–27, 174; and public school desegregation, 62–63, 65, 68, 145, 163, 166, 183; response to anti-NAACP laws, 85–91; South Carolina Conference, 11, 31, 113, 115, 128, 185; and teacher firings, 128–29; and teacher salaries, 31, 33–34; and voting rights, 13–17, 23, 29
Nash, Horace, 108
Nash, Shepard, 132, 139
National Review, 138
National Teacher Exam, 34–35, 131, 138–39, 157
Neal, M. T. (Mrs.), 83
Neal, Talmadge, 99
Nelson, J. Herbert, 105–06
Nesbitt, Mary, 105–06
New Kent County, Virginia, 163
Newberry College, 122
Newberry v. United States, 12, 191n10

Newby, I. A., 3
Newman, Anne P., 148
Newman, I. DeQuincey, 105, 127, 148–49
Nicholson, Francis B., 114
Nixon, Richard, 172–73, 185, 217n51, 219n73
Norris, Mary Elizabeth, 107–08
North Carolina, 30–31, 56, 62, 66, 76, 98, 100, 132

Oconee County, 124, 146
Office of Education, 145, 151–52, 159, 161, 167–68, 171–72
Olin Foundation, 103
Orangeburg, SC, 3, 39, 60, 70, 83, 84, 149, 189n1; citizens councils in, 69–70; desegregation of public accommodations in, 109, 115, 125–30, 142–43, 147, 149; public school desegregation in, 7, 115, 141–44, 147, 160, 162, 164, 167, 171–72, 182; racial violence in, 3, 98–99; and teachers' cases, 7–8, 85, 109, 125–30
Orangeburg Massacre, 3
Orangeburg Regional Hospital, 109, 127
Orangeburg Theater Corporation, 129

Palmetto State Teachers' Association, 31, 40, 64, 180
Panetta, Leon, 167
Parker, John J., 36, 56, 58, 62, 67, 70, 87, 89, 93, 173
Parks, Rosa, 73, 81
Pearson v. Clarendon, 54–55, 147, 198n3
Peltason, J. W., 1, 189n2
Perry, Matthew, 6, 94; and desegregation of higher education, 103–10, 115; and desegregation of public schools, 142–46, 154, 164, 166–74; and teachers' cases, 128, 130
Pettiford, Julia, 36–37
Pickens County, public school desegregation in; 145 and White primary, 24, 26
Plessy v. Ferguson, 1, 5, 7, 18, 22, 50, 58–59, 67, 71, 73, 75, 79–81, 93–94, 96, 136, 175, 201n4, 201n6
Plowden, Charles, 111
Poole, Robert F., 51, 103, 198n67
Pope, J. M., 75
Pope, Thomas, 91, 204n59
Porter, Gladys, 106
Pough, W. Newton, 78, 80

Presbyterian College, 66
Prigg v. Pennsylvania, 5
Price, James H., 43, 45, 47
Prince, Samuel, 43, 46–47
Progressive Democratic Party, 15, 17, 24–26, 63, 192n34, 197n55

Rackley, Gloria, 5, 8, 109–10, 115, 125–30, 133
Rackley, Jamelle, 109
Regional Education Board, 101, 104–05
Rembert, John H., 129
Republican Party, 29, 179–80, 220n87
Rhodes, W. S., 83
Ribicoff, Abraham, 114
Rice, Clay, 15, 17
Rice, John I., 17–18, 98
Richburg, J. H., 70
Richland County, 37, 42; and public accommodations, 105; public school desegregation in, 145–46; and teachers' salaries, 31–32, 34; and White primary, 15, 17–18
Riggs, Marion S., 167, 169–70, 173–74
Roberts, H. A., 170
Robertson, Evermae, 63
Robinson, Benjamin, 131
Robinson, David W., 181–82; defense of anti-NAACP laws, 89; defense of segregation, 170, 172, 175–77, 181–82; and desegregation of higher education, 42, 44–47, 102, 104; and desegregation of public accommodations, 106; and public school desegregation, 111–12, 114–15, 142, 147, 154–55, 157–58, 167–70, 173–74; as Gressettee Committee counsel, 5, 6; responding to *Brown v. Board of Education,* 65–66; and school funding, 64; and teachers' cases, 131
Robinson, Jackie, 95, 97, 205n8
Robinson, Klyde, 165
Rock Hill Evening Herald, 121
Rock Hill, SC, 66, 83, 98, 121, 128, 134
Roddey, Cynthia, 121
Rogers, Emory, 69, 135
Rogers, Joseph O., 111, 157, 167
Rogge, John, 12
Roper Hospital, 8, 178, 220n1
Rose, Peggy Ann, 90
Royster, W. B., 139
Rucho v. Common Cause, 180

Russell, Donald, 143, 149, 180, 214nn5–6, 218n54

St. Anne's School, 134
St. John's High School, 152, 165
St. Matthews, SC, 160
Saluda County, 184
Sampson, Donald James, 90, 108–09
Sapp, Claude, 15
Sarratt v. Cash, 132
Sawyer, Olin, 32
Scarlett, Francis Muir, 136
School equalization plan, 60–62, 75, 156
Seabrook, Thomas, 113
Sesquicentennial Park, 105–06
Sharper, H. P., 106
Shaw Airfield, 134, 143, 145
Shaw, Gerald, 108
Sherman, Joe, 118
Shirer, Pearl Green, 35–38
Simkins, Modjeska, 3, 99, 120
Simons, Charles E., Jr., 2, 124; and desegregation of public accommodations, 110, 148; and desegregation of public schools, 142, 144, 147, 153, 160, 162, 164, 170–74, 180, 183–84; and teachers' cases, 130
Sims, Hugo, 129, 142, 144
Sipuel, Ada Lois, 48, 196n32
Sit-in, 98–99, 101, 108, 128
Slochower v. Board of Higher Education, 87
Smith v. Allwright, 6, 16, 19
Smith, Ellison M., 37–38
Smith, Malissa, 31
Smith, Norman M., 42, 45
Sobeloff, Simon, 106, 118
Solomon, James, 120
South Carolina Conference of the Methodist Church, 121
South Carolina Education Association, 64, 67
South Carolina School Committee (Gressette Committee), 5, 6, 56, 64, 66, 70, 87, 104, 106, 115, 117, 120, 124, 128–29, 138, 144
South Carolina State College (and University), 3, 6–7, 33, 39–48, 50–52, 55, 70–71, 78, 82–84, 98, 103, 126, 176, 190n8, 203n39
Southern Education Foundation, 181
Southern Education Report, 175

Southern Manifesto, 71
Southern Regional Council, 156, 182
Southern Regional Education Board, 156
Southern School News, 68, 122
Spartanburg Junior College, 121
Sprott, W. C., 111
Stafford, G. Jackson, 70
Stanley v. Darlington County School
    District No. 1, 141, 183, 221n20
Stansfield, John, 27
Stell v. Savannah Chatham County Board
    of Education, 136, 140, 142
Stewart, J. G., 10
Stoddard, Hugh, 131–32
Strauder v. West Virginia, 59, 201n6
Strom, J. P., 105
Summerton Elementary School, 170, 174
Summerton High School, 170, 174
Sumter Movement, 130–32
Sumter, SC, 98, 105, 110, 126, 132
Supreme Court (South Carolina), 6, 184
Supreme Court (U.S.), 1, 4, 12, 20, 71, 78,
    87–88, 111, 117–19, 138, 144, 146, 150–
    51, 172, 180, 182; and anti-NAACP laws,
    90–91; and higher education, 6, 39, 44,
    48, 50, 52, 123, 134; and public school
    desegregation, 55, 58–59, 62–67, 70,
    139–40, 142, 162–63, 165, 170, 174–75;
    and public accommodations, 76, 80–81,
    93, 100, 107, 148; and White primary, 6,
    14, 16, 18, 21–22
Sweatt v. Painter, 52, 58

Tenth Amendment, 71, 136
Thompson, Albert N., 32–35, 38
Thompson, J. E., 152
Thornwell Orphanage, 66
Thurmond, J. Strom, 23, 29, 56, 67, 71, 145,
    165, 192n27, 217–18n51, 220n5
Till, Emmett, 68
Tillman, Benjamin, 17
Timmerman, George Bell, Jr., 60, 66, 68,
    70, 79, 82, 84, 139
Timmerman, George Bell, Sr., 2, 7, 21, 124,
    204n60; and desegregation of higher
    education, 41; and desegregation of pub-
    lic accommodations, 73, 80–81, 92–97,
    106, 110; and desegregation of public
    schools, 56, 58, 62; and teachers' cases,
    36, 89–90, 110

Tison, Sidney, 25–26
Tolbert, Mark, 95
Toomey, Robert, 111
Toth, Andre, 100
Travelstead, Chester C., 70
Trinity Methodist Church, 127
Truman, Harry, 21, 23, 204n60
Turner, Benner C., 51, 203n39
Turner, Sherwood, 84–85

U.S. News and World Report, 135
U.S. v. Ellis, see Gaffney, Lottie P.
U.S. v. Lovett, 88
United States v. Classic, 14, 18, 191n16
University of Georgia, 100
University of Mississippi, 100, 118–20
University of South Carolina, 39, 42, 120,
    123, 127, 149, 171; Law School, 39–42,
    44–48, 51, 64, 120, 176; School of Educa-
    tion, 70

Van den Haag, Ernest, 138
Verner, James S., 77–80
Vesey, Denmark, 185
Vickery, Kenneth, 101–02, 104, 207n37
Victory Savings Bank, 84
Virginia, 31, 34, 62, 65–66, 70, 100, 129,
    162

Wade Hampton Academy, 165, 181
Wade Hampton Hotel, 131
Walker, Classie Rae, 108
Wallace, George, 148
Walls, Dwayne, 181
Wannamaker, T. Elliot, 143
Ware, Archie, 28
Waring, Elizabeth, 21
Waring, J. Waties, 2, 6, 82, 84, 123, 193n49,
    204n60; and desegregation of higher
    education, 41–42, 45, 47–48, 50, 54; and
    desegregation of public schools, 55–62;
    and teachers' cases, 34–36; and vot-
    ing rights cases, 20–22, 24–28, 192n35,
    193n53
Waring, Thomas R., 67, 69
Warren, Earl, 118
Watkins, William L., 104, 118
Watson v. City of Memphis, 107, 139
Watson, Albert, 29
West Virginia, 38

White supremacy, 1–4, 9, 11–12, 16–20, 24, 27, 30, 41, 53, 67, 88, 96–97, 117, 125, 133, 177, 179, 182, 186
White, Harold, 105
White, Walter, 12, 55
Whitehead, Matthew, 56–57
Whittaker, Miller F., 42–46
Whittenberg v. Greenville, 183
Whittenberg, A. J., 95, 134, 145
Whittenberg, Elaine, 134
Wieman v. Updegraff, 87–88
Wilkins, Roy, 13, 68, 82
Wilkinson High School, 128
Williams v. Mississippi, 5
Williams, Ashton H., 2, 75–80, 89, 124, 179, 204n60
Williams, B. T., 110
Williams, Irene, 8, 125, 130, 132
Williams, Marshall, 87
Williams, Samuel, 37
Williamsburg County, 182
Wilson, John S., 139
Winthrop College (University), 120–21, 190n8

Wisdom, John Minor, 151
Wittenberg, Philip, 81
Wofford College, 121–22
Wofford, Thomas, see *Henry v. Greenville Airport Commission*
Workman, William D., 69, 122, 175, 182, 193n40, 200n50, 220n87
Wright, Alonzo W., 11
Wright, Delores, 113
Wright, Doris, 99
Wright, John E., 14
Wrighten v. Board of Trustees, 6, 40–56
Wrighten, John, 5, 6, 40–53, 75–77, 80, 176, 193n49
Wyche, Cecil C., 2, 204n60; and desegregation of higher education, 103–04, 117; and desegregation of public accommodations, 99, 108–09; and desegregation of public schools, 112, 115, 117, 134

York County, school desegregation in, 145, 152
Young, Charles F. 103
Young, T. B., 52